*Beyond Enchantment*

# Beyond Enchantment

## German Idealism and English Romantic Poetry

*Mark Kipperman*

uρρ  *University of Pennsylvania Press*

Philadelphia   1986

Library of Congress Cataloging-in-Publication Data

Kipperman, Mark.
  Beyond enchantment.

  Bibliography: p.
  Includes index.
  1. Idealism, German.  2. Romanticism—England.
3. English poetry—19th century—History and
criticism.  I. Title.
B2745.K56  1986     141'.0943     86–3368
ISBN 0–8122–8024–5 (alk. paper)

Printed in the United States of America

Designed by Adrianne Onderdonk Dudden

FOR

*Boris and Renee Kipperman,*
                *my parents*

# Contents

PART IV

*From Infinite Enchantment to Dialectical Imagination: Shelley's Maturing Quest*

PART V

*"Spirits Which Soar From Ruin": Byron's Pilgrimage from Idealist Quest to Heroic Stance*

# Introduction

This book is an attempt to develop a vocabulary for discussing romantic idealism, both in the strict sense of a formal philosophy and in the broader sense of a structural principle within romantic art. Critics have long assumed that some structural similarities might be found between idealist doctrines and poetic texts in the period, but too often philosophical ideas torn from their own texts have been compared only with abstracted "ideas" of poets to yield vague or general parallels. Yet, as Earl Wasserman had suggested ("The English Romantics: The Grounds of Knowledge," *SiR* [1964]), the epistemology of post-Kantian idealism—far more even than the native Berkeleyan tradition—seems to take as its central topic the same question that drives the psychological quest of English romantic poetry: what does it mean for a subject to conceive himself as the maker of his own circumstances? To what extent is this a meaningful philosophical and psychological assumption? In philosophical texts of the post-Kantian period, the philosopher must place the self at the creative center of the world, while avoiding on one side sterile and inarticulate self-consciousness and on the other side a world devoid of human presence. In the long poems we have come to call, after Harold Bloom, "internalized quest romance," the poet centers his text, too, on the creating mind, and for his part must navigate between debilitating self-enchantment with his own fictions and a desperate fear that the world is inherently incapable of responding to the questions of the human voice.

It was, of course, Immanuel Kant who insisted that the world, even in its most fundamental properties of space and time, answers our questions with our own voice. Idealism in the early nineteenth century took its form from the complex systems of self-consciousness initiated by the *Critique of Pure Reason*. The form of these systems is a constant questioning of the world as well as a questioning of what it might mean even to "question" a world at all, what it might mean to seek an answer. This systematic questioning (*quaesitus*) is a form of seeking (*quaerere*) that, when undertaken by an individual poet, assumes the form of psychological *quest*.

Because the Kantian texts ask their questions explicitly, I attempt to derive terms of the romantic quest for self-understanding directly from them. Although I do not claim any strict historical "influence" by Kant or the Kantians on particular texts, it is true that the philosophers both reflected and helped define the broader cultural idealism in which romantic art participates. If the transcendentalism of the Kantians was unknown to most romantic poets in England, it may nonetheless help us define the premises and questions of their idealist quest: Coleridge's need to find systematic form for his own idealism, after he had exhausted the possibilities of the native Lockean and Berkeleian tradition, is what led him to the Germans in the first place.

Since René Wellek's *Immanuel Kant in England* (Princeton, 1931), the literature relating Kant to English romanticism has been sparse indeed. Although limited in scope, the most useful works are Thomas McFarland's *Coleridge and the Pantheist Tradition* (Princeton, 1969) and Thomas Weiskel's *The Romantic Sublime* (Baltimore, 1976). (McFarland's most recent work, *Originality and Imagination* [Baltimore, 1985], includes a discussion of imagination in Kant and Fichte, pp. 148–78, that complements mine. It appeared as this work was in press.) I have limited myself to considering the dialectic of receptivity and spontaneity in the *Critique of Pure Reason* because I have found the structure of the argument in this text most useful for defining the course of later idealism. My purposes were not to trace the theory of art or imagination in Kant's work as a whole (there is considerable scholarly study of these issues), but rather to use the first *Critique* to establish themes that would evolve in many ways as idealism developed in J. G. Fichte and F. W. J. Schelling.

The literature on Fichte in English is virtually nonexistent, notwithstanding German scholars' sense that the *Wissenschaftslehre* is a crucial text in continental romanticism. (In good part this fact is explained by the lack of reliable translations.) Although good general introductions to Fichte may be found in Gian Orsini's *Coleridge and German Idealism* (Carbondale, 1969) and James Engell's *The Creative Imagination* (Cambridge, 1982), I have intended my own reading of the *Wissenschaftslehre* to provide specific definitions of the complex dialectics of mind and world that follow from the principle that the I creates itself and is its own place and time. I have tried to demonstrate the broad applicability of this reading to some common principles of the romantic "internalization" of quest.

By the time of the second generation of English romantic poets, the instabilities of an idealism that promised absolute self-autonomy had reached a breaking point. For Byron particularly, it became impossible to maintain that the mind drew its creative power from itself in complete isolation, or that the world was completely responsive to human desire. Byron, though no philosopher, is a survivor of many traps and enchantments of idealist premises, certainly committed to the power of the mind to overcome its circumstances in creative freedom, but equally aware of the price the world may exact and of the power of the world endlessly to surprise.

For all the epistemological implications of post-Kantian thought, the key psychological challenge for the romantics remained: what kind of *stance* does man as moral and as imaginative being adopt toward the conflicting currents of his own mind, his desires, and the world he must build and live in? In looking at a series of romantic long poems, I argue that the crucial romantic "mode" is neither lyric nor wholly reflective, but an evolving quest, a probing *activity*, in which the mind projects upon its stage the fragmented images of its own self-conception. But from these fragments the mind must uncover the stance in relation to itself that will permit it to become a moral actor on the stage it half creates, half perceives.

This book had its origin eight years ago, when I began to read Fichte and Schelling under the guidance of Mr. Bruce Foltz of the Department of Philosophy, the Pennsylvania State University. I alone am responsible for the success or failure of my application of these texts to poetry of the English romantic period; but my understanding of German idealism owes much to discussions with Mr. Foltz over a long period. I would like to acknowledge the long help and support of my adviser and friend Stuart Curran of the University of Pennsylvania, whose guidance extended over many years and reached from the dizzying heights of Kantian metaphysics to the (perhaps greater) complexities of English style. Frederick Garber, my first teacher of romanticism, continues to influence my work, through both his writing and his friendship. Lore Metzger and Timothy Corrigan have also read the manuscript, and I have benefited from their advice. For their patient guidance and helpful advice I would also like to thank David DeLaura of the University of Pennsylvania and my colleague at Princeton, Thomas McFarland.

I am grateful to the British Library and the Bodleian Library for providing me access to Coleridge and Shelley manuscripts. Portions of Chapters 4 and 5 have appeared in *Studies in Romanticism* (Summer 1984) and are reprinted by permission of the Trustees of Boston University. A portion of Chapter 9 appears, in slightly different form, in a volume of essays, *English and German Romanticism: Crosscurrents and Controversies*, edited by J. Pipkin (Heidelberg: Carl Winters Universitätsbuchhandlung, 1985), and is reprinted by permission of Carl Winter. For permission to quote from the recently discovered Scrope Davies MS of "Mont Blanc" I would like to thank the owner, Barclay's Bank, Pall Mall, London.

I was able to complete this book in the peaceful farm country outside Madison, Wisconsin, thanks to a year's leave from Princeton and funding from the National Endowment for the Humanities (Summer Grants) and the American Council of Learned Societies. My friends and hosts, Gordon and Carol Knopf, were most helpful and tolerant of the writer in their midst. To Sargent Bush and Phillip Harth of the English Department of the University of Wisconsin-Madison, I owe a debt not only for office and library access but also for their support and encouragement during my year's visit. And for keeping my feet sanely on the ground while my head was dizzy with idealism, thanks to Allen, Craig, Dave, and Nadine Weitermann, my dear Wisconsin friends.

*Sun Prairie, Wisconsin and Princeton, New Jersey*

# PART I

*Finitude and the Divided Self:*
*Kant and the Origins of*
*Romantic Subjectivity*

# 1

## Romantic Subjectivity and the Goals of Romance

It is an obvious and yet surprisingly overlooked fact that most romantic poems begin with something very wrong. So indeed do most of literature's long poems with central heroes, magical adventures, and ambitious quests, the poems we have come to call romances. But if we compare the major long poems of the romantic period with, say, *The Faerie Queene, Sir Gawain and the Green Knight, Perceval, Appollonius Prince of Tyre*, or *The Odyssey*, we find in the former no sickness blighting the land, no foul knights to be pursued, often no clear sense of what the hero is to do. The problem, in fact, is with the hero himself. The hero is no longer led through the forest of romance by the unifying intelligence of a bard; more often, the hero is the poet himself, who must in the course of the poem both define his own predicament and create his own heroic ideals. His task, completing the poem, requires overcoming his deepest anxiety—that he cannot even discover his task. His weapons are few—often only his tenacious will to survive—and his magic is his faith in the human imagination.

This task is most apparent in the famous sense of paralysis at the beginning of *The Prelude*. Paralysis, we might note, also afflicts Blake's Albion, Keats's Endymion and Saturn, Byron's Childe Harold, the transfixed Wedding Guest and the spiritually doomed Ancient Mariner, and (finally, as if to confront the motif visibly) the rockbound Prometheus. Wordsworth is "halted" even as *The Prelude* is about to begin by a sudden accession of self-consciousness, as Geoffrey Hartman has emphasized, but Wordsworth's immediate anxiety is the burden of the infinite freedom that romanticism claims for the creative mind:

> now free,
> Free as a bird to settle where I will.
> What dwelling shall receive me? in what vale
> Shall be my harbour? underneath what grove
> Shall I take up my home? and what clear stream
> Shall with its murmur lull me into rest?
> The earth is all before me . . . (1, lines 8–14)[1]

Wordsworth's search for guidance would ultimately lead him round to his own experience and to the source of freedom in the spontaneous, creative acts of the mind. The value of this freedom is not unequivocal. Even if one were free from received myths, from outworn cosmologies, what is one then free to do? To create one's own myth, we should recall, is paradoxical to begin with: a myth must be received as well as acted upon, must provide a guide to action. The hero of tradition does not usually know that he is the center of a fictive universe, although he may believe himself an actor in a large cosmic mystery. The reader, not the hero, is able to descry from his vantage point a tension between the hero's ignorance of the path and the reader's own knowledge that the labyrinth of completed myth encloses the path. The romantic poet-hero cannot assure himself or his reader that there is such closure. It may be that the thread the poet holds is itself the labyrinth—and this is no help. Anyone familiar with the literature of the romantic age will have sensed this burden of *consciousness*, that the artist is all too aware of himself as the spontaneous creator of myth. The problem continually arising for him is that the growth of the mind means the destruction of myth. It seems there can be no sure guides to meaningful action if the spontaneity of mind does not reach a stop, a saving remnant of *un*consciousness, something irreducibly given. Indeed, "meaning" itself implies otherness, a given ground.

Ultimately, romanticism comes to question even this dialectic: the larger critical question (which is a theoretical question also bequeathed to us, as critics) is, why does the mind *need* to think of itself as infinitely free, yet also need to be guided by otherness? This question makes freedom itself problematic and raises further questions. Why am I compelled to create personal myths that may provide no better guidance than old myths? Do I even have the freedom to adopt a self-created stance toward history or toward my role in human culture? Does the psychological process of adopting this stance, of becoming an integral self, limit or express freedom? And what is the role of psychological and "natural" determination: can man ever be meaningfully free from his memory or his desires? Finally, the moral question that remained as pressing for Shelley in 1814 as for Wordsworth twenty years earlier: In what sense can a romantic humanism be based on the creative mind's intuition that it and it alone is the spiritual creator of the world? How can the romantic quest of the mind unfolding itself to itself develop into a myth for all mankind?

These questions suggest that if the romantic quest begins with anxiety, this anxiety rises immediately from the assertion of subjectivity as the actual center and inevitable "topic" of poetry. Indeed, Freudian theory makes anxiety the *inevitable cause* of romance, that anxiety being produced by a *turning inward* of desire, by "strangulated affect," by a narcissistic devotion of energy to the subject himself. "Happy people never make fantasies," says Freud, "only unsatisfied ones."[2] R. D. Laing has acutely expressed the pathological state of subjective freedom carried to narcissistic lengths:

> The self, as long as it is "uncommitted to the objective element," is free to dream and imagine anything. Without reference to the objective element it can be all things to itself—it has unconditioned freedom, power, creativity. But its freedom and its omnipotence are exercised in a vacuum and its creativity is only the capacity to produce phantoms. The inner *honesty, freedom, omnipotence,* and *creativity,* which the "inner" self cherishes as its ideals, are cancelled, therefore, by a co-existing tortured sense of self-duplicity, of the lack of any real freedom, or utter impotence and sterility.[3]

The romantic poets did have to respond to this psychological danger, but in attempting to preclude it they evolved a notion of subjectivity radically at odds with the psyche of narcissism theory. To imagine that this involution describes simply an extreme, or pathological, outcome of subjectivity as the romantics understood it is seriously to misunderstand the goals of romantic quest. The subject of modern psychology is a fixed ego, bounded psychically by his repressed history, enclosed by his biology. But romanticism is the exploration of subjectivity as a transcendental process, as the unfolding of the mind to itself, as a dynamic, dramatic quest.

My task in this study is to explicate more fully this romantic subjectivity in its historical appearance in philosophical texts as the central theme of systematic transcendental analysis, and in some representative poems of the period as a recurrent theme to be articulated and explored through the structure, narrative strategy, and continuous redefinition of the poetry itself. In so doing, the inquiry must be narrowed from the usual broad attempts to trace the historical antecedents of romanticism. At one time or another, Plato or Plotinus, Leibniz or Locke, have been presented as spiritual ancestors of the romantic movement in Europe.[4] But the revolution in thinking about subjective awareness, its meaning and the ground of its possibility, was believed by most contemporary thinkers to begin with Immanuel Kant. Briefly, that revolution involved a turning away from the empirical study of mind and toward what came to be called the *transcendental* study of consciousness.[5] Despite the long history of the study of "imagination" as an element in psychological explanation—in writers such as Johann Tetens or Alexander Gerard—Kant's "Copernican Revolution" was seen as a decisive break. Kant offered not merely a new theory of mind or art but rather a new theory of man and the relation of "spirit" to the world.

Earl Wasserman, questioning the place of the English romantic poets in this vast cultural revolution, suggested that Wordsworth and Coleridge, Keats and Shelley each responded in characteristically different ways to the challenge of a new epistemology, a new discourse about mind that appeared in diverse forms among poets, philosophers, and psychologists. Without claiming any direct influence of Kant on the English poets, Wasserman nevertheless argues that "what Wordsworth, Coleridge, Keats and Shelley chose to confront more centrally [than the eighteenth-century poetry of psychological association] and to a degree unprecedented in English literature is a nagging problem in their literary culture: How do subject and object meet in a meaningful relationship? By what means do we have a *significant* awareness of the world?"[6] In their very different ways, the romantic poets explored the *ground* of the subject-object relation, the nature and possibility of true interchange. The activity establishing, defining, and creating this relation was the imagination.

The power of idealism to give us a new vocabulary for understanding the English romantic imagination has yet to be explored systematically, even though such scholars as A. O. Lovejoy, Earl Wasserman, M. H. Abrams, and Geoffrey Hartman have seen in the German movement the earliest attempts to deal discursively with the terms of the romantic quest for self-understanding. Can we arrive at some large enough cultural vision to comprehend the terms of the idealist philosophical movement as well as the "internalized quests" of the major romantic poets? How comprehensive can—or should— such a study be? It should, on the face of it, require no argument that the major long poems—epic or romance—of an age will always lead us back, as historians, to consider how the poem's hero embodies, discovers, or confronts his culture's dominant philosophical problems and articles of faith. Yet for a number of reasons, "comprehensiveness," even if we could agree on its meaning, is, I think, neither possible nor necessarily desirable in considering the effect of a broad cultural and intellectual movement on individual poets or artists. For one thing, the effect of what seem to us minor figures in the intellectual movement such as Johann Tetens and Jakob Fries, or poets like Heinz Otto Bürger, and August Kotzebue, is often extremely difficult to assess and is probably best left to fairly narrow studies of definite influence.[7] Another question, again, is the value of formulating detailed philosophical positions and imagining that poetry could, or should, recapitulate them.

It is my hope that one result of a study of idealism would be a clearer sense of the ways similar themes—self-consciousness, subjectivity, the ideality of the world—appear within very different kinds of discourse, philosophy and literature, and, as problems with similar facets, influence the structure of these texts in similar ways. Such a "history of ideas" (I would prefer to call them "themes") is open to the charge that it is itself a product of an idealist view of history. The history of ideas perhaps too readily assumes that texts are the simple product of authors responding at least at some level of consciousness and intention to ideas as cultural and historical forces.

Such history may even seem occult on the matter of the transmission and influence of "common ideas." Michel Foucault, for example (in *L'archéologie du savoir* [Paris, 1969]), attacks such history of ideas as merely a way of enshrining the "sovereignty of consciousness"; and much recent criticism is wary of assuming in the course of criticism the presence of any clear development of ideas in a progression of authors writing in some transparent but massive sea of common culture. I am not so suspicious of speaking about a climate of ideas or about texts as products of human minds or cultures. Nor am I persuaded that it must be more fruitful to eschew all critical discussion of psychological, moral, or political intent so as to privilege the study of textuality.

Nonetheless, in the face of the useful warning that the history of ideas in its frequently conservative practice too often displays a naively "romantic," idealist, or neo-Hegelian spiritual sense of history, my own history of themes will proceed with certain lowered expectations. I do not expect to find a unifying faith implicit or unconscious in heterogeneous texts that remains coherent through a historical era with clear beginning and end points. I do not expect to find a single master theme, such as the Hegelian homecoming. It would be eliding important differences to think of the romantic commitment to the freedom and spontaneity of human consciousness as static or unifying. I will indeed wish to define this commitment to a dynamic quest to make self-awareness the topic of philosophy and a good deal of literature; but though this topic is shared by many texts it is shared not so much as a common *faith* as a common *problem* or *question*.

When self-consciousness itself becomes a topic of theory or of art, it forces certain shapes onto texts. In order to define both the common commitment and the various modes of questioning, I will first examine some philosophical texts. Philosophical idealism in this period is most explicit about the various forces that are continuously at work as each level of its analysis forms and deforms those above and below it. In this sense its explicitness will at several points provide a model for the structures of other kinds of texts with analogous concerns—although certainly, as we will see, a poet's specific concerns even in facing similar questions will often diverge from a philosopher's. It is also true that idealism provides more than just a convenient model for critical study, that many of its formulations historically become clusters of concepts (such as "spontaneity of mind") that pass into the common specie of contemporary educated writers.

I do, then, believe that romanticism can be studied as a historical unity, but its unity is not that of a common set of results, theories, or transcendent faiths so much as it is a unity among heterogeneous responses to a common project. The project is neither narrowly literary nor speculative but broadly cultural, practical, and, finally, moral. It is to transfigure human self-understanding and so the world itself by a continuous questioning of consciousness as constitutive of its world. What romantic literary and idealist philosophical responses share is a commitment to establishing a new culture of humanism.

In this spirit, the thesis of this book is twofold: that the meaning of heroism itself is the question of romantic quest; and further, that this problem is in turn an outcome of the contemporary epistemological challenge: What does it mean that the hero is aware of himself and of his world? I will thus assume that the poetry and philosophy of the opening years of the nineteenth century constitute "cultural analogues," either systematic or poetic expressions of romantic quest.

Beginning with the challenge presented by transcendental idealism, I will inquire in what ways romantic poets used the romance to create a broad cultural humanism. Such a humanism aims at overcoming the alienation between man and world by asking the "transcendental" question: How does the mind come to construct a world for itself? Such a humanism aims beyond any simple psychological understanding of anxiety. Anxiety is not a natural psychological disorder, but rather is the threshold of a new self-consciousness; overcoming anxiety means grappling with the source of alienation in the gap between man's awareness of the vitality of his mind and his awareness of the otherness of the world. The humanism of romance aims at restoring man's faith that that gap can be bridged by his own mind, that the struggle is within humanity itself. At the same time, self-consciousness turned increasingly "inward" potentiates alienation and ignores the transcendental premise that "inward" and "outward" are not restricting givens, but are mental, human dimensions. Though nature seems given, it is the name we give to the "outward"; nature is given to and for us; it is a finitude that allows us to become fully ourselves. The quest to understand how and why the mind must divide against itself so as truly to know itself is the romantic response to alienation. The humanism of romance aims at the radical transformation of anxiety-ridden self-consciousness into self-fulfillment and of the rifts between the mind and its created ideals into new challenges for human growth and liberating social change.

"We have art," said Nietzsche, "in order not to perish from the truth." Art's illusions shield us from the bitter emptiness we must face and overcome in the continuing quest to realize the will. This is Nietzsche's response to the romantic tradition of thinking of art as the truest voice of humanity, the voice that articulates a world that is, far from being empty, the only true world. As Hegel put it—perhaps echoing J. C. F. von Schiller's *On the Aesthetic Education of Man*, a book he admired—"Only beyond the immediacy of feeling and external objects is genuine actuality to be found. . . . Art liberates the true content of phenomena from the pure appearance and deception of this bad, transitory world, and gives them a higher actuality, born of the spirit. Thus, far from being a mere appearance, a higher reality and truer existence is to be ascribed to the phenomena of art in comparison with [those of] ordinary reality."[8] Art is substance, not nothingness. In this strain of romantic theory art is the greatest "truth," the ultimate bridge between the self and the world it creates and inhabits.

Yet it is also arguable that the romantic poets feared the illusory power of romance as often as they expressed faith in the truthfulness of beauty. Recent critics have debated whether "organicist" or "self-deconstructing" strains predominate in romantic texts. The organic component of romance assumes that the being of mental creation is continuous with the being of nature; but in the deconstructionist theory, the romantic text contests its own claims to fill the void between mind and nature. Or, more exactly, the language of romance in suggesting its own negation undermines the poetry's claim to create a substantial self.

Typical of the latter view is the recent assertion of Tilottama Rajan that much romantic "sentimentality" is an evasion, an expression of bad faith, in which the poet asserts the creative power of art to elide a more central truth, the unreality of poetic language: "Because it is a product of consciousness rather than a reflection of external nature, it shares in the nothingness of consciousness rather than in the substantiality of things. As an attempt to transcend its own nothingness, the poetic image is doomed in advance."[9] Romantic texts often do confront the presumed nothingness of their discourse, but any resorting by the poet to an ideology of organic harmony is a strategy of repression. Implicit in this view is the Husserlian notion that consciousness is unable to be one with itself, unable to achieve the self-identity of an object.[10]

But if it is true that the organic unity of word and world is questioned by the darker side of romance, the romantics were not yet ready to see consciousness (no matter how self-divided) as a nothingness, or its products as the negation of a more real "something" in the world. They recoiled from carrying disillusionment to the point of attributing a more real being to an object-world void of human engagement, a world existing unperceived, a vision of the most profound absence of all, the absence of human beings. In this they found support from the philosophical culture of their day, as we shall see. It is not that Rajan is incorrect about the paradox and aporia intrinsic to a poetry that seeks to comprehend its own processes of idealization. It is, rather, that "romanticism" describes a broader field of discourse, whose concepts as I study them in this book—"the self," "self-consciousness," "idealism," "freedom," "nature"—are dispersed in texts that do more than question their own adequacy. Uncanniness, absence, the sudden dissolution of reality into dream or dream into nothingness: these are moments in a complex culture that also includes Shelley's struggle to articulate an idealist politics; Byron's "redemptive gestures," self-disclosures that are self-constituting for the narrator at the level of the text and its narrative rhythms; and Wordsworth's quest for a self autonomous enough to affirm its openness, or "availability," to being as more and more is taken from it.[11] For every moment of self-conscious alienation from the various projects of building a self, an ideal, a text, there is a moment of precarious but affirmative availability.

Romanticism tended to see self-consciousness not as merely a formal unity or self-negation but rather as an *act* in which the self asserts its being in the world. Certainly a self-consciousness that does not engage the world remains merely formal, enclosed, or, in the language of idealism, a bare possibility of freedom. But the self becomes real only as it sees itself in encounter with the world.

The question, of course, was how an act such as the creation of fictions or poems could constitute either a self- or world-disclosing movement. Are dream, reverie, fantasy, memory, reflection, or gestures of self-autonomy truly acts of world-making? It is precisely the nature of romantic (and idealist) faith that they are, but not in a simple or unambiguous way: the question is continually being re-posed from increasingly keener vantages. Some of these points are well known for their expressed anxiety over this need to idealize: "Whither is fled the visionary gleam? / Where is it now, the glory and the dream?"; "O Lady! we receive but what we give, / And in our life alone does Nature live"; "Was it a vision or a waking dream? / Fled is that music:— Do I wake or sleep?" Romantic literature shares with philosophical idealism not a univocal optimism that makes the world transparent, unifying world and mind, but a probing stance that redefines world-making and questions the contours of the world as the scene of our creative encounters.

Again, if the romantics do not commit themselves to any ultimate vision of a higher reconciliation of nature and spirit or to any final knowledge of the "real" unity of world and mind, neither are they forced to reject art as only deception, thus asserting the greater reality of some dehumanized object-world. The present examination of both poetic and philosophical texts will show that for romanticism generally, the being of self and world cannot be determined apart from each other. No object of its discourse rests in itself; all things— the self, the moral and social world—are questions because all things exist only *for* and *within* a probing dialogue with a human quester.

In part, this indeterminability stems from Enlightenment skepticism about the ultimate status of things and of mind. But even more it is a result of the romantics' dialectical experience of the self, which demands to be self-determining but continuously finds that it becomes itself only in encountering a world, which in its turn becomes a more meaningful place. Indeed, it seems that in certain romantic poems, such as *Childe Harold's Pilgrimage* or "Ode: Intimations of Immortality," disillusionment is a far more creative state than we moderns are accustomed to understand. For disillusionment does not always lead to the artist's denying the power of art or self, or even to the internal subversion of the text, but rather to an acknowledgment of self-enchantment and a turning toward the world in order to reestablish creative power. It often appears, in fact, that romantic poets *sought out* moments of disenchantment as their most fertile *topoi*; but they did this not to display (or even to test) the nothingness of poetry or imagination. On the contrary, we might find it remarkable that from the time of *The Prelude's* composition to *Childe Harold IV,* an accepted, even expected subject of great poetry was the strengthening of the poet's own imagination through crisis, disenchantment, and renewed faith in the mind's power to transform a world recognized as not entirely its own.

We ought not to confuse a rejection of self-enchantment with a rejection of the creative imagination. At the same time, embracing imagination need not mean embracing a mystical final homecoming or an ultimate reconciliation of subject and object. Between the ideal and the real the finite mind remains divided. The goal of imagination is not the static self-identity of an object or the quiet repose of nature; the positive recompense for the mind's self-division is not an edenic state but its own freedom, its endless capacity to create and recreate itself within the world. Disillusionment becomes a precondition of growth, and if we think of moments of great emotion in romantic poetry—Wordsworth's Mount Snowdon ascent in *The Prelude,* Prometheus's self-transformation in *Prometheus Unbound,* or Byron's "curse" of forgiveness in *Childe Harold IV*—we find that although both nature and human history seem to be bound in predictable cycles, the mind retains some core of denial, a freedom to destroy its own self-conceptions and emerge renewed.

We might note, too, that typically it is some "timely utterance" that has the power to transform, words giving form to powerful emotions and enabling them to be discharged. Prometheus must call up the words of his curse in order to dispel it. Language, particularly poetic language, was not for the romantics an evasion of the nothingness of consciousness, insofar as that implies the mind's "estrangement" from the world. Rather, speech more often reflected emotional engagement in the world, in the manner of myth. For Etienne Condillac, Johann von Herder, and Schelling, for example, poetry was the language in which, as Ernst Cassirer has said, "the word not only preserves its original creative power, but is ever renewing it"; far from reflecting the nothingness of consciousness, the poetic word "recovers the fullness of life."[12] Words may indeed seem impotent to recreate a world so fallen (from a romantic perspective) as to be untouched by a human presence; but it is begging the question to assume that romantic language proceeds from the repression of this latent vision of nothingness. Language was also the medium of questioning the human presence in the world, of reinjecting it through a range of personal, cultural, and political transformations.

I have implied that self-transformation and a renewed faith in the power of imagination are the goals of the quest romance in the romantic era. The anxiety I have spoken of at the beginning of the romance might be more profitably understood, then, as the apprehensiveness of mind at the threshold of transformation; that transformation must also involve the continuous resurrection of the real world into a world that is the mind's own. Yet through this transformation, somehow neither the mind nor the world is to lose its integrity. The quest itself, the poem, becomes the vehicle of transformation because through the quest the world becomes *symbolic*, by which I mean that the mundane discloses its *spiritual value* to the mind.

I take this to be the large context of nineteenth-century romance: that the mind seeks to create, on its own terms, a world of evolving spiritual revelation or significance. This is, to use a Kantian term, the *practical* goal of romance. The *theoretical* goal is the continuous self-revelation of mind. To put it another way, the practical goal is the humanizing of the cosmos. From this perspective the world is the stage of the human drama, or the magic forest of romance. The theoretical goal is the overcoming of the mind's estrangement from itself. Here self-consciousness is not stultifying or narcissistic, but rather implies that mind freely determines the conditions of its experience—its experience of the world and, through that world, of itself. To paraphrase Coleridge, the former goal is to make the objective subjective; the latter goal is to make the subjective objective.[13]

In art itself, Coleridge (following Schelling) believed, these two goals harmonize and become two aspects of the same interchange between the creator and the aesthetic object.[14] This was Coleridge's stated ideal in his prose, but it is another question whether this ideal was capable of vitalizing his own imaginative efforts. Other romantic poets sought the unity of practical and theoretical in very different ideals: Shelley, for example, in *Prometheus Unbound* envisages a total interchange between the human and the natural, in which the mind evolves through renovating the cosmos, and in which an increase in knowledge is an increase in the bond of love that underlies all the mind's interactions.

The case of Wordsworth is more complex, since in his long life he experimented with many possible relations of the two impulses of romance, to see nature as humanly meaningful and to bring the mind into harmony with its memories and desires. This is the explicit ideal of "The Prospectus" section of *The Recluse* fragment: "my voice proclaims / How exquisitely the individual Mind . . . to the external World / Is fitted:—and how exquisitely, too— / . . . The external World is fitted to the Mind."[15] Hartman has chronicled Wordsworth's long struggle with the "apocalyptic" imagination, the power that continuously impels man beyond what nature can provide.[16] Wordsworth seeks out a renovated nature on behalf of his own creative imagination, and in that sense the theoretical seeks to subsume the practical. Wordsworth's "anxiety for continuity is too strong for him," Harold Bloom remarks, "and he yields to its strong enchantment . . . the final vision of *The Prelude* is not of a redeemed nature, but of a liberated creativity."[17] In the early days of the romantic revolution, it was William Blake who most clearly understood the implication of this anxiety for continuity: for him there could be no truly liberated creativity without a redeemed nature. Imagination and nature are moments in the life of the man who is the cosmos. Blake proclaims the whole theoretical/practical distinction a "Cloven Fiction" from the start, the anxiety-ridden mind-world dualism an error of fallen vision. Hence the waspish response to Wordsworth's "Prospectus": "You shall not bring me down to believe such fitting & fitted I know better & it Please your Lordship."[18] The world needs only as much renovation as the eye that sees it is fallen: a Last Judgment is available each moment to the imagination willing to identify itself with the body of the world: "The Last Judgment is an Overwhelming of Bad Art & Science. Mental Things are alone Real what is Called Corporeal Nobody Knows its dwelling Place [it] is in Fallacy & its Existence an Imposture" (*Vision of The Last Judgment*, p. 555).

Despite this great variety in romantic approaches to the problems of romance, I believe we can define a unity of theme with some broad historical validity and applicability: to see the two goals of the romantic quest as in some sense ultimately one is the moral mission of romantic humanism. The moral ideal is a world infinitely responsive to a renewed imagination. Yet this humanistic vision approaches this "responsiveness" and this "renewal" in a dialectical way.

For there would be no impulse to renewal, no "progression" in Blake's terms, if it were not the case that, in the finite world, the growth of the mind often takes place at the expense of the real, or, similarly, if often the world did not present itself as an opaque boundary to the mind. Wordsworth had spoken of both poles: the overleaping imagination that meets disappointment at the reality of the Alps in Book VI of *The Prelude* and the encroaching prison-house of the world that (providentially) humanizes the imagination in the "Immortality" ode. The practical goal and the theoretical goal begin to coalesce, as the mind begins to see the world as its own embodiment; practical and theoretical diverge as the world becomes alien, the opaque boundary of mind. But even in this divergence, this disenchantment, the mind recognizes in the world at least the material necessary for its creation of form; no matter how far the world falls it always retains the potential to be taken up again into the human. Even the most passive mind encounters the world in perception, and this very act transforms it: "The eye—it cannot choose but see; / We cannot bid the ear be still."[19]

The finite mind oscillates or "hovers" (the word—*schweben*—is J. G. Fichte's) between the theoretical and the practical, between the world as symbol needing to be understood and the mind as freedom, asserting itself in creation. This oscillation is the dynamic subject of romantic quest; it is the human imagination:

> It is quite true that if there is no sense that the mythological universe is a human creation, man can never get free of servile anxieties and superstitions, never surpass himself, in Nietzsche's phrase. But if there is no sense that it is also something uncreated, something coming from elsewhere, man remains a Narcissus staring at his own reflection, equally unable to surpass himself . . . it is through the maintaining of this struggle, the suspension of belief between the spiritually real and the humanly imaginative, that our own mental evolution grows.[20]

# 2

## The Context of Romantic Subjectivity and Transcendental Idealism: Kant's First Critique

I will argue that we should study the context of German idealism to illuminate the structure of striving and quest in romanticism. But I will not attempt to show that idealism is a doctrine that in itself provides a substitute theology or an implicit agenda for all romantic poetry. Rather, it provides an explicit and dynamic model for the evolution of self-awareness central, in many forms, to romantic long poems. The idealist text proceeds dialectically, searching like so many romantic texts for some satisfactory model of the creative mind's relation to its world.

In their development, the philosophical texts of post-Kantian idealism seek to demonstrate that aspects of the mind's "situation"—temporality, sensation, limitation—are somehow modes of its own activity. Yet in the process it becomes obvious that even to begin this argument depends upon a self-contradiction: the activity of consciousness is apparently inexplicable apart from the mind's awareness of itself *within* its situation. And is not any "model" of mind suspect, being itself the creation of mind? Unlike poetic texts, the philosophic texts confront the inevitable paradoxes and contradictions of their idealism by pushing thought itself a stage higher at each impasse. In fact, the confines of a single text may not provide sufficient closure for a "system" of idealism, the system evolving over an entire career—and so it was that Hegel could accuse Schelling of carrying on his philosophical education in public.

In poetic texts, on the other hand, we do not find systems or attempts at such closure: the romantic poet, begin as he may with certain idealist assumptions, must learn to acknowledge paradoxes and contradictions as he attempts to live his life concretely and to develop as a creative artist. As we shall see, in the second generation of English romantics, the tension between idealist traditions and the actuality of the individual's experience becomes a source for creative probing of what had become dominant cultural assumptions. And yet the goal, as in idealism, remained the expansion of mind into the world along with its simultaneous self-revelation.

Not all romantic poems or poets consistently maintain idealist positions, of course. It is natural to associate contemporary idealism with a poetry so centrally concerned with self-consciousness, but other philosophical, cultural, and theological traditions have long been seen as influences on English romanticism. And though I believe the case has been overstated, other scholars have argued for the determining influence of post-Lockean empiricism and associationism on both aesthetic theory and poetic practice.[1] In responding that the romantic quest is fundamentally idealist I do not mean to deny the contextual importance of other intellectual movements: indeed, idealism itself does not appear in a vacuum and is usually adopted in defense of some moral, political, or theological position. I do wish to argue that an understanding of the structure of idealist argument will lead us to some central principles of any romantic quest whose goal is the evolution within the text of the narrator's self-awareness.

It may be objected that the parallels between any epistemological theory and a work of poetry or a poet's career are always difficult to delineate. I agree, and I think this is true even of the romantic period, when poetry and speculative philosophy seem particularly close: precisely because this was an age of vital and competing paradigms, a poet may have attended to conflicting theories of experience without necessarily perceiving any dissonance. Or it may be that the scholar tries to fit the work to one or another contemporary theory. Perhaps the interpretive problem lies in the abstractness and absoluteness of an older scholarly method. When scholars try to view a particular poem too narrowly within one or another speculative paradigm they may well produce contradictory readings. It is notoriously difficult, for example, to place Wordsworth unambiguously within a single intellectual tradition. Wordsworth's quest is unusually complex because his greatest poems, from 1797 to 1805, can be seen to support a number of epistemological positions, all within the larger secularist framework of the human mind's dependence only on itself in contact with nature in the project of developing a virtuous and harmonious life.

It would be a mistake to identify this secularism, as critics often do, with idealism alone, since a kind of radical meliorism is an element also of other influences on Wordsworth, like John Locke, David Hartley, and William Godwin. The question of transcendental idealism is not only the hope for a harmony between man and nature, but more fundamentally a probing of the mind's ability to know itself as the free and undetermined source of its own experience. From *Tintern Abbey* and *The Prelude I* and *II* to the "Immortality" Ode and *The Prelude XIV* Wordsworth's attitude toward this transcendentalist project is neither uniform nor simple to trace. An historical method that does not begin with a thorough reading of transcendentalist epistemology risks generalizations about Wordsworth's poetry, or ideas abstracted from that poetry, that may seem incomplete or artificial.

I do not, then, join critics like Melvin Rader and M. H. Abrams in proclaiming Wordsworth's thorough affinity with transcendental idealism. Rader, for example, sees Wordsworth as fundamentally an idealist, changing his beliefs at most to modify his early pantheism to "immanent theism" under Coleridge's tutelege. But Rader's discussion of transcendental idealism depends heavily on Coleridge, tending to equate his rejection of Locke and Hartley with Wordsworth's more tentative and slowly developing idealism. Abrams—whose Hegelian analysis of idealism I will discuss in Chapter 4—believes that "Wordsworth's thinking frequently parallels that of his philosophical German contemporaries." This is true, but Abrams's main point of convergence is Wordsworth's belief that "unity with himself and his world is the primal and normative state of man, of which the sign is a fullness of shared life and the condition of joy." Indeed, idealists would maintain this view, but so too would Hartleyan meliorists and a number of eighteenth-century radicals.[2] At issue here is what generalizations we can make about Wordsworth's epistemological positions over his long career. A persuasive argument is made by Alan Grob, who describes a complex evolution from the early radical empiricism and optimism of *Tintern Abbey* and the first books of *The Prelude* to a transcendentalism that, after 1802, increasingly expresses itself in the more traditional language of religious faith and the moral imperative.[3]

I hope in these pages to offer a reading of idealism that will clarify the ways in which analysis of idealist texts may be applied to the study of certain "internalized" quest romances. The romancer's faith is that the evolution of a self through fictions parallels the growth of the self in life—that life, in fact, displays the same plasticity and responsiveness as texts. Wordsworth was deeply attracted to the notion that the autonomous self can determine the conditions of its relations with the world. And yet his poetry displays a curious reluctance about romance. His overt praise of romance in *The Prelude*, Book V, ends with the paen to the "Visionary Power" that "Attends the motions of the viewless winds, / Embodied in the mystery of words" (lines 595–99).[4] But in defining the role of romance Wordsworth implies its own negation. Romance had provided the young boy, confronting the image of the drowned man in Esthwaite, a continuity with a past sense of wonder and natural piety that can elide the horrific vision (lines 426–59). Yet at the same time the purpose of romance is to reenergize a past from which the self is now ruptured. Even the vision of the drowned man is seen not "now" but in a displaced past, more open to romance. Romances "Charm away the wakeful night / In Araby" (lines 496–97). The charm of romance is in nostalgia. Book V broods with the anxiety of loss. Its central episode, the Dream of the Bedouin Arab, prophesies the deluge that will engulf "books" of romance and by metonymy will engulf the young boy's own power of romance.[5]

The Bedouin's search to preserve the energy of romantic quest is maddening. He is the young Wordsworth's dark double, expressing overtly Wordsworth's fear of the loss of the mind's power of wonder but covertly his fear of a regressive attachment to romance:

> I to him have given
> A substance, fancied him a living man,
> A gentle dweller in the desert, crazed
> By love and feeling, and internal thought

Protracted among endless solitudes;
Have shaped him wandering upon this quest!

. . . . . . . . . . . . . . . . . . .
          yea, will I say
Contemplating in soberness the approach
Of an event so dire [the deluge], by signs in earth
Or heaven made manifest, that I could share
That maniac's fond anxiety, and go
Upon like errand. (lines 143–49, 156–61)

Wordsworth's questers are often such lonely wanderers, border figures like the Leech Gatherer, who seem to reflect the poet's anxiety
that the pursuit of romance is destructive to the carefully articulated
continuities of the maturing self. Tilottama Rajan remarks that in
these encounters with border figures, "Wordsworth seems to question and see through his own view of poetry as a unifying commu-
nicative act, and to feel himself thrust back into the privacy, indeed
the irrelevance, of his vision. . . . They represent a certain recalcitrance of the universe of things toward penetration by the light
of imagination: a limit at which poetic representation finds itself ex-
posed and unable to insist on itself as truth."[6]

In the face of this recalcitrance, romance offers—as we shall
see—a continuing excursion into the world, with the poet armed
with the active power of the mind. The question of the activity or
passivity of the mind is, of course, a constant topic in Wordsworth's
poetry. And even in the explicit rejection of romantic fictions in
*Home at Grasmere*, Wordsworth does not turn away from the actively
self-creative mind.[7] But the goal of that activity is not the recreation
of romance but a revision of the world *as it is* into an adequate context for the autonomous self. The goal is, in a word, tranquillity.

          Paradise and groves
Elysian, fortunate (islands) fields like those
In the deep ocean wherefore should they be
A History or but a dream, when minds
Once wedded to this outward frame of things
In love find these the growth of common day. (lines 800–805)

But as Frederick Garber has shown, as romance recedes in *Home at
Grasmere* the world becomes increasingly recalcitrant. Increasingly,
the center of gravity shifts to the active self, and that activity turns

inward to the constitution of its own inviolability: "The self is finally immune to the world's uneasiness, unassailable even when old fictions do not quite mesh with current reality. . . . A consciousness so organized transcends the need for consonance because it is self-consonant, and it is so in such a way that it can never be disturbed by man, his fictions, and his inadequacies."[8]

For Wordsworth the recession of romance introduces a recalcitrant world; the continuity and tranquillity that nature once provided will now be supplied by the self, which constitutes its own world in its commitment to its vocation: "Yet 'tis not to enjoy that we exist, / For that end only; something must be done" (lines 664–65; also see 666–702). But Wordsworth's vocation, particularly as he defines it in *The Prelude*, is the poetic ordering of a visionary excess that works against tranquillity. This tension between vocation and tranquillity produces the anxiety that surfaces in poems like *Resolution and Independence*. The demand for tranquillity is strong in Wordsworth and continues even after nature has receded into a memory, or a model, of equilibrium. Indeed, the famous commitment to vocation that concludes *The Prelude* of 1805 is preceded in the 1799 *Prelude* by a more explicit farewell to nature—or to the "one life" the poet saw in her: "If, mingling with the world, I am content / With my own modest pleasures, and *have* lived with God and Nature communing . . . the gift is yours [Nature's]" (lines 474–78).[9] Nature will provide the model of continuity that enables vocation to mature. But at the same time, that visionary excess at the source of vocation (cf. lines 445–65) is deliberately rejected here.

Wordsworth's youthful vocation had been to reenergize poetry in a secular world transformed to a fit dwelling place by personal vision. As he grew older he needed to find a source of authority for his vocation more public and more traditional than the activity of his own creative powers.[10] For younger poets this was a deeply disappointing turn. Urbane, skeptical, secular, they were struck by the older Wordsworth's pomposity or by the reactionary nostalgia of his quest—troubled though it certainly was—to revise natural experience into a model for mature spiritual tranquillity. Because they knew their debt to Wordsworth they felt all the more betrayed. For Shelley, Wordsworth had raised the idealist issue of the mind's activity in experience only to turn away from a nature become opaque to vision. Shelley took this as an offense, not to nature, but to the power of the mind to embark on a renovation that is not merely self-defensive. His sense of betrayal by Wordsworth and his need to re-vise romantic quest in response to Wordsworth are surely factors in his creation of his own wandering border figure, the Poet of *Alastor*.[11]

Other romantics responded to the opacity of the world by pushing back the borders of vision. The project of the transcendental idealist philosopher is the unfolding, within the idealist text, of a new awareness of the meaning of the spontaneously creative mind, an awareness evoked by the dialectics of the text itself. The mind's capacity for self-revision will be revealed in the evolution of the text. This faith in the transformative power of self-articulation is similar in many ways to the faith of the romancer: even as the ro-mance may become an ongoing questioning of its own fictionality, the mind grows in its power of self-revision. It does so precisely in its assertion of its freedom to be self-determining through the nega-tion and repositing of order. This, in turn, requires an idealist's faith in the plasticity and responsiveness of the world.

Such an ambitious project has its successes and failures, its re-treats, reactions, and reassertions. The purpose of this book is to delineate its contours. In focusing on Coleridge's idealism and on some key "internalized quests" of the second generation, I will ex-plore the ways in which the Wordsworthian theme of the active mind becomes increasingly "transcendentalized": that is, the very mean-ing of a recalcitrant world is tested, as are the meaning, purpose, and direction of the mind's free activity. Further, as the resistance and the activity come to be seen as mutually interdependent, the dangers of a fallen, deromanticized world or a self-defensive isolated mind begin to subside. Finally, I will note that at the very borders of idealism, the world's opacity becomes a saving grace, a source of de-mystification and of the joy of surprise and encounter to a mind se-cure in its own integral powers.

## Introspection, Psychological and Transcendental

I have said that a careful study of transcendental idealism is neces-sary before one can reach conclusions about the idealist structure of any romantic text. In the conflict between empiricist and idealist interpretations of a poet's epistemology, what exactly is meant by "transcendentalism" and "associationism"? Such a study should begin with Kant, both for his intrinsic interest to students of the romantic movement and because the later (and to us even more useful) developments of idealism owe their terms to him.

Kant's inquiry into mental activity was markedly different from the essentially psychological models common in the eighteenth century. Although recent scholarship has disclosed Kant's indebtedness to such psychologists as Tetens and Gerard, Kant's own purposes were not to add new models to the faculty psychology of his day. The aim of the transcendental idealism he initiated was both broader in scope and radically different in its epistemological and metaphysical assumptions.

Explaining this distinction will clarify the often misunderstood romantic reaction to the Lockean tradition of empirical study of the mind's contents ("ideas"). According to this tradition, the objects of our awareness are ideas only, and they are the only possible objects the mind can know. Experience is the aggregate of associations of these ideas, and the laws of these associations follow the relations inherent in nature. The activity of philosophy is to make evident these laws, or natural relations, which are immediately evident to the faculty of mind that judges relations, "Reason."

Until about 1790, some version of this "subjectivist" viewpoint, a development of Cartesian introspection, prevailed as the dominant mode of speaking about mental activity. The philosopher can only reasonably be expected to perform a kind of natural history of the legitimate relations of ideas and to explain under what circumstances these ideas come to be (e.g., sensation, intuition, logic). With only slight differences in method, metaphysics, or temperament, this is the purview of Locke, David Hartley, David Hume, and George Berkeley. As late as 1791, new editions of Hartley's associationist *Observations on Man* (1749) continued to be used as philosophy texts in Britain, and admiration for Hartley persisted far into the romantic era.[12] According to Hartley, "All our internal feelings may be called *ideas*. Some of these spring up in the mind of themselves, some are suggested by words, others arise in other ways. . . . The ideas which resemble sensations, are called *ideas of sensation*: all the rest may therefore be called *intellectual ideas*." Hartley, who is said to have introduced the word "psychology" into English, has in a single sentence epitomized the *subjectivist*, or psychological, view of how conscious experience comes about: "Any sensations, A, B, C, &c. by being associated with one another a sufficient number of times, get such a power over the corresponding ideas a, b, c, &c., that any one of the sensations A, when impressed alone, shall be able to excite in the mind b, c, &c., the ideas of the rest."[13] In other words, the unity of experience is given by the laws of the associations of sensations or ideas, and the mind is the aggregate of associated sensations in the nervous system and their corresponding associated, interlocking intellectual ideas.

Philosophers disagreed about the source of sensations: according to Locke, they are materials impinging upon the nervous system; for Berkeley the source is mental, a Divine Mind; for Hume the sources are impossible for the mind (confined as it is to *ideas*) to discover. But consciousness itself is no mystery. The mind's contents are ideas, and these ideas, on the analogy of a visual image, are always immediately available to introspection.

It is quite otherwise for Kant. To the subjectivist, there are "objective" sensations, a series $s_1, s_2, s_3, \ldots$ , and subjective ideas $i_1, i_2, i_3$, related through some mechanism, $R$. But the question is, for whom is this objective/subjective series evident? The mind observes the ideal series, but how does it become aware of this series? And if the awareness is something distinct from the series of ideas, or images, can the philosopher say he has explained "mind" if he has explained only the images and their association? Further, how can he know what role the mind might have in *forming* the images if he is aware of only the images themselves? If the mind only passively receives impressions, it remains a mystery how the philosopher was able to create the larger idea of himself as passive. How can the mind have become aware of the relation $R$, and of itself as an "internal" series observing "external" facts? Finally, how can the philosopher understand the role that the "objective" world might have in forming the ideas: if we are aware of only images, how can we know that they image anything real at all?

In other words, the subjectivist's psychological method must either ignore or beg the question of how awareness of either the "real" series $s_1, s_2, s_3 \ldots$ , or the ideal series, $i_1, i_2, i_3,$ becomes possible to begin with. Robert Adamson, in his introduction to Fichte's transcendental idealism, has summarized this turning point in philosophy:

> English philosophy thus starts with a definite conception of the nature and limits of speculative inquiry. Experience, inner and outer, is equally matter for scientific treatment. . . . It is not putting the matter too strongly to say that the categorical rejection of this psychological method is the very essence of the critical (Kantian) philosophy, the keynote of the critical spirit in speculation. . . . The psychological method has simply thrown out of account or neglected the fundamental fact, that of self-consciousness. . . . The speculative method proposes, by an analysis of self-consciousness and of the conditions under which it is possible, to clear up the significance for the conscious subject himself of these important differences [between the real and ideal series] which characterize his experience.[14]

In transcendental idealism, the mind is no longer immediately explainable to itself through images or ideas. For Kant, philosophy must explore the extremely complex relations between both subjective and objective experience and the unitary consciousness for which these experiences appear. The *transcendental* questions are these: How does the mind come to think of itself as aware of objects, and how can the philosopher elaborate the conditions through which objects become objects for us? These conditions are a priori principles that are "transcendental" in the sense that they are "outside" our knowledge of objects, underlying that knowledge. Yet these conditions can be found only within us. In other words, the philosopher seeks the *meaning* of consciousness from within consciousness itself. The reflexive nature of this task is, as we shall see, one reason that the philosophical text becomes an unfolding activity of progressive self-questioning. In Norman Kemp Smith's summary, "Kant is led to the conclusion that consciousness must be regarded as an activity, and as determining certain of the conditions of its own possibility."[15]

Consciousness of nature, with its laws and regularities, is intimately bound up with our awareness of ourselves as conscious. Yet Kant teaches that the ultimate nature of self-consciousness is completely beyond our knowing—it is "transcendent," not "transcendental." Unlike Fichte and later idealist philosophers, Kant believed that we cannot say whether the mind itself is *wholly* responsible for

all its knowledge. Some conditions of knowledge lie outside or beyond our knowing. Although Kant believes that logically we must
begin to know the world through self-consciousness, this does not
mean that self-consciousness itself is actually an ultimate condition
of all things. Any transcendent conditions of awareness *precede* self-
consciousness just as they precede objective experience, and these
conditions, Kant taught, can never be known cognitively. Kant believed that we do know that these unknowable conditions operate on
us in some sense, but he wished to preserve their independence from
the laws of knowledge. In fact, because these conditions *underlie*
knowledge, they are free from its laws, and so Kant hoped to preserve the radical freedom of man's mental and moral life. The problem of the exact nature of self-consciousness in Kant's system has
been called, by Gottfried Martin, "one of the most difficult problems in the interpretation of Kant." He goes on to emphasize, however, that Kant believed consciousness a free, spontaneous activity;
for this very reason its ultimate, real nature can never be known:
"Precisely because the knowing subject is spontaneous in its own
being, it cannot know itself in this specific being. Pure spontaneity
cannot know itself as spontaneity. If it knows itself, it is no longer
something spontaneous but something known." [16]

Kant's transcendentalist response to subjectivism impelled European thinkers toward new systems, symbolic revelations of thought
itself. The Kantian effort to delineate the logical ground of any possible consciousness spurred the development of a thoroughgoing
transcendentalism, particularly in Germany. This *transcendental idealism*, represented most notably by J. G. Fichte and F. W. J. Schelling,
proceeded along very different lines from the Kantian program—
despite the frequent protests from idealists that they were "completing" Kant's work—but the systematic analysis of self-conscious
awareness became the philosopher's quest for meaning. If the mind
cannot know its deepest nature directly or immediately, and if ideas
are not the mind itself but its products, then self-awareness can only
be a process of continuously relating the products of mind to their
hidden sources.

The romantic poets stood in the midst of this new cultural stream,
which was to swell to a major tributary of nineteenth-century art
and philosophy. For we should remember that the nineteenth was
the century that sought the appropriate language whose symbols

could reflect the relation of mind reflecting upon itself. The history of philosophy records here the growing estrangement between empirical psychology, which continued to think of mind as immediately known relations of ideas, and the transcendental philosophy, which sought the ground, or meaning, of consciousness as an active principle of self-awareness.[17]

The former tradition saw mind as somehow determined by nature, or natural law; the latter tradition saw mind struggling to *create* a nature of human meaning through art, the moral law, or the spiritual evolution of human history. The psychological tradition is familiar to us in the work of Hartley, James Mill, Alexander Bain, and William James. Aside from Fichte and Schelling, the "transcendentalists" best known to English readers are Thomas De Quincey, Thomas Carlyle, Ralph Waldo Emerson, and the idealists J. H. Stirling, T. H. Green, and F. H. Bradley. Less familiar is a group of thinkers who developed psychologies based on unconscious "drives," variously mental or natural or a mystical identity of the two: most notable, especially for his influence on Freud, was Goethe's friend C. G. Carus, whose great work *Psyche* (1846) was perhaps the first psychological text to identify mind and nature specifically through natural unconscious drives that, when conscious, we call "sexuality."[18] Thinking along similar lines were psychologists such as Maine de Biran and Eduard von Hartmann, who based consciousness on a world-principle of unconscious will, striving through human awareness to unfold itself.[19]

Common to these idealists is the doctrine that nature acquires its identity, becomes what it is, through the presence of human awareness. The origin of this doctrine was Kant's conclusion that nature in what he believed was its most primordial form, spatiotemporal relations, is a product of mental activity. However we may today judge Kant's drawing conclusions about nature's being from such rarefied and scientific abstractions as "space" or "time," we cannot deny the revolutionary impact of his argument on a culture bent on testing the true scope of the mind's power.

## The Human Mind in Space and Time: Spontaneity, Receptivity, and the Background of Kant's Idealism

Coleridge, who was apt to parade his more arcane insights before his presumably bewildered friends, announced a triumph to Thomas Poole early in 1801: "If I do not deceive myself, I have not only *completely extricated the notions of Time and Space*, but have overthrown the doctrine of Association, as taught by Hartley, and with it all the irreligious metaphysic of modern Infidels—especially, the doctrine of Necessity."[20] It is even now a point of contention exactly what Coleridge meant by his italicized words: A. O. Lovejoy, for instance, propounded the view, in a closely reasoned article, that Coleridge meant he had extricated time from spatiality, that he came to the Bergson-like conclusion that time as inner intuition was not a spatial series of moments but rather a nonextended "moment" somehow transcending serial time.[21]

This is a possible reading, based on later remarks in the *Biographia*, but it is not clear how this interpretation is related to the Kantian doctrine Coleridge told Poole he had been "attentively perusing" in 1801. According to this doctrine, time and space are appearances, not transcendently real entities, and their "extrication" means that spatiotemporal phenomena do not, as in Locke and Hartley, determine the mind and its judgments, but are themselves forms of human sensuous intuition ("sensibility"). Space and time are the conditions of sensibility itself, and the sensibility supplies the Understanding with sensory material in the form necessary for Understanding to operate upon it and organize the natural relations we know. In other words, the mind supplies to itself the phenomenal order of space and time. Phenomena, or appearances, are not real in themselves and do not determine mental activity. Phenomena appear to us in forms determined by our mental organization. Lovejoy summarizes the importance of Coleridge's discovery of Kant, as reported in his famous letter:

> It is, then, probable that it was the Kantian exclusion of space and time from the real, or non-phenomenal, world, that was the logical instrument of Coleridge's final and complete conversion from necessitarianism; and it is . . . certain that in his published writings, it was this that

provided the usual philosophical basis of his own doctrine of freedom
and of his most cherished religious & moral convictions.[22]

Coleridge had been reading Leibniz as well, and indeed Kant's
arguments about the ideality of space and time can be traced to the
lively debate early in the eighteenth century between Sir Isaac Newton, his spokesman Samuel Clarke, and Leibniz over the foundations
of a mathematical physics. It has been said that "the Kantian philosophy is in intention and in achievement a fundamental discussion
with Leibniz"; and, more to the point here, Thomas McFarland has
stressed the importance of seeing Leibniz as the true fountainhead of
the crucial romantic responses to the Enlightenment.[23] The issue,
most broadly, was not simply the rather dry speculations, so scho-
lastic sounding to us, over whether space was an attribute of God or
a substance; what was at stake was the choice of very critical metaphors for the relation between the ordering mind and the order of
the natural world. Both Coleridge and Blake, however disparate
their temperaments, metaphysics, and theology, recognized here a
vital and exciting challenge, and for both, Newton and Locke were
the bêtes noires of a debilitating, unhumanistic, indeed loathsome
world-view. To see the transcendentalist view of nature in its fullest
relevance to romantic concepts of mind, we must, then, glance
briefly at the interesting and suggestive discussion about the natural
world into which Kant stepped as systemizer, logician, and moralist—the discussion between Leibniz and the English philosophers.

What is surprising, given the vehemence of the romantic response to Locke and Newton, is how really vapid the English speculative tradition had been. Locke, for example, does not venture a
true definition of space, or what it means to be able to perceive spatially. Instead, he offers only the *psychological* observation that our
idea of space is abstracted from our being able to touch extended
objects; conceiving of a body in motion, we are able to imagine that
the "place it deserted gives us the *idea* of pure space without solidity,
whereunto another body may enter without either resistance or pro-
trusion of anything." But the philosophical issue, it would seem, in-
volves how we are able to understand *place, solidity,* and *extension* in the
first place. Locke becomes petulant about such metaphysical issues:
"If anyone asks me *what this solidity* is, I send him to his senses to
inform him. Let him put a flint or a football between his hands and

then endeavor to join them, and he will know."[24] Locke similarly refuses to explain *"what* this *space* I speak of is," since space is an idea
abstracted from our sensation of extended bodies.[25] The experience
of extension is taken as a primitive *datum.* Yet it is clear that Locke
does *not* mean that space is ideal in itself; extension is a primary
quality of real bodies, and so presumably absolute space is a physical
reality. The nature of Locke and Newton is a grid of fixed contours
independent of the observing mind. Locke was apparently persuaded by the Newtonian view, which required a static, absolute
space, to provide a reference grid to distinguish one mass-point from
another and make possible the mathematical description of motion.[26]

What is interesting for our purposes is Newton's metaphor, his
image, of the absolute. "Absolute space," said Newton, "in its own
Nature *without relation* to anything external, remains always similar
and immovable."[27] The absolute is external to the mind, is static, is
material, and determines physical change. Indeed, Newton had
come close to identifying absolute space with infinite substance and
so to identifying absolute space with God. Bishop Berkeley was
among the first to attack the dangerous identification and even attempted to dispute Newton's examples of circular motion to argue
that "if we sound our own conceptions, I believe we may find all the
absolute motion we can frame an idea of to be at bottom no other
than relative motion thus defined."[28] Three years after this attack,
Newton prepared a second edition of his *Principia* (1713), adding a
"General Scholium to Book III" in which he attempts to clarify: absolute space is not a substance, but an attribute of the infinite, all-
present God.[29]

The response to Newton that is most important for establishing
Kant's view of space, however, is that of Leibniz. "We deceive ourselves in wishing to imagine an absolute space," he said; "the idea of
the *absolute* is in us internally, like that of being."[30] Leibniz had several philosophical motives for combating the Newtonian view of
space, a combat waged in a famous exchange of letters with Newton's
pupil, Samuel Clarke, in 1715–16. He objected to Newton's doctrine of atoms and void, of motion in absolute space, because for
Newton an object becomes an *individual* only because of its unique
position in space; in other respects atoms are indiscernible. This
theory violates Leibniz's metaphysical principle of the Identity of In-
discernibles, as well as, by its arbitrariness, the principle that God

must act with Sufficient Reason in ordering the universe.[31] For Leibniz, space was an ordering of *relations*, and as such space—and time—were not real. Only the monads are real entities, and the relations between them are not real but mental. Leibniz wields a powerful metaphor in the course of his argument—the analogy of spatial relations to a genealogical table (and also to mathematical ratio), which no one would think to reify:

> I have demonstrated that *space* is nothing else but an *order* of the existence of things . . . *space* in itself is an *ideal* thing, like *time*. . . . In order to have an idea, of *place*, and consequently of space, it is sufficient to consider these relations [of situated objects], and the rule of their changes, without needing to fancy any absolute reality outside the things whose situation we consider. . . . [Space] can only be an ideal thing; containing a certain *order*, wherein the mind conceives the application of relations. In like manner, as the mind can fancy to itself an *order* made up of *genealogical lines*, whose bigness would consist only in the number of generations. . . . And yet those genealogical *places*, *lines*, and *spaces*, though they should express real truths, would only be ideal things.[32]

As Gottfried Martin summarizes, "[Space and time] are not things but representations, and do not have real existence but ideal existence." Yet, although ideal, space and time are nevertheless objective for Leibniz, not subjective, since their objective existence "is expressed by saying that the thinking for which space and time, taken as relations, are representations, is God's thinking."[33]

The next development of the argument was by Kant, for whom space is an appearance to *human* thought: "Space is nothing but the form of all appearances of outer space. . . . It is, therefore, solely from the human standpoint that we can speak of space, of extended things, etc." (A26 = B42).[34] The absolute can no longer be thought of as simply "out there," since in Kant's analysis the concept of externality is itself provided by the mind as an a priori condition for determining objects (see A47–49 = B64–66, A267 = B323). Indeed, the thrust of Kant's mature philosophy was to make impossible the subsuming of the absolute under any concept; rather, the absolute is realized only as a *task* of Practical Reason, as the infinite freedom to actualize the ideal Kingdom of Ends. The absolute in Kant's later thinking is seen not as a fixed and external being but rather as a demand that sets in motion new relations between the mind and the world. In the first *Critique*, though, the problem of space as human

intuition develops into a discussion of the *finitude* of human knowledge—in what sense, Kant asks, can the mind be said to create its
world "spontaneously"; in what sense does the very concept of an
objective world limit and determine that spontaneity?

I take this to be, historically, the single most important point for
understanding the dialogue between Kant and later idealism, as well
as for unraveling some of the immense confusion over Kant's relationship to later romantic themes. It is not the case, for example,
that Kant's "Copernican Revolution" in philosophy implies that the
mind creates the world; it creates only the conditions (space, time,
the categories) for reconstructing on its own terms what is given by
the senses. Two important implications of this reasoning developed,
contrapuntally, into the major concerns of transcendental idealism.
On one hand, the mind is no longer a passive recipient of the given,
but actively constructs what it beholds. This was a crucial discovery
for Coleridge, who wrote to Poole later in March 1801:

> Newton was a mere materialist—*Mind* in his system is always passive—
> a lazy Looker-on on an external world. If the mind be not *passive*, if it be
> indeed made in God's Image, & that too in the sublimest sense—the Im-
> age of the *Creator*—there is ground for suspicion, that any system built
> on the passiveness of the mind must be false, as a system.[35]

On the other hand, the mind must also be thought of as in some
sense passive. As Martin Heidegger emphasized regarding the demands of Kant's metaphysics, "Finite intuition of the essent [the
thing] is not able by itself to give itself an object."[36] And in his own
annotations to his copy of the *Critique*, Coleridge wonders if the
mind constitutes objects in pure spontaneity how it consistently applies this category to this object: what accounts for the sense of a
given order in experience?

> The perpetual and unmoving cloud of Darkness that hangs over this
> work to my "mind's eye" is the absence of any clear account of—Was ist
> Erfahrung [experience]? What do you mean by a *fact*, an empiric real-
> ity, which alone can give solidity (*inhalt*) to our Conceptions? . . .
> I apply the categoric forms to a Tree—Well! *What* is this Tree? How
> do I come by this Tree? Fichte I understand very well—only I cannot
> believe his system. But Kant I do not understand.[37]

Coleridge certainly came to understand Kant well, as his later *Logic*
manuscript shows. He would come to see that Kant does not mean

to answer "what" the tree is; Kant asserts only that the tree's identity for us is organized and determined by the mind. I do not "apply" categories to a tree, but to the intuition that I will construct into a tree. Yet Coleridge's larger question, the meaning of the *givenness* of experience, would remain a persistent difficulty for idealism.

Precisely because human knowledge is finite, it depends upon intuition to "give" it the matter it forms into objects. And because intuition—the forms of space and time—creates for us the phenomenal world, the object that reveals itself cannot reveal itself to us as it would be to a pure intellect, an intellect that knows through intelligence alone, apart from space and time. Such an intellect would be aware of a wholly "intelligible" world, or (using the Greek form) a "noumenal" world. Human intuition does create objects, phenomena, but it does not create the noumenal beings-in-themselves, which we know only mediately, on our own terms. A divine understanding alone can intuit things as they are in themselves, because such an infinitely spontaneous mind would create things in the act of knowing them, not merely create conditions for constructing objects from the manifold of sense (see B145). Sensibility is receptivity: it provides the matter of experience. Intellect is spontaneity: it constructs the formal conditions of experience. The contours of the relationship between mind and world can no longer be clearly defined; but for Kant, philosophy must attempt to obtain clear answers to a new question, "What is the relationship between receptivity and spontaneity in the activity of human awareness?"

## The Ideality of Space and the Finitude of Human Knowledge in Kant's Transcendental Aesthetic

We know that, despite his enthusiasm for Kant's Copernican Revolution, Coleridge considered the dualism of receptivity and spontaneity as central to the plan of the first *Critique*, yet very puzzling. In his marginal notes to the *Critique*, he finds it hard to believe that Kant "in his own conception confined the whole plastic power to the forms of the intellect, leaving for the external cause, for the materials of our sensations, a matter without form. . . . [Kant's] is clearly not the system of Receptivity, like that of Epicurus and Hartley, it is not the system of innate Aptitudes or preformation, or any form of pre-established Harmony, and so on."[38] Exactly what Kant's system was, and how he dealt with this radical dualism in the human mind, eluded Coleridge, at least at the time he wrote these annotations.

By so dividing mind into receptive and spontaneous aspects, and insisting that such forms of a priori knowledge as geometry and physics have to do only with human intuition, not things-in-themselves, Kant broke consciously and decisively with Leibnizian rationalism, in which sensibility does not receive anything from "without" but is rather a confused form of mental activity. For Leibniz, the real nature of all Being is mental; for Kant, its real nature cannot be known: "The philosophy of Leibniz and Wolff, in thus treating the difference between the sensible and the intelligible as merely logical, has given a completely wrong direction to all investigations into the nature and origin of our knowledge. . . . It is not that by our sensibility we cannot know the nature of things in themselves in any save a confused fashion; we do not apprehend them in any fashion whatsoever" (A44 = B61). What man *can* know, and know with apodictic certainty, is the contribution of a priori forms given by his own mind. As early as the 1770 *Inaugural Dissertation on the Form and Principles of the Sensible and Intelligible World*, Kant saw the need to distinguish sensibility as the passive aspect of knowledge and space and time as the forms of sensible intuition necessary for all human knowing.[39] The activity of our intellect is wholly dependent upon the forms. The task of the *Critique of Pure Reason* is to determine how far this split between the receiving mind and the creating mind limits what we can know; the task of the three *Critiques* as a whole is to seek some principle of *unity* that will enable us, despite our intellectual limitations, to judge and to act.

Kant carries the key distinctions of the *Dissertation* into the *Critique of Pure Reason*, placing them at the opening of the "Transcendental Aesthetic" and the "Transcendental Logic," corresponding to the "two stems of human knowledge, namely *sensibility* and *understanding*, which perhaps spring from a common, but to us unknown, root" (A15 = B29). Again, by "transcendental" Kant means an inquiry into the principles a priori by which we are able to know objects; by "aesthetic" Kant refers to the root αἰσθητὰ "having to do with sense-experience." Hence a "Transcendental Aesthetic" is an inquiry into the a priori conditions of sense-experience. He begins with these definitions:

> In whatever manner and by whatever means a mode of knowledge may relate to objects, *intuition* is that through which it is in immediate relation to them, and to which all thought as a means is directed. But intuition takes place only insofar as the object is given to us. This again is only possible, to man at least, insofar as the mind is affected in a certain way. The capacity (receptivity) for receiving representations through the mode in which we are affected by objects, is entitled *sensibility*. Objects are given to us by means of sensibility, and it alone yields us *intuitions*; they are *thought* through the understanding, and from the understanding arise concepts. (A19 = B33)

The finitude of human knowlege requires thought to work upon intuition before we can have knowledge of beings. That aspect of sensible intuition which is only receptive and supplies us the empirical matter of appearances Kant terms "sensation." But he argues that that which enables sensations to be ordered in a particular form "cannot itself be sensation"; this pure form of all possible sensibility Kant calls "pure intuition." How can we arrive at this pure intuition? It would be possible to remove from a body such empirical sensations as color, size, and hardness, but it is not possible to imagine an object not in space or time. The mind itself can imagine, say, that a blue book is painted brown, or that my paperbound books will in the course of time become yellow; but the mind cannot construct for itself a nonspatial book. Though I can think of space without objects, the very notion of an object's presence seems to entail presence-in, or spatiality. Further, I cannot think of myself *thinking* the outer object and that thinking not taking place in a moment of time.[40] Space, then, Kant identifies as the pure form of outer sense, time as the pure form of inner sense.

Kant's procedure here was subjected to vigorous criticism by Fichte: can we, by thought alone, arrive at the "given," the sensory manifold that must be given apart from time and space? There is legitimate reason to question Kant's method, and indeed he does not attempt to prove either that sensations themselves cannot have spatial attributes or that we can in fact imagine space abstracted from sensation.[41] Yet Kant insisted that his system rested on a real distinction between matter, which is a posteriori and given in sensation, and form, which is a priori and lies within us. We do not, he maintained, "think" the manifold of sense-data; but we must posit it as necessary to explain the givenness of phenomena. We do not have any a priori knowledge of sensations because they do not originate with us; we do have a priori knowledge of space, however, in the apodictic necessity of geometry.

This is one of Kant's major arguments for the subjective, a priori character of space. For it is not logically contradictory to think that, for example (given the Euclidean space of our perceptual experience), two straight lines can enclose a figure: given only a knowledge of "two" and "straight line" we could not arrive at any conclusion about the possibility of enclosing a figure. Yet with apodictic certainty we say that two lines will not bound a plane figure. Similarly, no amount of experience will teach us that space necessarily has three dimensions (see B45). We can explain the necessity of geometric propositions only if these are a priori formal conditions of space. They could not be certain if we built them empirically from experience; they are certain only because they originate in us.[42]

Space is thus an a priori condition for apprehending objects as "outside" of us. There could be no intuition of objects as "outside" us if we did not already have within us the transcendental (a priori) capacity to intuit spatially. Space (and time) are not themselves "outside" us, not objective; they are transcendental idealities which enable us to synthesize a given manifold under the outer and inner forms of human intuition. The primordial forms of nature, for Kant, originate with us.

But this does *not* mean that space and time are illusions (*Schein*). They are necessarily involved in all empirical presentation and are *real* in the sense that all objects as we perceive them ("appearances," *Erscheinungen*) must appear to any human awareness under the forms of space and time. Space and time are thus "empirically real" but "transcendentally ideal." They are real in the sense that they must always apply to objects, that is, in their *applicability*; they are ideal and subjective with respect to their *origin* in us, not in the world as it is in itself. Space and time are subjective just as sensations of color, taste, and the like, but differ in an important way: they are a priori necessary conditions of our subjective awareness.

Kant would seem, then, to accept the Lockean distinction between primary and secondary qualities, but like Berkeley he sees primary qualities as originating in the subject, not in the thing itself. Unlike Berkeley he refuses to conflate primary and secondary qualities so that all appearances are subjective states, or ideas. The secondary qualities—color, taste—are the result of a certain state of receptivity, a certain particular and unknown interaction between a being and an individual sensibility. But primary qualities—space and time, for Kant—are universal and necessary modes of synthesizing objects from the given manifold. Hence it is possible to give mathematical descriptions of a coherent reality that will be true and valid for any human consciousness (B69–71).[43] The doctrine of the transcendental ideality of space and time thus represents a significant response to the British Empirical tradition: space and time, though ideal, cannot be thought of as "built up" by the mind from the original empirical ideas of "alongside" or "consecutive." Instead, they are the formal conditions a priori for our intuitions of "outside" and "inside."

Kant has thus placed the activity of the mind prior to our awareness of the internal and external. For "internal" and "external," the dynamic and logical terms "receptivity" and "spontaneity" become base images in a new mental topology. Truth, or certainty, can no longer be thought of as a correspondence between mental image within and world without. Truth will emerge from a study of the a priori conditions through which the mind synthesizes its objects. Because of the finitude of our knowledge we cannot know things as they would be to an intelligence that created the *being* of a thing simultaneously with its knowledge (representation) of it. Our knowledge comes, rather, from a series of synthetic relations through which we construct a unified object from what is given us in sensibility. We can attain a scientific certainty about these relations, but the creative spontaneity of the intellect has a less comforting aspect in Kant. The unity which the mind constructs is synthesized from the manifold as we receive it. It is built, as Heinz Heimsoeth reminds us, only from those aspects of beings ("substances" in the old metaphysical language) which are directed at us, which are in relation to us (the "accidents").[44] In finite knowing, then, we do create a world, but we also have created a unity removed from the original unity of being itself.

In the next section of the *Critique*, "The Transcendental Logic," Kant addresses both the positive and the negative aspects of the mind's created syntheses. In the first case, he explores the faculty of thinking which unites intuitions in the higher synthesis of concepts, that is, the *Understanding*. In the second case, he will identify the "higher" faculty of *Reason* as a mode of thinking which illegitimately attempts to apply the highest unities of concepts—God, the Universe as a Whole, the nature of the Immortal Soul—to the unity of beings in themselves. We are prohibited from knowledge of this real unity by the finitude of the human mind.

# 3

## Nature, Imagination, and Self-Consciousness: Kant's Transcendental Deduction

The mind reaches after higher unities than the mere forms of space and time provide. Perception produces only a representation of the spatiotemporal object; the object of the higher synthesis of Understanding is the interconnected system of *nature*. Nature, for Kant and for idealism generally, meant not only the empirical or historical environment of man, but more "the synthetic unity of the manifold according to rule," or the conformity of appearances to law (A127). No matter how "absurd and exaggerated it may sound," Kant further insists that these laws of nature are laws of the human mind. The initial justification for this result is similar to that of the "Aesthetic": objects appear to us under certain formal necessities—for example, those of substance and accident, or cause and effect—and if we ask how we could arrive at a priori *knowledge* of that necessity we must conclude that our empirical experience of nature could never itself be the source of our feeling of a priori conformity to law. Just as this reasoning had led Kant in the "Aesthetic" to affirm the subjectivity of space and time, so here he is led inexorably to the famous conclusion, "the order and regularity in the appearances, which we entitle *nature*, we ourselves introduce. We could never find them in appearances, had not we ourselves, or the nature of our mind, originally set them there" (A125).

It might seem, then, that in this most intimate creative relation of mind and nature, Kant revokes the finitude of the mind in cognition. To see that this is not in fact unambiguously true, we must examine the rather technical section of the *Critique* that holds Kant's conclusions about mind and nature. Although the following discussion will be at times far removed from the particular philosophical and cultural terms of romanticism, we must bear in mind that idealist philosophy grapples in its own ways with terms first introduced in the architectonic mazes of the *Critique of Pure Reason*. The central romantic issue I will examine is the spontaneity of mind in relation to nature, and a useful (as well as historically influential) vocabulary may be found in those faculties that were introduced by Kant in his exploration of the creative Understanding. We must clarify the technical relations among Kant's key terms in his deduction: the Understanding, or system of a priori concepts which gives us knowledge of nature; apperception, or the self-consciousness that is the condition for any consciousness at all; and imagination, or the synthesizing power that creates objects out of sensible intuition according to the categories of the Understanding.

Kant asks not only how the imagination synthesizes objects, but how we can become *aware* of objects as constituting a uniform nature? The imagination, that is, we understand as the spontaneous creator of images; but we do not identify the image or representation with the object, nor can we ascribe that a priori necessity of natural law to image-making alone. If in fact we create the regularity of nature, from where does the feeling of necessity arise?

Kant is here responding to Hume, for whom all "ideas" are only subjective images, and judgments about nature are matters of habit and feeling. But Kant replies that Hume's skepticism about natural law robs judgment of its essential feature: it claims to be true for all consciousness. There is a decided difference between the belief "that sound makes me think of rain" and "that sound is caused by the movement of air." For Kant, no order of nature could emerge from empirical association within the empirical ego. The order of nature must arise from a synthesis taking place in advance of the empirical ego, that is, at the transcendental level which conditions the empirical ego and makes judgments valid for all consciousness. Here Kant stands at the source of one crucial and characteristic goal of later romantic speculation: to see the organization of mind and the organization of nature as aspects of an organic continuity, such that the mind discovers aspects of its own order in pursuing relations within the world of its experience (see below, Chapter 5).

Further, Kant sees more clearly than Hume that the necessity of judgments about nature is required for us to have any unified consciousness at all. We could not become aware of ourselves as single consciousnesses unless our loose and separate experiences had the uniformity of law: "No fixed and abiding self can present itself in this flux of inner appearance. Such consciousness is usually named *inner sense*, or empirical *apperception. . . .* But there can be in us no modes of knowledge, no connection or unity of one mode of knowledge with another, without that unity of consciousness which precedes all data of intuitions, and by relation to which representation of objects is alone possible. This pure original unchangeable consciousness I shall name *transcendental* apperception" (A107). Kant thus finds the question, "how do I become conscious of a lawful nature?" bound up with the question, "how do I become conscious of myself *as* conscious?" Indeed, our knowledge of nature and our awareness of ourselves mutually imply each other.[1] What is the role that knowledge, or judgment, plays in the generation of unified, lawful experience?

## A Model of Mind: Transcendental Logic

Kant's task is to explain how appearances are unified in the object. In general, he will show that appearances appear as objects through the application of pure concepts of the Understanding (see A85–92). How does the Understanding produce knowledge through concepts? A "concept" is a representation of the unity that comprehends the many, a general abstraction from given perceptions. "Judgment" is knowledge arrived at through a comparison and unification of concepts, a kind of representation of representation, as "this object is a red object," or "ghosts must be invisible objects." In Kant's words, "all judgments are functions of unity among our representations; instead of an immediate representation, a *higher* representation, which comprises the immediate representation and various others, is used in knowing the object, and thereby much knowledge is collected into one" (A69 = B94). Traditional logic describes judgments as they operate in abstraction from all contents, assuming contents to be simply given. Kant introduces a *transcendental* logic, which, rather than describing only the operations of the Understanding on given objects, will seek to discover how the Understanding itself constitutes those objects as objects. Traditional logic is concerned only with the Understanding's operation in itself, abstracted from any relation to objects; transcendental logic asks how the Understanding can make a priori judgments about objects within the synthetic unity of nature.[2]

Kant believed that both kinds of logic arose from a single function of judgment and that the forms of traditional analytic logic would provide the clue to revealing exhaustively the a priori forms of any synthetic judgments, most simply called "the categories." Thus, to the twelve categories of traditional logic correspond twelve categories of Understanding. For example, to the Universal judgment of analytic logic ("All men are mortal"), the corresponding category of synthetical judgment is Unity; to the Particular ("Some men are mortal"), the category of Plurality; to the Singular ("Socrates is mortal"), Totality. Similar correspondences complete the Table of Judgments (A80 = B106).

Few commentators today would accept this artificial architectonic of a synthetic logic. As A. C. Ewing makes clear, Kant relies upon at least three unquestioned premises in his Table of Categories: first, that Aristotelian logic exhausts all the forms of judgment; second, that his categories of Understanding are somehow deduced with logical certainty from the Table of Judgments; and third, that in some way *the same kind* of systematic process involved in making the formal judgments of analytic logic operates in the synthetic thinking that produces nature and the unities of natural law.[3]

The importance of Ewing's last point leads us to consider a key tension in Kant's Transcendental Analytic, that between the topology of the mind and the dynamic functions of mental activity.[4] How can Kant know that the map, or Table, of formal categories adequately represents the spontaneous creative function of Understanding? The empiricism and faculty psychology of the eighteenth century certainly encouraged "mappings" of the mind, models of systematic images representing the law-governed faculties of representation themselves. The governing metaphor here is the visual image: the mind seems to reflect "given" objects like a mirror or *camera obscura*— why not represent the mind's activities *to itself* through images? Locke, indeed, used the word "idea" in its root sense ('ιδεῖν, "to see") to refer equally to images of objects, sensations, and internal activities of the mind (doubting, willing, reasoning), as well as to the activity of understanding reflecting upon itself—an enthusiasm for a metaphor which can be said to have caused nearly endless confusion for three generations of philosophical discourse in English. The mapping of mind in the eighteenth century combines this fascination with static pictorial form with the traditional Aristotelian mental metaphor, mind as logical process. (Note the English "mapping" of Kant in the 1812 *Encyclopedia Londiniensis*.) Finally, in Hartley, to this systematic mapping is superadded the system of natural biological organization (the doctrine of cerebral "vibrations").

But with Kant, this tendency reaches a breaking point: the mind creates the objects it images, and the search is to reveal not *more* images but the source of the mind's capacity to form images in the first place. For we are no longer merely passive reflectors and cannot rest on the glib assumption that mind mirrors objects; to direct ourselves to the mind's imaging power now is critical, for it will reveal to us clues to the creation of the orderly nature we once assumed was merely mirrored by mind. This faculty, or process, will resist any easy representation in a rigidly schematic picture of the mind. Hence, alongside Kant's architectonic is a *transcendental activity of synthesis*, which operates outside of consciousness to produce the object. It is *not* the Understanding's categories, derived from judgment, that produce the object in time and space; it is rather the activity of imagination. Kant's imagination does not synthesize mere airy nothings, but rather engages in the production of actual experience (a result, we will find, reached by many pathways in romantic thought; see, for example, below, Chapter 9).

Kant did recognize the difficulties explicitly raised by Ewing's third objection (see A78 = B103). How, indeed, can the synthetic categories of a priori natural law be derived from the categories of analytic logic if these are not aspects of a single faculty—judgment—

# SENSE.

A Receptivity or *Passive Faculty,*
*divided into two parts.*

Internal Sense
*receives a*
Variety
*in succession.*

External Sense
*receives a*
Variety
*which coexists.*

# UNDERSTANDING.

A Spontaneity or *Active Faculty,*
*which produces* Form or Unity *by connecting* Time and Space *according to*
*the* CATEGORIES *of*

Quantity.　　　　Quality.　　　　Relation.　　　　Modality.

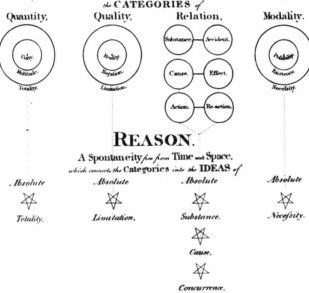

# REASON.

A Spontaneity *free from* Time and Space,
*which connects the* Categories *into the* IDEAS *of*

*Absolute*
⛤
*Totality.*

*Absolute*
⛤
*Limitation,*

*Absolute*
⛤
*Substance.*

⛤
*Cause,*

⛤
*Concurrence.*

*Absolute*
⛤
*Necessity.*

*Thomas Wirgman invenit.*

*Henry Richter excudit.*

*For the Encyclopædia Londinensis_____ Vol.II. page 608.*

*1st January 1812.*

*London Pub. as the act directs by Adlard & Jones.*

Diagram by Thomas Wirgman, author of one of the earliest English Kant commentaries, *Encyclopedia Londiniensis,* 1812.

but belong to two different activities? Kant will conclude that it is not the abstract categories that produce our concrete experience but the unifying activity of imagination. As Kemp Smith notes,

> There is no real identity—there is not even analogy—between the processes of comparison and abstraction on the one hand and those of synthetic interpretation on the other. The former are merely reflective: the latter are genuinely creative. . . . Kant eventually realized that there is no proof that these two types of activity are ascribable to one and the same source. The synthetic activities—as he himself finally came to hold—are due to a faculty of imagination.[5]

Yet although Kant may not have proved that he can deduce a table of specific categories, it is nevertheless possible that some categories or categorical functions are operative in creating experience. The question Kant must address is how these abstract concepts operate in producing our actual experience of objects in time. How can the categories be said to create our temporal, sequential consciousness, consciousness of a real world?

Kant's answer to this, the core problem of his philosophy, constitutes his most brilliant and most influential discussion of the relations of imagination, Understanding and self-consciousness. It is not exaggerating to say that the terms of later philosophy in Germany, particularly its preoccupation with the creative imagination, would have been impossible without Kant's chapter "The Transcendental Deduction of the Categories." As Coleridge wrote in his annotations to the *Critique*, the Deduction contains the "most difficult and obscure passages of the Critique, or rather the knot of the whole system."[6] The difficulty of the chapter is not eased by its divisions into subjective and objective deductions, whose relationship is not always clear, conclusions of the first argument often presupposing conclusions of the later argument. Worse still, though most commentators would agree that the subjective deduction is far more important to the argument than Kant himself believed, it is omitted and the chapter entirely rewritten for the second ("B") edition. The Deduction contains some of Kant's most obscure prose, some of his darkest doctrines, and statements which are, at times, simply contradictory.

Yet the Transcendental Deduction also contains some of his most lucid and compelling arguments, provoking almost at once serious and fundamental philosophical inquiry and weighty tomes of critical exegesis. I will not attempt any resolution of the many scholarly and critical issues still being debated but will try to give some account of the Deduction's structure and basic doctrine. I will consider the two Deductions, for the most part as given in the first edition, taking subjective and objective as mutually interrelated, although not in any simple or always consistent way.

## Self-Awareness and the Production of Nature

Kant, beginning with a subjective deduction grounded upon facts of psychology, seeks to explore the activity of Understanding as it constructs the object. The objective deduction, which Kant believed was freer from the merely contingent facts of empirical psychology, seeks to explain how consciousness of objects is necessarily related to the possibility of consciousness at all. Kant's elimination of the subjective deduction in the second edition probably derives from his uneasiness at its contingent, descriptive quality, but he thus complicates and confuses much of his argument. For the analysis of transcendental faculties depends upon his early psychological analysis of the empirical activities of time-consciousness.[7]

Kant analyzes time-consciousness as a threefold synthesizing of the object of intuition in activities of apprehension (empirical), reproduction, and recognition. In apprehension, the manifold of space and time first becomes a unified spatiotemporal intuition. Here we see an important and easily overlooked point: that space and time are not constituted as unities until thought grasps them as such. Kant does not make clear why space and time do not themselves provide sufficient unity for us to become conscious of the object, but he suggests (A99) that objects are presented in intuition as in a spatial *manifold* yet somehow must also be held in the mind as a uniform series. In the case of a succession *a, b, c, d*, we must be able to hold *a, b, c* in consciousness as a unity before *d* can be joined to them.[8] But this synthesis, in turn, depends upon the mind's *imaging* power as a mode of temporal memory. We must be able to remember and reproduce the series if we are to have consciousness of it from one moment to the next. Hence the *reproductive imagination* is essential to our experience of objects in time. Kant's reproductive imagination, allied to memory, rescues the mind from dissolving into a pure spontaneous

flux of images by holding and ordering them, giving them boundaries and formal order (thus leading Fichte to develop more fully a
concept of imagination as the "mediator" between infinite spontaneity and human finitude; see below, Chapter 5).

> For experience as such presupposes the reproducibility of appear-
> ances. . . . But if I were always to drop out of thought the preceding
> representations (the first parts of [a] line, the antecedent parts of [a]
> time period, or the units in the order represented), and did not re-
> produce them while advancing to those that follow, a complete rep-
> resentation would never be obtained: none of the abovementioned
> thoughts, not even the purest and most elementary representations of
> space and time, could arise. The synthesis of apprehension is thus in-
> separably bound up with the synthesis of reproduction. (A102)

Finally, there must be a synthesis of *recognition* through which an
image becomes for us an image of *something*. Memory can produce a
series, but not a unified object. In recognition, we unite the series of
representations under a concept, by which Kant means "under a
rule." Only in this way do I unify the representations not merely
through memory but as moments in a single, connected act. I not
only remember *a*, *b*, *c*, and *d* as images but also can conceive them as
constituting a single series of four.

This may all sound dark enough, but in fact it is here that Kant is
led to the most crucial and fertile of results, the unity of empirical
*self*-consciousness and the transcendental unity of apperception.
Kant has deduced that, however unified our representations, they
would not be representations of *objects*, but perhaps mere discon-
nected reverie, were they not unified under rules:

> Now we find that our thought of the relation of all knowledge to its
> object carries with it an element of necessity; the object is viewed as
> that which prevents our modes of knowledge from being haphazard or
> arbitrary, and which determines them a priori in some definite fash-
> ion. . . . It is only when we have thus produced synthetic unity in the
> manifold of intuition that we are in a position to say that we know the
> object. But this unity is impossible if the intuition cannot be generated
> in accordance with a rule by means of such a function of synthesis as
> makes the reproduction of the manifold a priori necessary, and renders
> possible a concept in which it is united. Thus we think a triangle as an
> object, in that we are conscious of the combination of three straight
> lines according to a rule by which such an intuition can always be repre-

sented. This *unity of rule* determines all the manifold, and limits it to conditions which make unity of apperception possible. (A104–05)

Moreover, the unity of recognition of objects must rest upon my awareness of *myself* as the identical consciousness which experiences a regular series in time. Otherwise, I might perceive a unified series but could not make the step from the unity of a counted series to the unity of an *object*.[9] This identical consciousness, in turn, can become aware of itself only through the unity of its experience of objects. Thus, for Kant and the idealists who followed him, the mind and the world of its experience are interdependent, both consciousness and self-consciousness arising from the unifying activity of the imagination. In Kemp Smith's words, "Such an act of recognition [of synthetic unity] is, indeed, merely one particular form or concrete instance of self-consciousness. The unity of the empirical concept in and through which recognition takes place finds its indispensable correlate in the unity of an empirical self."[10]

But so far, Kant has only arrived at the empirical self. Kant asks what transcendental conditions are necessary for empirical consciousness to unite experience with unconscious regularity and necessity under a single "I think," a unified self as opposed to a jumble of images and memories. The necessity that governs experience can never be derived from experience but must take place a priori, as the condition of unity. This formal unity through which all concepts are united in *one* consciousness is the *transcendental unity of apperception.*[11] The empirical self has representations as its content; the *transcendental* apperception has no real content at all. It is the "I think" which must accompany all my representations if they are to be mine (B131). The transcendental unity of apperception is a form, or logically necessary unity. Further, for this self to experience objects as a necessary unity, the associations of reproductive imagination must be guided by rules a priori, must take place at a nonconscious level. This faculty must "act in the manner required to yield experiences which are capable of relation to the unity of self-consciousness, i.e. of being found to conform to the unity of the categories."[12] Kant calls this faculty, which produces not just unified images but a nature in conformity to the rules of the Understanding, *productive imagination.*

The imagination is thus a mediating faculty between the empty rules of the Understanding and the manifold of sensible intuition. Under the unity of apperception, imagination provides Understanding with a nature conformable to its rules, and Understanding raises us to conscious *knowledge* (through judgment) of nature.[13] In Kant's words, "the transcendental unity of apperception thus relates to the pure synthesis of imagination, as an a priori condition of the possibility of all combination of the manifold in one knowledge. But only the *productive* synthesis of the imagination can take place a priori; the reproductive rests upon empirical conditions. Thus the principle of the necessary unity of pure (productive) synthesis of imagination, prior to apperception, is the ground of the possibility of all knowledge, especially of experience" (A118). Kant argues (A123) both that the transcendental apperception is a condition for the possibility of the imagination's synthesis taking place in one consciousness and that in turn imagination's synthesis of temporal experience under rules is itself a precondition of the transcendental unity of consciousness.

Thus imagination and transcendental apperception mutually imply each other. It is essential to emphasize that Kant does not take apperception as an *ontologically* prior principle. That is, he does not assert that the transcendental ego creates the world. Apperception is a formal principle, the unity of the "I think." It is not a thinking *of something* but is the transcendental possibility of unified thinking. It is dependent upon experience of objects just as much as that experience is given meaning only through the unity of apperception. Consciousness of nature is inseparable from consciousness of oneself as conscious being. It remained for Fichte to take self-consciousness as a separate ontological principle of spontaneous creation. In Kant, we must remember, it is meaningless to speak of self-consciousness apart from its formal relation to consciousness of the synthetic unity of nature (cf. A108). This spontaneity of consciousness is bound up with the imagination's synthesis of experience in space and time.

Yet in the productive imagination we seem to find an irreducible spontaneity. Although it creates only appearances, does it not provide the order and regularity of the nature through which we "live and move and have our being"? If man defines himself through his relation to nature, does not imagination constitute a spontaneity that has real meaning to me, as a man in the world? We return to the opening question: In this relation of mind and nature, has Kant revoked the finitude of the knowing mind?

A brief response to these questions would be that man in fact does not, for Kant, define himself solely as a being in nature but also as morally free. To preserve this moral freedom, Kant must retain the finitude of knowledge. Nonetheless, the question of the true creativity of imagination is a difficult one and is the point at which we must examine Kant's relation to romanticism as a broad cultural movement.

## Finitude, Spontaneity, and Romantic Quest

To see the problem of the spontaneity of mind in Kant more clearly, let us summarize the reasoning of the Transcendental Deduction which led to the conclusion that "the order and regularity in the appearances, which we entitle *nature*, we ourselves introduce" (A125). Kant identifies the power of mind that produces the unity of experience as image as the *productive imagination (Einbildungskraft)*. The Understanding is "a unity self-subsistent, self-sufficient, and not to be increased by any additions from without," purely spontaneous, creating an ordered matrix out of the unified images synthesized from the sensible manifold by the imagination (A65 = B90). This ordering is such that in its lawfulness it is capable of being comprehended, known, by a unitary consciousness. Finally, Kant argues that the very possibility of a unified consciousness depends, in its turn, on the orderliness and unity of nature as given by the mind (see A108, B134).

Thus, in a real sense, the power of imagination makes possible the lawful unity of nature on the one hand and the higher unity of consciousness on the other. In this doctrine Kant carries to its conclusion, even redeems, the Enlightenment's fascination with natural lawfulness, a fascination that threatened to overwhelm the spontaneity of mind. For Kant, "law" is in fact the result of the mind's need for unity and order, and the more one comprehends nature, the more one comprehends the activity of the human mind. As one commentator is led to conclude, Kant's Transcendental Idealism represents "a positive step towards breaking down the man-nature dualism which underlies all empirical philosophy, by making experience depend upon what Coleridge called a 'reciprocal concurrence' of the 'conscious being' and 'that which is itself unconscious.'"[14]

Yet despite the creative spontaneity of imagination, it would be going too far to say that Kant has unambiguously revoked the finitude of human knowing. This is not the case. It is interesting that Coleridge's quoted words about a "reciprocal concurrence" between conscious and nonconscious being do not refer to any doctrine of Kant's and are in fact not Coleridge's words, but Coleridge in the *Biographia* translating verbatim from Schelling.[15] For Schelling there was indeed such interaction, but this is far more problematical in Kant. For Kant, man has no clear or cognizable interchange with nonconscious being-in-itself. For man to have knowledge of beings at all, he must know them through *concepts*, which are representations of representations: "No concept is ever related to an object immediately, but to some other representation of it" (A68 = B93). Thought is purely spontaneous in a dynamic sense, but in the overall topology of the mind in the *Critique of Pure Reason*, thought remains in service to intuition. If thought were not linked in some way to finite intuition, it would not in fact be thought *of* something. Human knowing, Kant makes very clear, is mediate, not directly intuitive. As Heidegger reminds us, the function of imagination in Kant is to mediate between the pure concepts of Understanding and the appearance of objects in intuition, specifically their appearance in time. The Understanding requires the synthesis of imagination in time, and so "it is by means of this relation [of imagination to Understanding] that the true nature of the Understanding, namely, its finitude, is most clearly revealed." Heidegger even argues, in a controversial opinion, that Kant "recoiled" from the position that imagination, "the disquieting unknown," despite its apparent creativity, actually revealed the *finitude* of man's being, man's inevitable bondage to time.[16]

In a cogent response to Heidegger, Ernst Cassirer argued that in the context of the three *Critiques*, clearly the imagination—indeed, the whole cognitive function—cannot be said to constitute the central informant of man's relation to being. Rather, the faculty of Reason demands the unconditioned, and although it cannot know this through cognition or theory, Reason does reach the unconditioned through practical freedom. The infinite in man, though not

susceptible to cognition, reveals itself through his freely constituting himself under the moral law. Man's being in Kant's mature
thought is a dualism, an unconditioned freedom within the finitude
of knowledge.[17]

I cannot but agree with Cassirer's larger perspective. My own
purpose, however, is not a philosophical estimate of Kant's thought
but an account of his relation—which is not only historical by way
of some terms that were influential in and out of philosophy, but also
structural by way of addressing common questions—to key themes
of romantic quest. I have confined myself to the *Critique of Pure Reason*, the work that became a cultural archetype of the philosophical
quest for the source and meaning of knowledge. I have so limited
this study so as to concentrate on Kant's epistemological rather than
aesthetic or moral terms, which (except in the case of Coleridge)
have received less attention from critics interested in Kant's relation
to romantic themes.

In the first *Critique* the emphasis is on Theoretical Reason, and so
Reason appears, for the most part, in its negative aspect. The emphasis of this work is not on the infinitude of human freedom; historical romanticism understood not only moral freedom but also the
dynamic creativity of imagination to be potentially able to revoke in
some sense the finitude of receptive sensible intuition. Cassirer, too,
argues that even within the first *Critique*, Understanding is not merely
passively "in service under" intuition but spontaneously *creates* sensible intuition as a definite being, *as* space and *as* time: intuition
depends for its definiteness on Understanding as much as Understanding must take its material from intuition.[18] That is, the mind
would not be *aware* of its receptivity *as* receptivity, were it not simultaneously active in consciousness—a result in Kant that, as we
shall see, develops into some of the thornier dialectics of idealist
philosophy.

In the context of the first *Critique* alone, it is probably impossible
to resolve the issue of how far the infinite spontaneity of imagination
in a dynamic sense mitigates the radical finitude implied by Kant's
mental topology. There are, nevertheless, two comments we can
make about Kant's theory of knowledge in the context of later romantic themes. First, it is clear that from the historical point of view,
Kant's "Copernican Revolution" upset the entire course of Enlightenment rationalism, unifying mind and nature in such a way that the

organization, the very beauty and truth of nature, reflects the unity and spontaneity of human consciousness. Here indeed was a revolution as important to the development of romanticism as that which beheaded a king, perhaps far more so, as Heinrich Heine's whimsical words imply: "You French are tame and moderate compared with us Germans. The most you could do was kill a king, and he had already lost his head before you beheaded him. . . . Truly, it does Maximilian Robespierre too much honor to compare him with Immanuel Kant."[19] Second, it is also clear that Kant himself insisted upon the finitude of theoretical knowledge, insisted that the unities created by the spontaneous mind are nonetheless not the unities of Being itself. Indeed, man *needs* to create the unities of discursive thinking, to unify the object under concepts, precisely because he cannot intuit directly the unity of things in themselves. Despite the unity of mind with nature, this unity is in no sense ontologically final, in no sense represents a unity of mind with being in itself. For Kant the expression of the infinite, of noumenal reality, in man never emerged in Theoretical Reason, but only in the fact of human freedom, in Practical Reason and the actualization of the moral law. It can be argued that the entire motive of the first *Critique* was to restrict theoretical knowledge to nature alone, so that man's moral life would be free from the determinism of a fully comprehended system of natural law.[20]

These general remarks should clarify Kant's usefulness to this study of the terms of romantic quest. He has, first, completely reinterpreted subjectivity, making it the creative first principle of human knowledge, insisting that the first priority of metaphysical inquiry must be an investigation of the structure and meaning of human awareness. Second, he has at the same time made problematic the theoretical investigation into the highest unity beyond consciousness and the nature it creates, into man's destiny, into the real relationship between man and being. As the *Critique of Practical Reason* (1788) makes clear, it is not through knowledge but through moral worth that man stands in authentic relation to being. Even in the first *Critique*, man's freedom is said to exalt him above the mechanism of nature and unite him with the supersensible, but no conceptual knowledge of this freedom is possible (A798–804 = B828–32). Freedom, to be truly free, must choose to obey the moral law unconditionally, and this actually requires theoretical ignorance of any "conditions" of moral freedom. But the "mechanism" of nature is a creation of the human mind—inescapably, the dualism of theoretical and practical is locked within us, as a product of our own intellectual constitution.

Indeed, our sense of the infinite spontaneity of mind impels us to demand knowledge of the infinite itself; but in creating nature we confine our cognition to finitude. The infinite appears only as a demand, as a continuous *activity*. This dialectic would ramify throughout idealism and romanticism.

The faculty Kant calls "Reason" is an aspect of the Understanding as it seeks the highest unities, the unconditioned ground of its categories. Reason seeks synthetic knowledge of freedom, God, the origin of the temporal universe, and the true nature of the soul. It would know, not merely nature, but a *world*. This ambition can never be realized. Reason becomes tangled in hopeless contradictions, Kant thought, when it tries to reach a synthesis that would reflect the true nature of being itself. We cannot know things-in-themselves, ultimately, because to do so would be to arrive at the highest synthesis, between the mind's conditions and the unconditioned "out there" that affects us. Reason's positive function, in the first *Critique*, is to provide unattainable ideals of higher syntheses, but these only guide Understanding in its quest for the truths of nature (cf. A408 = B435ff.).

For Kant, this fall into duality was the necessary condition of moral life. For romanticism, nothing could more cogently express the source of the anxiety noted earlier that alternatively hinders or impels the romantic quest. We are now in a position to view this psychological anxiety from a "transcendental" perspective: *anxiety is a psychological expression of radical separation from a certain kind of being, the being of unity.*

Our finitude, Kant believes, forbids our seeking within ourselves any ground of unity between the sensible and the supersensible. We might ask, then, to what end the mind *begins* the quest to understand itself as the creator of nature, only to find its speculation trapping itself in its own creation and forced to kneel before the irreducibly given (the moral law) rather than pursue the spontaneity of thought to its own real source and true being? Between the real being of the world and the real being of man stands the finitude of human thought. Here, with Kant, begins the striving to define this finitude, not from the point of view of a transcendent infinite God or an immanent rational cosmic order, but from the point of view of man's awareness of himself as conscious being.

It was Fichte who insisted upon giving real being to the spontaneity of thought. Spontaneity of thought is a clue to man's true being, freedom. From a real grasp of this being-as-freedom, Fichte sought to deduce all theoretical knowledge. All knowledge will proceed from this first principle of human being and so will form a self-sufficient system, a science of knowledge Fichte calls *Wissenschaftslehre*. Nothing could be more opposite to Kant's critical procedure as he understood it, yet clearly (as Fichte claimed) Kant's own system seemed to require the "completion" of a science of knowledge. Kant declared that what the *Critique* had put asunder, thought and being, no man could join. But what was the being of thought? What was the meaning of this division, and could man ever understand a unity that had true being, a being that was a unity? How does thought, as act, relate to being as limitation or the "objective"? Kant's critical philosophy was an overture whose motifs would evolve, sometimes with an almost perverse life of their own, into the high music drama of historical romanticism. In the words of the Kant critic H. J. de Vleeschauwer, "The Aufklärung was succeeded by a romanticism of which Fichte is one of the most powerful protagonists. . . . The *Critique* and the *Wissenschaftslehre* are not two books and two doctrines which conflict with one another; they are two epochs which face one another. Kant and Fichte, the master and the pupil, are the two actors who embody on the stage of history the cultural and sentimental spirit which animates these two epochs: the one silent like all ends, the other noisy like all beginnings."[21] We turn now to this beginning, to Fichte and his lectures on the science of knowledge at Jena in 1794.

# PART II

*Cultural Analogues of Quest Romance: Fichtean Striving and Romantic Irony*

# 4

## Fichte and Romanticism

Johann Gottlieb Fichte arrived at the University of Jena in the warm spring of 1794. Europe had seemed to be washed clean by a life-giving revolution, but now the storm had turned fearsome and everyone waited anxiously for more news of the Terror in France. In the last two years, peasants had revolted in Saxony and the Rhineland; intellectuals had aggressively defended the rights of man, forming Jacobin clubs across Britain, Holland, Germany, and Italy; Geneva had proclaimed itself a republic; the German city of Mainz actually asked for annexation to France. Now, however, the intoxication with universal liberty was checked by growing reaction, confusion, and fear. It was to prove a portentous year for those writers and intellectuals who would find themselves caught up in the fervor of a movement that would be called "romanticism." In 1794, Goethe, at Weimar, met and began his famous correspondence with Schiller at nearby Jena, who encouraged him to take up *Faust* again. Also in 1794, Coleridge met Robert Southey, and the two men, united by their common enthusiasm for the French Revolution, began their plan to found a utopia on the banks of the Susquehanna River, the plan they called "Pantisocracy." Between 1792 and 1794, William Blake would write *The French Revolution, The Marriage of Heaven and Hell, America: A*

*Prophecy*, and *Songs of Experience.* Wordsworth watched with growing dismay as events in Paris shook his youthful faith in dawning political and spiritual liberation. Separated from his ideals and from Annette Vallon, a gloomy Wordsworth wandered through the Lake District with his sister and composed *Guilt and Sorrow.* The year had begun with Mary Wollstonecraft's report from Paris, on New Year's Day, of Tom Paine's arrest by the Committee of Public Safety. And in July came news of Robespierre's death on the guillotine. It was a volatile time.

In this extraordinary period, Fichte found himself in an extraordinary place. The University of Jena was the undisputed center of speculative philosophy in Germany, and perhaps nowhere in Europe could a faculty more illustrious or intellectually daring be found. The Jena–Weimar region, once called a "modern Athens," was alive at the end of the century with the writings of Goethe, Schiller, Schelling, Hegel, Fries, Schlegel, Herbart, Oersted, and Hölderlin.[1] Fichte's arrival was anticipated with much excitement because he was both a brilliant young protégé of Kant and the author of two pamphlets philosophically defending the French Revolution. A friend wrote to Fichte that "in Jena there has been for some weeks past an indiscernable [sic] joy over the triumvirate of professors due at Easter . . . but your name resounds above all, and expectation is strained to its utmost—doubtless in part because you are regarded as the most valiant defender of the rights of men."[2] In this stormy age, bright flashes of the intellect seemed to follow the rumblings of the Jacobin armies and the echoes of the *Marseillaise.*

Within five years Fichte would be forced to leave Jena, embroiled in a controversy over his alleged atheism. He reacted to the charge with indiscreet petulance and lost the support of Goethe and Kant, but the issue was genuine: complete freedom of thought and expression. In his years at Jena, Fichte developed the radical idealism that declared—in the spirit of his age—that freedom is the birthright of men and women as self-conscious beings.

## Fichte and the Dialectics of the Romantic Ego

In the words of the great Goethe scholar Hermann Korff, "The early romantic movement (in Germany) is a spiritual forest fire [*Geistes-*

*brand*], sparked off by Fichte's philosophy. The fire only really burned when abstract thought was fanned by the wild winds of liberated fantasy and produced a blaze of poetic-philosophic ideas."[3] Indeed, although he is little read today among English-speaking scholars, Fichte had a direct or indirect influence on writers of his day— through Goethe, Schelling, the Schlegels, Novalis, Tieck, Cole- ridge, and finally, Carlyle—certainly as great as that of any specu- lative philosopher upon a literary movement. Though Kant was clearly the father of transcendentalism, romanticism in the arts drew special inspiration from Fichte and his circle. Fichte has suffered in English from poor translation. In fact, no translations appeared until the 1840s, and only in 1970 was a generally reliable translation available of his great theoretical work of 1794, the *Wissenschaftslehre*.

From Fichte we can learn more than the details of a historically influential doctrine; we can also watch one of the keenest theoretical minds of the age define the terms and grapple with the paradoxes of living in a world after Kant, a world of radical idealism. As much as Wordsworth, Coleridge, Keats, or Shelley would in their long poems, Fichte explored in the *Wissenschaftslehre* the question: What does it mean to live in a world where man is his own creator and defense? In giving the mind such creative freedom what is gained and what is lost? How do we explain man's finitude, his temporality, his desires? In this subjectivist world of infinitely expanding dimensions, how can man take the measure of his own true being?

The being of man is act. By this Fichte means not only an action or deed (*Tat*) but the free activity (*Tätigkeit*) of conscious self-assertion as well. The beginning point of Fichte's philosophy is the undeter- mined, ungrounded assertion, or "positing" of the I: "That whose being or essence consists simply in the fact that it posits itself as existing, is the I as absolute subject. . . . To *posit oneself* and *to be* are, as applied to the I, perfectly identical."[4] We cannot say what the I is, only that it acts: "When all existence of or for the subject is taken away, it has nothing left but an act" (2d Intro., *GWL*, p. 33). It is not simply empirical self-consciousness with which Fichte begins; for the I is not to be defined as the simple identity of a series of thoughts, "I who think *A* am the same who thought *B*." This would lead to an infinite regression, and we would never be able to explain the "I think" at all (see 2d Intro., *GWL*, p. 49). Rather, the I is a mental activity, the unconditioned "I think I" whereby the Ego becomes aware of itself *as* aware. The transcendental idealism of the *Wissen-schaftslehre* seeks to ground all phenomenal being in this primary mental act. As Coleridge understood Fichte's significance, the *Wis-senschaftslehre* "was to add the keystone of the [critical idealist] arch: and by commencing with an *act* instead of a *thing* or *substance*, Fichte assuredly gave the first mortal blow to Spinozism, as taught by Spinoza himself; and supplied the *idea* of a system truly metaphysical, and of a *metaphysique* truly systematic (i.e. having its spring and principle within itself)." As Goethe, who boasted of an early enthusiasm for Fichte, more dramatically asserts in *Faust*, "In the beginning was the Act [*Tat*]."[5]

To begin with this act is to take the spontaneity of the I as prior to its existence as the empirical individual representing I. Like Kant, Fichte must somehow account for the feeling of dependence, of receptivity in the I which images a world. Fichte, however, will ask a higher critical question: not how we are affected by things-in-themselves, or even *whether* we are affected by things that are not mental, but why we come to believe that we are. The end of the Science of Knowledge will not be a glib skepticism about the existence of "external" objects but a complete history of the meaning of human finitude from the standpoint of undetermined, self-conscious activity. The *Wissenschaftslehre*, far from presenting an absolute idealism, will develop a truly systematic transcendental idealism: Fichte does not maintain that the world exists fundamentally as a mere idea in the mind of the Self. Rather, he will proceed dialectically, beginning with the absolute identity of the I, and progressively deriving the world as its boundary. This critical dialectic seeks to understand how the I can know itself both as infinitely active and also as bounded. As one critic summarizes Fichte's problem:

> Representation is only able to be thought under "the presupposition that a check [*ein Anstoss*] happens to the I's activity which is reaching out infinitely and indeterminately" [*GWL*, p. 220]. The I as intelligence is dependent upon a "not-I."
>
> [But] how can an absolute I with its unlimited activity contain a dependence? What prevents the destruction of the unity of the I by this dependency? How is it possible that the I be both absolute and an intelligence? The task is to maintain both the unlimited activity of the I and its representing, but at the same time to deny the dependency. What does it mean to deny this dependency and what are the consequences of such a denial?[6]

The origin of the *Wissenschaftslehre* in an absolute self-consciousness, for which the I and its object are one and the same, may tempt us to see an analogue to the romantic theme of a state of Innocence, a state prior to the division of consciousness against itself. Indeed, the *Wissenschaftslehre* of 1794, M. H. Abrams has noted, is the first chapter of a developing romantic "plot," the story of the fall and redemption of mankind. For Abrams, however, that story must end in the reintegration of the mind with itself; he must then see Fichte only as raising problems that will be resolved, ultimately, by Hegel's completed history of self-consciousness.[7] But a close study of the *Wissenschaftslehre* will, I believe, show that it has conceptual and historical importance for understanding the romantic quest precisely because the final relationship between mind and world is left problematic in the sense that thought alone cannot (as in Hegel) return to the absolute. Thought alone cannot stand outside itself to discover the central mystery of consciousness: How do we come to think of ourselves as passive receptors of a finite world? For Fichte, only in action, in striving, in quest is there a fit response to this question—not in any conceptual resolution, but in an embodiment of the rhythms of the I reaching out to encompass the world and of the world acting to impress itself upon the I. From the theoretical point of view, however, the question remains: How do we come to know this interchange if we cannot stand "outside" of ourselves, if indeed—as Kant would have it—the very notions of "inside" and "outside" originate with the mind?

As we have seen, Kant's Transcendental Deduction argues that consciousness (of objects) is unthinkable without a unifying self-consciousness, the transcendental unity of apperception. Both Kant and Fichte agree that "dogmatic" philosophers, realists and idealists, cannot explain how we become conscious of ourselves as conscious beings. That is, both the transcendent realist and the transcendent idealist—Kant and Fichte call their positions "dogmatisms"—differ from the transcendental critical idealist in their assertion that all being is essentially either material or mental. But the realist must explain consciousness as the effect of an external material object on the subject. As Fichte points out, this explanation relies on a causal chain, on an object causing a presentation in a subject. The intellect is, however, fundamentally different from the object: the object exists only for an intellect, but the intellect exists *for itself*, reflects upon and observes itself. The object belongs, Fichte says, to a "single series," a chain that does not reflect upon itself; in the mind, however, we find not only the appearance of a real series but also the observation of this real series. "In the intellect, therefore—to speak figuratively—there is a double series, of being and seeing, of the real and the ideal; and its [intellect's] essence consists in the separability of these two (it is synthetic); while the thing has only a single series, that of the real (a mere being posited)" (1st Intro., *GWL*, p. 17). Causality belongs only to the single series; it is a "mechanical" power. Hence dogmatic realism cannot explain this doubleness in consciousness, how a series can reflect back into self-awareness: "Mechanism is unable to apprehend itself, precisely because it is mechanism" (2d Intro., *GWL*, p. 79).

The dogmatic idealist is equally unable to explain self-consciousness. The idealist attempts to avoid the problem of causality by assuming that there is only a single, *ideal* series and that the object is presented by the mind to itself. But again, as Kant's Deduction had shown, self-consciousness derives its unity from consciousness of the object as given in finite intuition.[8] The idealist cannot explain how we come to believe in the presentation of objects as finite and given. Unity of self-consciousness requires that the I must reflect upon itself thinking the unified, finite, presented object. To the absolute idealist, the I gives *itself* its objects: How then does the I "give" itself an object it feels determined by? Where does this finitude come from? Without the presented object, no self-consciousness is possible (*GWL*, pp. 140, 147).

Kant and Fichte agree on this problem of dogmatism and on the critical philosopher's response: a transcendental idealism denies that the subject is causally affected by a transcendent, external object, but also denies that self-consciousness is possible without our thinking ourselves determined, or limited, by a thing-in-itself. The thing-in-itself is the noumenon, or that which we imagine appearances are appearances "of."[9]

But in what sense can the mind know that it is limited by a thing-in-itself? Fichte believed that his response to this question was completely in the spirit of Kant's system, but Kant himself thoroughly repudiated the philosophy of the *Wissenschaftslehre*.[10] There was no more hotly debated philosophical issue in the decade following the *Critique* than Kant's doctrine explaining the receptivity of human knowledge through the activity of the thing-in-itself, the noumenon that cannot be thought but must be somehow posited "out there" behind appearances. It has long been argued—indeed, was argued as early as the generation of Tieck, Novalis, and Friedrich Schlegel—that the final rejection of the thing-in-itself was the crucial moment in which a floodgate opened, and a tide of romantic "enthusiasm" threatened to engulf speculative philosophy and carry its ideas downstream throughout the culture of the day. Kant himself saw the doctrine of the thing-in-itself as a bulwark against what he considered a philosophical reverie, that is, the notion that phenomena are merely appearances dreamed by the mind.

To understand Fichte's idealism, we must see him as trying initially to reconceive the whole problem of the thing-in-itself, attempting to clarify the doctrine against Kant's critics, even against some of Kant's own statements. Briefly, Fichte agrees with the general objections of the critics F. H. Jacobi, K. L. Reinhold, and G. E. Schulze but wants to argue that they have mistaken the spirit and tenor of the critical philosophy and that, properly understood, a coherent system can be made of the idealism to which the first *Critique* was only propaedeutic.[11]

The criticism of Jacobi was the earliest, most stinging, most thorough, and most influential. Jacobi's attack on Kant was as shrewd as it was relentless; he was the first major thinker to ask what the ultimate result of the *Critique of Pure Reason* was: in what position does it leave man in relation to real being?[12] According to Jacobi, Kant's account of the spontaneity of the mind leaves us in complete ignorance of any real being beyond appearances. The thing-in-itself cannot be intuited or thought, so how can it be said to be responsible in any way for phenomena as they appear to us? "Without the supposition that objects make impressions under the senses," Jacobi could not enter the Kantian system; with that supposition, he "could not remain in it." Further, the mind that creates the phenomena is itself unknowable: the mind presents to itself in thought "neither itself nor other things, but solely and alone that which is neither what the mind is itself, nor what other things are."[13] As Kant's Deduction itself purported to show, the concept of affection (causality) is a category of the Understanding's synthesis: how then can we know that anything "outside" the Understanding is affecting it? Jacobi argues that the *Critique* undercuts itself, demanding that the mind undertake a quest for self-comprehension that it can neither complete nor, on its own terms, even begin.

What could such a starting point be? Other critics of the early 1790s, such as Schulze and Reinhold, had complained that Kant does not systematically deduce the categories from some single principle, but rather seems to "come upon" them. How can the mind discover laws—categories—within itself and determining its activity, which the mind has not deduced from its own nature? Since Kant had shown that these laws do not come from outside the mind, from what principle can he deduce them? Fichte accepts this criticism, for if Kant correctly saw that self-consciousness is the essential condition for consciousness, then for the unity of the intellect to be preserved the conditions of thinking—both the forms of intuition and the categories—must be derivable from self-consciousness alone (2d Intro., *GWL*, pp. 48–52). Responding to Kant's critics, Fichte asserts that a true starting point for a systematic deduction of consciousness does appear in the first *Critique*, though Kant himself may have been unaware of it. That point is the transcendental unity of apperception, "the highest principle in the whole sphere of human knowledge."[14]

Kant had argued that we cannot begin to know ourselves through transcendental apperception, since this is only a logical postulate of thought—the subject simply cannot immediately intuit himself. For Kant such an "intellectual intuition" was repugnant, smacking of a mystical, nonrelational, immediate contact with Being. Intuition was sensory or it was nothing. The unity of apperception, the *I think*, is wholly dependent upon representation: "Inner experience is itself possible only mediately." Kant wished, moreover, to prove the very existence of permanent Being through this "negative way," by denying that the mind bounded within and without by mere images could ever discover Being, a "permanent something," within itself: "But this permanent [something] cannot be an intuition in me. For all grounds of determination of my existence which are to be met with in me are representations; and as representations [they] require a permanent [Being] distinct from them."[15]

Fichte asserts, boldly, that we at once *do* have a direct intuition of self-consciousness and also that this intellectual intuition is *not* Kant's proscribed contact with a transcendent substance or being. Fichte purges Kant of the last vestiges of eighteenth-century epistemology, the triad "Being-of-Mind / Being-of-Image / Being-of-Object." He agrees that we are not conscious of the I as a being; but we are always conscious of the I as an *activity*:

> This intuiting of himself that is required of the philosopher in performing the act whereby the I arises for him, I refer to as *intellectual intuition*. It is the immediate consciousness that I act, and what I enact; it is that whereby I know something because I do it. We cannot prove from concepts that this power of intellectual intuition exists, nor evolve from them what it may be. Everyone must discover it immediately in himself, or he will never make its acquaintance. . . .
>
> I cannot take a step, move a hand or foot, without an intellectual intuition of my self-consciousness in these acts . . . whosoever ascribes an activity to himself, appeals to this intuition. The source of life is contained therein, and without it there is death. (2d Intro., *GWL*, p. 38)

Fichte's "romanticizing" of Kant consists in this, that instead of beginning with static images or systems, he begins with the I as a self-creating activity.[16]

What is the meaning of this starting point, this "act"? The act of the I, we must first understand, is not a thought or a concept. It is the ground, or possibility, of self-conscious thought. Nor ought we to confuse—as so many romantic authors did—this I with the empirical I. The absolute I is not a thing that acts, it *is* act, an ungrounded activity. In the *Wissenschaftslehre* the thing studied coincides, initially, with the one who studies. Only in reflection does the philosopher later *conceive* of the I as a thing acting. But primordially the I is the self-reverting act, the fundamental possibility of self-awareness. This act belongs not to the philosopher alone, but equally to any man who will reflect upon himself in the act of thinking.

It is difficult to resist, at this point, retelling the famous anecdote describing Fichte's explanation of this intuition to his students at Jena in 1799. As retold nearly forty years later by Heinrich Steffens, Fichte began, "'Gentlemen . . . collect yourselves—go into yourselves—for we have nothing to do with things without, but simply with the inner self.' Thus summoned, the auditors appeared really to go into themselves. . . . 'Gentlemen,' continued Fichte, 'think the wall' (*Denken Sie die Wand*). This was a task to which the hearers were all equal; they thought the wall. 'Have you thought the wall?' asked Fichte. 'Well then, gentlemen, think him who thought the wall.' It was curious to see the evident confusion and embarrassment that now arose. Many of his audience seemed to be utterly unable to find him who thought the wall."[17] We could go on like this, of course, "think him who thought him. . . ." And in this infinite recursive activity we see a type of the romantic sublime, we see that whenever the I attempts to become an object for itself it slips from itself, receding down mirrored corridors of endless activity. It was this activity—far more than simple organic unity or growth—that romanticism identified with "Life."

Fichte's meaning was not lost on Coleridge, who had heard this anecdote and written in his notebook in 1801: "—By deep feeling we make our *Ideas dim*—and this is what we mean by Life—ourselves. I think of the Wall—it is before me, a distinct Image—here. I necessarily think of the *Idea* and the Thinking I as two distinct and opposite Things. Now let me think of *myself*—of the thinking Being—the Idea becomes dim whatever it be—so dim that I know not what it is—but the Feeling is deep and steady—and this I call I." Above this, Coleridge has quoted from Wordsworth's *Lines Composed above Tintern Abbey*: "—and the deep power of Joy / We see into the *Life* of Things—."[18] This life of things is, in Coleridge's idealist reading, the life of the actively self-creating mind.

The I, then, is not simply "there," a thing that suddenly performs a self-reverting act. The I is the activity and nothing more. It is not an idea, or a thing, but only an act, a "positing" that posits itself as positing (see 2d Intro., *GWL*, pp. 31, 64–70). If this is the original unity of mind with itself with which Fichte's quest is to begin, it is also true that this source of life is not itself living. That is, this I as such is not conscious of itself. The self-reverting activity is, as it were, "empty," a contentless recursiveness beneath or within consciousness. For consciousness to arise, there must be a halt, or a limitation placed on the "I think myself thinking. . . ." This halt cannot be within the I to begin with because we have seen that the I is pure act: the not-I does not appear within the absolute self-reverting assertion. Yet for the philosopher reflecting upon this act, what the I asserts *becomes* a not-I; indeed, the assertion itself, he realizes, could not take place unless there is something asserted.

This asserted something is identical to the assertion, from the point of view of the Absolute I. "The absolute," said Coleridge, "is neither singly that which affirms, nor that which is affirmed, but the identity and living copula of both."[19] But for the philosopher reflecting upon the activity, there is a gap, or discontinuity; the I cannot be *thought of* as asserting without a distinct asserted, a not-I. This not-I is not to be seen as a thing or a being, but rather as simply an opposition, the primordial possibility of objecthood. As Fichte explains:

> How does the I exist for itself? The first postulate: Think of yourself, and notice how you do it. Everyone who does no more than this . . . will find that in the thinking of this concept his activity as intelligence reverts into itself and makes itself its own object. . . . The philosopher can thereupon proceed to his demonstration that this act would be impossible without another, whereby there arises for the I an existence outside itself. (2d Intro., *GWL*, pp. 33–34)

"The Absolute I," one commentator points out, "reveals itself in [philosophical] discourse, but in so doing conceals or alters itself."[20] The task of Fichte's *Science of Knowledge*, then, is to account for this paradox, that the not-I should at once seem impossible in, and necessary to, the assertion of the I. His method will be dialectical, showing under what conditions each case is, in its way, true, arriving at further and further syntheses. Yet because the paradox of the not-I arises *with* and *for* thinking, we cannot expect that thought alone can do more than explain how it is possible for experience to arise from this paradox. Thought cannot subsume the paradox itself. As we shall see, the power that unifies the Absolute I and the not-I is a dynamic oscillation that Fichte identifies as the imagination.

## Idealism and Romantic Criticism

So begins what J. N. Findlay calls Fichte's "remarkable myth."[21] There is a long tradition in romantic criticism of failure to understand this dialectic of paradox and the mystery of alienation that makes romantic myth a dynamic quest. It has seemed to some critics that in the absolute assertion of Fichte's beginning there is also a redemptive ending, that in intellectual intuition consciousness returns to its source, to the timeless Absolute. Yet for Fichte—and, I hope to show, for the major achievements of romantic myth—this cannot be so, because the Absolute is empty and cannot occur in consciousness without the (inexplicable and ineluctable) intrusion of the not-I. The dual irony of Fichte's doctrine is that without man's capacity for direct intuition of the Absolute, he would not understand his finitude; yet without that finitude the absolute source of his self-conscious life would be—though indeterminately free—empty and unconscious. It has been said that here, with Fichte, is the central intellectual expression of romantic irony.[22]

In certain traditional readings of romantic quest by literary critics, this paradox of finitude is often "overcome" by the act of criticism itself, which seeks to complete the quest and "bring consciousness home to itself." The critic may attempt to reach a closure that the poet never achieves. Even when particular poems resist any "sublation" of contrariety and paradox, critics may seek such resolutions across a poetic canon, or through endless reachings after definitions of "romanticism" as the coherent myth of an intellectual epoch. Finally, the historian may find a mythic resolution by seeing the period as a whole as a lost age in which the alienated artist still valued the quest after unity and to some degree achieved it through his art.

It is not difficult to document this point of view as one element, or mood, in the age's complex understanding of itself. What is interesting and highly relevant to our discussion is the source of this modern reading of romantic quest in the many nineteenth-century attempts to assert some clear relation between the finite mind and its intuition of the Absolute. The twentieth-century analyses of these attempts may be divided into two large and interrelated schools of interpretation. One is the tendency to see romanticism as secularizing the traditional religious experience of the Absolute, denying that our experience of the Absolute is the experience of a transcendent world, or of some realm whose dimensions are not those of the human mind. Historically related to this is a second tendency to read romantic quest, backward in time as it were, from the standpoint of Hegel. For Hegel—who directly opposed Fichte on this point—the "rift" in consciousness between finite and infinite can be healed by consciousness alone, by the Absolute realizing itself through progressively higher syntheses of thought.

Among the first modern exponents of the "secularization" theme was A. O. Lovejoy, who argued that romantic poets identified (rightly or wrongly) "intellectual intuition," a transcendental capacity, with states of dream, reverie, precognitive awareness, and other psychological processes. In this state of intuition "the Ego *knows* eternity at first hand, and lives in the eternal."[23] For Lovejoy, the myth of a timeless realm of ideas is secularized to become an actual experience in the temporal life of the sensitive mind. He quotes Schelling:

> In all of us there dwells a mysterious and wonderful power to withdraw ourselves from the changes of time into our innermost self, freed from all that comes to us from without, and to intuit the eternal in us under the form of immutability. . . . In this moment of intuition time and duration vanish for us; we are no longer in time but time is in us—or, rather, not time, but pure, absolute eternity.[24]

Echoing Lovejoy, George Poulet generalizes that romantic poets "wanted to reflect in their poetry not the fixed splendor of God's eternity, but their own personal confused apprehension, in the here and now, of a human timelessness . . . they brought eternity into time."[25] He quotes from Shelley's note to *Queen Mab*, 8.203: "Time is our consciousness of the succession of ideas in our mind. . . . If, therefore, the human mind by any future improvement of its sensibility should become conscious of an infinite number of ideas in a minute, that minute would be eternity."[26] Both these examples, however, are taken from very early, youthful works. Neither Schelling nor Shelley had as yet begun to examine the full consequences of this particular faith, and both men would soon realize that such essentially psychological intuitions lead to the transcendental problem: *how* and *why* does the finite mind demand a certain relation to the Absolute?

The case of the influence of Hegel is more complex because he directly confronts the problems raised by Fichte for his generation. Hegel's earliest response to Fichte, in *The Difference between the Fichtean and Schellingian Systems of Philosophy* (1801), was that the I of the *Wissenschaftslehre* is incurably alienated from itself. Hegel argues that, in intellectual intuition, the pure "I = I" is inevitably different from the experience of the empirical I that thinks the objective world, the "I + not-I." In the basic Fichtean intuition, Hegel argues, "where I = I is set up as one among other axioms, it has no other meaning than pure self-consciousness as opposed to the empirical. . . . The pure consciousness I = I and the empirical consciousness I = I + not-I, remain opposed. . . . [But] I = I as the principle of speculation or of subjective philosophical reflection, a principle opposed to empirical consciousness, must objectively validate itself as the principle of philosophy by sublating [this] opposition to empirical consciousness. . . . This is the question: Can the absolute identity, insofar as it appears as the theoretical capacity, also abstract entirely from subjectivity *and* from the opposition to empirical consciousness and objectivity become itself, A = A, within this [purely theoretical] sphere [itself]?"[27]

In other words, Hegel calls for speculation, thought itself, to reach the highest synthesis possible between the Absolute I and the empirical I, between subject and object. For Hegel, Fichte's Absolute self-consciousness not only is empty but also implies an absolute sundering of mind from itself, an *alienation* of self-consciousness from consciousness of the world. "But this position of severed life has in its turn to be overcome," Hegel says in the 1817 *Logic,* "and the spirit must, by its own act, achieve concord once more. . . . The principle of restoration is found in thought, and thought only: the hand that inflicts the wound is also the hand that heals it."[28]

Various modern critics have seen romanticism as the triumphant march toward this new, higher unity. Indeed, in a survey of modern criticism, René Wellek—reviewing the work up to 1960 of Poulet, M. H. Abrams, Albert Gerard, R. A. Foakes, and E. D. Hirsch— proclaimed that "a convincing agreement has been reached: they all see the implication of imagination, symbol, myth, and organic nature, and see it as part of the great endeavor to overcome the split between subject and object, the self and the world, the conscious and the unconscious. This is the central creed of the great romantic poets in England, Germany, and France."[29] Not all critics, however, have been so convinced. Geoffrey Hartman, in a crucial essay, argued that "Shelley's visionary despair, Keats's understanding of the poetic character, and Blake's doctrine of the contraries, reveal that self-consciousness cannot be overcome; and the very desire to overcome it, which poetry and imagination encourage, is part of a vital, dialectical movement of 'soul-making.'" Quoting Hegel's famous remark, in the *Logic* above, Hartman counters that the Hegelian myth of consciousness redeeming itself was a problem for romanticism, not a solution. However effectually Hegel may have responded to Fichte, Hegel's myth of unity will help us far less to understand romantic irony, paradox, and alienation. "The romantic poets," Hartman affirms, "do not exalt consciousness *per se.* They have recognized it as a kind of death-in-life, as the product of a division in the self. . . . The attempt to think mythically [in Hegel's manner] is itself part of a crucial defense against the self-conscious intellect. . . . Whether myth-making is still possible, and whether the mind can maintain something of the interacting unity of self and life, are central concerns of the romantic poets."[30]

As Findlay succinctly puts it, Fichte "demythologizes himself." The *Wissenschaftslehre* struggles with its myth of a world that blocks the infinite assertion of the I; yet the work's idealism demands that this blocking be seen as also part of the Ego's assertion of itself. "The Ego," says Findlay, "posits a resistant environment precisely because it *requires* such an environment to elicit its own activities, and to bring them to consciousness."[31] Having asserted that the I confronts an alien not-I, Fichte asks why the I *believes* that this is so. Can both an infinite assertion and the infinite resistance in any sense be attributed to the same Ego? What can it mean that "the I is infinite in its finitude and finite in its infinity" (*GWL*, p. 228)? The paradox that seems to disable in Fichte's quest exists for the I only when it attempts to think of itself as a fixed being; but for the I as an activity of infinite *striving* the paradox becomes a dialectic of self-discovery. At a certain point, as we shall see, Fichte's speculation must overcome itself, since further theoretical forms cannot break through the circle it creates. At this point the conscious ego finds its reason-for-being in infinite practical striving, in moral quest.

Commenting on the essential romanticism of Fichte's self-consuming myth, H. A. Korff remarks,

> If the prime act of the Ego involves it in a polarity with world, and thus limits it, curtailing its freedom, this act must have some further significance if it is to be true to the Ego: for that limitless activity which is the essence of the Ego is also by its nature free. . . . The Ego may need the objective world to attain self-realization, but it needs it in order to overcome it. . . . It creates such limits for itself in order to free itself from them. This act of self liberation is what we call consciousness.[32]

## The Circle of Finitude: The Structure of Idealism in the Wissenschaftslehre

For Fichte, the "I am" grounds all being, since it is the ground of the logical principle of identity, which states that if A is, then it is the same with itself (A = A). This is a fundamental principle of post-

Kantian idealism, that the unity of all beings should be grounded on the unity of the I am I. But the absolute subject, the I = I, is, unlike the "if . . . then" principle, not merely conditional. The "I am" is both existing and the same with itself, is both the agent and product of itself, comes into existence by asserting itself. The absolute I am does not "come to self-consciousness," but exists only to the extent that the I thinks itself (*GWL*, p. 98). "The I's positing of itself is thus its own pure activity. The I *posits itself*, and by virtue of this mere self-assertion it *exists*; and conversely, the I *exists* and *posits* its own existence by virtue of merely existing" (*GWL*, p. 97).

If I should think of myself as an object, it must be as the object of an absolute subject, whose object, of course, is itself; in this sense I cannot escape subjectivity, cannot escape the fact that I exist for my-self. "From your self-consciousness you can never abstract" (*GWL*, p. 98). Generally, Fichte concludes, the absolute subject, the I am, is the identity of subject and object, is "that whose being or essence consists simply in the fact that it posits itself as existing. . . . The I is that which it posits itself to be; and it posits itself as that which it is. Hence *I am absolutely what I am*" (*GWL*, pp. 98–99).

At this point began the creative misinterpretation of Fichte by ro-mantics in Germany (Novalis for example) for whom this free and ungrounded assertion of the Absolute Ego was in a manner of speak-ing "symbolized" by the boundlessly self-reflexive activity of the in-dividual creative mind, the Absolute and the finite differing only in degree.[33] In fact, Fichte's Absolute I is not the self-consciousness of any one mind; it is rather the infinite self-reflexive act that makes any consciousness possible and cannot be restricted to any one thing or person. The Absolute I can be intuited in us only as the continuous synthetic activity that enables us to be conscious of ourselves as sub-jects, but it cannot be brought under a concept or intellectually con-ceived. For though Fichte has indeed transformed the Kantian unity of apperception from a merely formal requirement to a dynamic self-creating being, the Absolute I is not conscious of itself as such: con-sciousness for Fichte (as for Kant) requires boundaries, categories, the presence of something not-I. The philosopher reflects upon his intellectual intuition, "by an act upon an act itself," and reports, as it were, on the absolute activity by uttering the "I = I." This I = I expresses the intuition and provides the philosopher with the cer-tainty of the absolute synthetic activity:

[The original act of the absolute I] is not a *conceiving;* this it only becomes by contrast with a not-I. . . . By the act described [the intellectual intuition], the I is merely endowed with the possibility of self-consciousness; but no true consciousness comes into being as yet. The act in question is only a part . . . to be separated by the philosopher, of that entire enterprise of the intellect whereby it brings its consciousness into being. (2d Intro., *GWL,* pp. 34–35)[34]

This brings us to a crucial point in the *Wissenschaftslehre,* one Hegel believed devastating to the intellectual unity of Fichte's system. The I = I expresses, indeed, a unifying first principle in which the I as subject sees itself as one with the I as object. As we have seen, above, the absolute subject licenses this identification. But if there was something to unify—the I as posing and the I as posed—there must be a *difference* to begin with. The absolute I accounts for the unification; what accounts for (or "grounds") the original difference?

Hegel complained that Fichte's idealism could not explain this duplicity as it should, by the absolute I completely conceived through philosophical reflection:

But the I = I is not a *pure* identity, i.e. not an identity which has arisen through the abstraction of reflection. If reflection conceives of the I = I as unity, it must also conceive of it at the same time as duplicity. . . . I = I is the absolute principle of speculation, but this identity is not exhibited by the system. The objective I is not equivalent to the subjective I and both remain absolutely opposed.

Hegel goes on to charge that Fichte does not deduce his second principle, the principle of difference, from the first principle, the principle of unity.[35]

In the sense of systematic deduction, Hegel is correct. But although Fichte finds he cannot deduce his second principle from the first, it should be seen as nevertheless following immediately from the *utterance* of the I = I, since this affirmation of unity implies an affirmation of original duality. He finds that there is, in fact, no possible systematic derivation of negation from the I = I; hence he "comes upon" this primordial negation as a fundamental act of the Ego, negation "is posited absolutely, *as* such, just *because* it is posited" (*GWL,* p. 103). Fichte finds in the very articulation of the principle of unity (A = A) a dualism inherent in our coming to *consciousness* of unity: this awareness underlies the basic logical form of negation, namely that not-A $\neq$ A. The not-A could not be counterposed unless the I posed itself to begin with. Hence the counterposing does take place *within* the I; yet since in the original absolute positing the I poses itself, if there is to be a counterposing it must be something absolutely opposed to this I, a *not-I*. From this negation Fichte arrives at the second principle of human knowledge: that within the I, a not-I is opposed absolutely (*GWL,* pp. 104–5).

Fichte had now articulated the fundamental dilemma of transcendental idealism, and his manner of grappling with it would have far-reaching implications both for the articulation of his system and for its place in the history of thought. It is also a problem, I will argue, that has parallels throughout the culture of idealism and self-assertion in the romantic era. "I am I" has led to an evident though complex contradiction. The absolute activity becomes conscious of itself through an act of self-position. But in so doing—for reasons Fichte maintains are unknowable—the Absolute has *created,* has opposed a creation to itself. Only the I is active, only the I posits; the not-I, then, is posited only so far as the I originally posits. Yet the not-I is posited absolutely against the I, so that insofar as a *not-I* is posited within the I, that I does *not* posit itself. To the extent that the I posits, it posits absolutely a not-I; to the extent that it posits a not-I absolutely, the I does not posit itself. What is the meaning of this strange circle, and is it possible to escape from it?

In fact, this circle can never really begin, for if opposition is asserted absolutely in the I, then the I divided against itself would be annihilated, and consciousness as we know it could not arise (*GWL,* pp. 106–7). Yet experience shows us that we are, or think ourselves to be, affected by a "not-I" even if philosophy cannot explain the origin of this otherness.[36] What we are seeing here is a direct and systematic confrontation with the dilemma raised for idealism by Kant, which was examined in Chapter 3. The "not-I" represents not nature but the mind's capacity to receive nature, to be passive; transcendental idealism, Fichte insists, demands that the not-I be not something abstracted by mind from its experience of objects, but *a receptivity given by the mind to itself* (*GWL,* p. 105). If this receptivity is asserted absolutely (as in Fichte's second principle), then the mind's absolute capacity for *self*-determination (the first principle) would be destroyed, and self-consciousness would be impossible. Fichte needs some third principle that can reconcile the first two, proceeding from them and preserving both the facts of self-consciousness and that we feel ourselves determined by a not-I.

Opposed to the Absolute is negation; but also opposed to the Absolute (from another perspective) is the finite. The act of the I that will allow both absolute principles to be asserted without anni-hilation, while preserving their opposition, is *limitation*. Both the I and the not-I will be posited *to the degree* that the other is not. For this to be so, both the I and the not-I must be finite, or divisible into parts. The third principle of human knowledge, then, is the prin-ciple of finitude: "In the I, I oppose a divisible not-I to the divisible I" (*GWL*, p. 110). No philosophy, says Fichte, can go further in articu-lating the fundamental principles of consciousness.

Here a new opposition has been created—between the absolute I and the finite I. The absolute I can become conscious of itself only through this act of limitation or *reflection*. "Consciousness," says Fichte, "is possible only through reflection, and reflection only through de-termination" (*GWL*, p. 237). A new, more clearly defined circle hereby arises. The I opposes a divisible I to a divisible not-I. Yet simply finding that "the not-I in part negates the I" does not explain how the I—which is originally pure activity—can "posit" this nega-tion in itself. And finding that "the I in part negates the not-I" does not explain how the not-I comes originally to have *any* reality for an I that began by positing all reality within itself. As the I becomes aware of itself as conscious, it cannot explain the "givenness" of the world; as the I becomes conscious of the world as given, it cannot account for how it becomes given for the I, how the I becomes *aware* of itself as affected by a world. Fichte's explanation of this dilemma is lucidly paraphrased by Robert Adamson:

> So soon as we reflect upon the activity of the Ego, the Ego is neces-sarily finite; so soon as the Ego is conscious of its finitude, it is con-scious of striving beyond those limits, and so of its infinitude. Were the question raised, Is the Ego, then, infinite? the Ego, by the very ques-tion, is finite. Is the Ego finite? then, to be aware of finitude, it is neces-sarily infinite, and so on, in endless alternation.[37]

This "endless alternation" we may call *the circle of finitude*, and the main body of Fichte's work is devoted to the immensely complex task of its systematic analysis and reconstitution within the synthetic unity of the absolute I. For the purposes of my argument only the major results of this difficult reasoning need to be discussed. At this point, we can see clearly that these fundamental principles illuminate that dialectic which stands at the beginning of romantic quest: the fall from absolute self-affirmation (the identity of the affirmer and the affirmed) into finite self-consciousness (the division of alienated self and opposed world).

Though some critics have, like M. H. Abrams, noted Fichte's account of alienation and its cultural parallels, few have understood his creation of a system of imagination to explain and to justify human finitude. That system will be a unity, but not a static one. It will evolve by antithesis and synthesis, dynamically, from its own principles. Its goals will be nothing less than the articulation of finitude—the boundary of the not-I—as the necessary revelation of absolute consciousness. This revelation will not overcome or "sublate" finitude, but will display the Absolute—the *ideal*—in its relation to the finite human imagination. Fichte's work, like many romantic texts, resembles both theodicy and quest for self-revelation.

That revelation, for Fichte, must be an activity of moral quest, or *striving*, and in this he diverges from much in romantic culture that resisted subordinating the creative imagination to the moral imperative. Yet Fichte's system of imagination is nonetheless a profound, radical, yet characteristic statement of an essential component of this culture. Though Blake, for example, is quite distant from Fichte on many doctrinal points (Fichte believes, for instance, that intellectual not sensuous intuition is our only intimation of infinitude), his cosmology in *The Book of Urizen* and elsewhere closely parallels in mythic image the phenomenological analyses in *The Science of Knowledge*. In Blake's myth it is the voice of the once "silent, dark Urizen" who complains that in the Absolute, without form nothing is certain; there are no articulate words as yet in what, to him, are "bleak desarts." In the beginning, from the narrator's perspective,

> Earth was not: nor globes of attraction
> The will of the Immortal expanded
> Or contracted his all flexible senses
> Death was not, but eternal life sprung
> (*The Book of Urizen*, pl. 3, lines 36–39)[38]

But for Urizen, "Dark revolving in silent activity. . . . A self-contemplating shadow," assertion will mean the creation of an absolute negation, "a solid without fluctuation":

> First, I [Urizen] fought with the fire; consumed
> Inwards, into a deep world within:
> A void immense, wild dark and deep,
> Where nothing was; Nature's wide womb[.]
> And self balanc'd stretch'd o'er the void
> I alone, even I! The winds merciless
> Bound; but condensing, in torrents
> They fall and fall; strong I repell'd
> The vast waves, and arose on the waters
> A wide world of solid obstruction.
>     (Pl. 4, lines 14–23)

For Urizen the creation of form is a chance to destroy relatedness through absolute negation; for Los, it will appear, this fall is an opportunity to create a system of imagination, a living synthesis of oppositions (cf., for example, *The Book of Los*, pl. 4, lines 43–53). To grant the not-I its integrity as finite form, the ground of human intelligence, and also to see it as an imaginative creation is the task of Fichte's system. Or, as Blake says of the creative work of the Sons of Los,

> every Natural effect has a Spiritual Cause, and Not
> A Natural: for a Natural Cause only seems, it is a Delusion
> Of Ulro: & a ratio of the perishing Vegetable Memory.
>     (*Milton*, pl. 26, lines 43–46)

# 5

## Interdetermination, Imagination, Striving: Fichte and Some Principles of Quest Romance

How does it come to be that the mind knows itself, poses itself, as determined by a finite not-I? This central question expresses the circle of finitude: if the I poses *itself*, then it is not finite; if it poses itself as *determined*, then it must be finite. This circle, we have seen, follows from Fichte's third principle, which itself harbors two propositions: that "the I posits the not-I as determined by the I," and that "the I posits itself as determined by the not-I." The first proposition is the foundation of the Practical *Wissenschaftslehre* and assumes that a real not-I exists for the I to determine; at this point, however, it is precisely this question of existence that is at issue. Fichte must postpone considering this proposition until the Theoretical portion of his system can make sense of the contradictions implied in the second proposition. The problem for Theoretical Reason is to explain the mind's belief in the "natural causality" of its mental images, to explain the sense of a "real" not-I. Initially, the I posits all reality in itself. How, then, can the I that "posits itself" believe, too, that it is *affected* by a real not-I that *causes* mental images (presentations)? Can idealism account for our conviction that we are acted upon by a real not-I, by an independently active nature?

Transcendental idealism meets this challenge through organic *system*. Fichte will attempt to show that these very questions derive from the unity of the first principles of human consciousness. The entire articulated system of knowledge, of a *Wissenschaftslehre*, represents in its development of the relations between mind and world a single reflection of the I upon itself. The absolute character of the I demands that this system evolve dialectically, uncovering contradictions and finding synthetic resolutions, only to reach a new boundary implying new contradictions.[1]

Even the form of this organic system Fichte derives from the principles of consciousness. The third principle, for instance, states that "A in part = $\sim$A," and vice versa (*GWL*, p. 110). Fichte calls the principle of divisibility the "grounding" principle: if A and $\sim$A are opposed, it must yet be possible to find some *ground* on which they are alike. And if A is the same as A, it must nonetheless be possible to find some ground on which they are opposed (this is demonstrated in *GWL*, pp. 110–11). The first movement is that of synthesis, the latter of analysis. The *Wissenschaftslehre* contains within itself the principle of its own form, the evolution of dialectical synthesis popularly associated with Hegel.

Moreover, this demand for organic unity is not derived from any analogy with nature or biological organization, but rather proceeds from the essential demand of consciousness to evolve a self-comprehension that is one with itself. It is only by evolving such a system that man comes to conceive organism and purpose in nature. In other words, though most critics of thought recognize the romantic quest as a striving after organic unity, they tend to see this as stemming from a naturalistic urge to identify the mind with nature.[2] But Fichte's analysis, properly understood, provides a more fundamental theory of the urge to organic system: that it is in fact the creation of the mind formulating to itself its unity through a series of confrontations with division and finitude. It is for this reason that we are able to conceive or value organic teleology. This essentially spiritual interpretation of organicism became typical with Hegel and Schelling; extended throughout romantic culture, it constitutes an important structural principle not only in philosophical texts but also in the major literary forms of the period from Bildungsroman to quest romance.

The demand for organic unity is for Fichte, however, just that— a demand. At a certain point in the system, what is disclosed is a circling, a contradiction, that can only be fully determined and defined but not overcome. The circling is between realism and idealism, between the world as thing-in-itself and the mind as free and creative. The central deduction (Section E) of the *Wissenschaftslehre* is a continuing oscillation between a realism that can account for the givenness of the world and an idealism that can account for the freedom and self-consciousness of the I.[3] Yet Fichte will conclude that this oscillation, or opposition, is necessary to the finite mind: "From the very fact of absolute opposition there follows the entire mechanism of the human mind" (*GWL*, p. 202). The opposition is created to make *real* for us both the I and the world; the power that creates, sustains, and unifies these theoretical opposites within a single consciousness is the *productive imagination* (*GWL*, p. 201).

Understanding how Fichte arrives at this extraordinary doctrine will deepen our sense of its meaning and its applicability to romantic practice. I can give here only the basic outlines of his conclusions, and I will do so specifically to offer clear definitions to three principles of quest romance: striving, imagination, and the dialogue between the real and the ideal. In the central deduction Fichte is at his most brilliant and suggestive, and these three doctrines taken together imply an overarching and comprehensive theory of romantic irony as the continuous creation and endless overcoming of world upon world, concept upon concept, by the striving creative imagination. According to Nicolai Hartmann, "The doctrine of the productive imagination rightly ought to be valued as the masterpiece of the *Wissenschaftslehre*."[4]

Yet even so astute a reader as Hartmann also believes that Section E is "among the most difficult texts ever written."[5] Without questioning this dubious honor, I will nevertheless attempt a brief summary of the stages of synthesis between the I and the not-I, understanding that Fichte's system serves tentatively as an analytic model for the psychological dialectics of imaginative quest in romantic culture.

## *The Fichtean Ego and the Enchantment of Romance*

Stripped of Fichtean jargon, the question so central for romantic thought is, Can the mind see itself as somehow the ultimate source of its own limitation in the real world? If it can, the real becomes a function of the ideal; if it cannot, the real is something *other*, alien, and its action upon us—thought and image—is as mysterious as a dream. Romantic culture saw dangers and possibilities at both poles: it asked whether a mature wisdom could find a dynamic third position, a true mediation?[6]

Grasping the possibility of such mediation is the elusive goal of Fichte's struggle in his theoretical deduction. He begins by analyzing the basic principle of theoretical reflection, "The I posits itself as determined by a not-I" and finds within this a paradox. If the I posits itself, it is active; if it is determined by a not-I, it is passive. How can both principles be maintained? Fichte introduces a third principle, the notion of limitation. The I will posit itself *in part*; the reality the I does not posit of itself, it must therefore posit of (or attribute to) the not-I. In other words, for every negation of reality the I posits in itself, it posits just so much positive reality in the not-I. For example, the I posits itself as "thinking," but does not also attribute to itself "not-thinking." The I therefore attributes "not-thinking" to the not-I.

In this synthesis, then, the I attributes a certain degree of reality to itself, but precisely to the extent it attributes reality to itself, so much reality does it deny to the not-I. To the extent it attributes reality to the not-I, so much reality does it deny to itself. The apparent paradox is thus resolved: from one point of view the I determines itself (it posits a negation in itself); from another point of view the not-I determines the I (its reality opposes that of the I). Yet these are only two ways of expressing the same relation, that the I and the not-I mutually determine each other. Fichte calls this synthesis *reciprocal determination* (*Wechselbestimmung*), or, as it is usually translated, *interdetermination*.[7]

Although this synthesis, it will appear, is only a tentative result, a landing place, an unstable dialectical moment, it nevertheless has the most profound implications for a theoretical study of the culture of romance. The principle of interdetermination belongs to a transcendental deduction, a history of consciousness that commences with absolute self-affirmation. Fichte's is not an analysis of the psychological subject but of the grounds for the possibility of any consciousness at all. Yet we may "translate" interdetermination along psychological axes, just as so many romantic artists were eager to understand transcendental discussion about consciousness as discussion about the particular psychological subject. Such a translation reveals at once a parallel *structural* matrix between Fichte's idealist analysis of consciousness and the principles of quest in romantic poetry. So translated, the reciprocal determination of I and not-I in Fichte reads as a fundamental postulate of romance: *that I exist only so far as the world I create does, and the world exists only so far as I permit it to.* The first half of this proposition defines the I as *dreamer;* the second defines the world as a *symbol* of mental (spiritual) activity. Fichte's philosophy, Novalis believed, could justify a "magic idealism"; although Novalis's word applies only to this first stage of Fichte's work, this desire for absolute transparency remains one of the most primitive principles of romance. The priority of this principle of *magic* is of course logical and not historical: any number of romances in this period begin with anxiety over magic that has fled.[8]

Such a loss is inevitable because the principle of magic is inherently unstable. The facts of human experience seem to contradict both halves of the principle of magic. If the I in some way creates the not-I it does so without consciousness. Why would the I obscure from itself its own creative power? A theoretical question also intrudes, a question familiar in theology: *why* does the I need to create, and why does that creation seem alien to it? In Fichte's analysis, the principle of interdetermination only raises further questions. How can the I, which originally is all reality, come to posit reality in a not-I and deny any reality to itself (*GWL,* p. 128)? Both in the *Wissenschaftslehre* and in the structure of romance, these instabilities impel further development and dynamic syntheses. Fichte sees the issue as between an absolute ("dogmatic") idealism in which the world is only one aspect of the I's activity and an equally absolute realism in which the I is made a passive recipient of the world's activity. In his search for a coherent synthesis of these absolutes, Fichte articulates further principles of human consciousness, and these too, we will find, have their counterparts in the psychological and literary principles of romance.

Fichte proceeds through a series of immensely intricate syntheses of realism and idealism, at each stage defining intermediate positions and discovering contradictions or limitations therein.[9] The final synthesis must show that the I's positing of itself is impossible without a check (*Anstoss*), but that this check is also dependent upon the I.

Thus the I may assert itself as infinite but could not do so without a boundary: "The check occurs to the I insofar as it is active in the I; its possibility is conditioned upon the I's activity: no activity of the I, no check [an idealism]. Conversely, the activity of the I's own *self-* determining would be conditioned by the check: no check, no self-determination [a realism]" (*GWL*, p. 191). This crucial synthesis goes beyond simple interdetermination to assert that in *a single act* the not-I permits the I to assert, and the assertion of the I is to pose a not-I. In this synthesis, the not-I does not have independent reality; this "critical realism" maintains only that the I defines *itself* through its assertion, and that in order to do so there must occur a check to the I's act which enables it to limit itself.

Thus the not-I is the product of the self-assertion *and* self-limitation of the I. Yet this does not deny the I's ultimate *finitude*, for the I could not become self-conscious were it not for this boundary to its activity. This boundary is in one sense produced by the I's act, but in another sense it is not: the act itself is made possible by the boundary. Does the boundary, then, exist or act independently of the I? We seem caught in another circle. But from this circle, Fichte finds, no theoretical philosophy can escape (*GWL*, p. 247). Further, this circle itself is what makes possible all human awareness, what generates the world in space and time and enables us simultaneously to appropriate that world as knowledge.[10]

The conflict between the boundary as real and the boundary as the product of the I must be synthesized in a single act, and that act must produce consciousness as a synthesis of the real and the ideal. In a striking conclusion, Fichte identifies this primary synthetic activity as the *productive imagination* (*GWL*, p. 193).

For Fichte, it is the imagination that binds man to finitude (time) even as it discloses his creative infinitude. As Thomas Hohler points out, "The production of time [for Fichte] is at the core of the imagination."[11] To clarify this point, we must understand what and how the imagination synthesizes. It is useful here to quote Fichte's summary:

> The activity of the I consists in unbounded self-assertion: to this there occurs a resistance. If it yielded to this obstacle then the activity lying beyond the bounds of resistance would be utterly abolished and destroyed; to that extent the I would not posit it all. But for all that, it must also posit beyond this line. It must limit itself, that is, it must posit

itself to that extent as not positing itself; it must set the indeterminate, unbounded, infinite limit . . . and if it is to do this, it must be infinite.
— Moreover, if the I did not bound itself, it would not be infinite.
— The I is only what it posits itself to be. That it is infinite, is to say that it posits itself as infinite; it *determines* itself by the predicate of infinitude. . . . This infinitely outreaching activity that it differentiates from itself must be *its* activity. . . . But in thus being received, the activity is determined, and so not infinite. . . .
This interplay of the I, in and with itself, whereby it posits itself at once as finite and infinite . . . this is the power of *imagination*. (*GWL*, p. 193)

This is the single most important result of Fichte's deduction and undoubtedly was the most well known and influential. In a single act, the I asserts both its finitude and infinitude, and the paradox is synthesized through the imagination.[12] This is possible because the Fichtean imagination creates spatial images and temporal series: in these, the *boundary*, or check, is made real. At the same time, these boundaries of space and time can be extended indefinitely by endless division. The present moment, as Hohler notes, is undefinable and indeterminate (infinite); yet it is *also* bounded, dependent upon the past series. The imagination brings the infinite to man through a synthetic act of *preserving* and *binding*. It holds up the past to the awareness of the present moment and carries these both forward to the next element of the series.[13]

Through this realizing of the boundary, the I is enabled to assert itself as infinite and as real—in a sense, the imagination "rescues" the I by enabling it to turn back upon itself from the finite boundary. The finite boundary, made real by imagination, *enables* the I to assert itself—as infinite. The synthesis of imagination, Hohler concludes, "expresses the continual holding together of the opposed, and in its circular movement nothing is fixed. . . . This unity consists of the temporalizing imagination which is guided by the I's interest to be itself. Time as the fundamental unity of the I is the originary, horizonal unity whereby the I can *be* in its own meaningful world."[14]

The synthetic, productive imagination "hovers" (*schwebt*) between the real and the ideal. Through the real, the ideal comes to know itself as a striving toward infinity. This is Fichte's dynamic resolution to the problem of the thing-in-itself. When the mind attempts to assert the independence of the world *or* the independence of the I, it becomes caught up in a circle created by the imagination. The circle becomes a trap only if the mind demands to know absolutely, infinitely, whether the world or the mind is the only reality. This question cannot be answered, because—as we have seen—we cannot know the one without somehow presupposing the other. If the mind poses the thing-in-itself as independent, immediately it is clear that this thing-in-itself was posed as independent *by us*. But if we assert that the thing-in-itself is "only" a product of the mind, we must still posit "farther out" another boundary to explain consciousness. "The Science of Knowledge," Fichte asserts, "is therefore *realistic*. It shows that the consciousness of finite creatures is utterly inexplicable, save on the presumption of a force existing independently of them." Yet Fichte's is also a transcendental idealism because that independent force, when reflected upon, "again becomes a product of its own power of thought, and thus something dependent on the I. . . . But in order for this new account of the first explanation to be possible, we again presuppose that something on which the I depends." Any philosophical system that pretends to transcend this circle is a dogmatism that ignores human finitude. "This fact, that the finite spirit must necessarily posit something absolute outside itself (a thing-in-itself), and yet must recognize, from the other side, that the latter exists only *for it* (as a necessary noumenon), is the circle which it is able to extend into infinity but can never escape" (*GWL*, pp. 246–47). The alternative to dogmatism is a system of imagination, which deduces the source of this circle in the imagination. Further, the *purpose* of the imagination's activity is to provide the I with the means to realize itself through the finite. At this point, having defined the theoretical circle, the *Wissenschaftslehre* becomes a practical wisdom, a philosophy of moral *striving* (*streben*).[15]

## Imagination and Human Finitude

We see, then, that Fichte's system is far from the absolute idealism it often is portrayed as being, far from the "Crude Egoismus" Coleridge branded it.[16] The not-I is brought forth not by a magical ego but by the imagination in its continuous oscillation between finite and infinite, between the real and the ideal. From the first principle of romance—the magical interplay of the I and its created world—we have arrived at the second principle, one that takes further account of the independent action of the real world while simultaneously granting it reality only as it is taken up into the human mind. This psychological principle directly parallels Fichte's deduction and is fundamental to the evolution of romance: *The world is an other that discloses itself to me, becomes real to me, only through my own creative act; this act can only transform what it first encounters as something "other."* The first half of this proposition defines the I as *creator,* or in some versions of romance, as *artist;* the second defines the world as alien, or more optimistically as the dormant material of symbolism, necessary to the ego's creativity. Taken together, this second proposition of romance is the principle of *imagination.*

The romantic imagination is the subject of enough study that it may not seem profitable or enlightening to add yet another formulation or derivation. What I would emphasize here, however, is that this Fichtean analysis reveals a little-understood structural continuity among the terms of romantic quest—organicism, self-assertion, imagination, magic, quest, infinitude, irony, alienation. This continuity, I hope to have shown, discloses itself through a careful unfolding of the implications of an organic system of idealism. This is not to argue, however, that every romantic poet or poem evolves the *same* continuity: an imaginative dialectic with the world is generally valued over a simply magical one, for example, but there may be struggles and contradictions between poets or within a single canon. As Earl Wasserman emphasized, the challenge to the critic is to articulate the diversity and particularity of each poet's response to a common cultural problem—the radically redefined relations of subject and object implicit in the new idealism.[17] Fichte's conclusion that "our doctrine here is therefore that all reality . . . is brought forth solely by the imagination. . . . [Imagination] is not a deception, but gives us truth, and the only possible truth," is strikingly congruent with Keats's faith that "what the imagination seizes as Beauty must be truth."[18] Through a clearly articulated system of idealism, that congruence is comprehensible and neither surprising nor facile. Yet even more important is the opportunity to trace with deeper insight the ramifications of diverse responses and developments in their particularity (why does Keats, for instance, add the element of *beauty,* and how does this affect the development of his romance?).

Moreover, Fichte assuredly did not have the last word in developing a system of idealism. Fichte, unlike others, saw the system of imagination as subordinate to a further principle, a principle of moral striving and practical activity. Again, this final position of the *Wissenschaftslehre* is illuminating in defining a third principle of romance. But it was not true that for every romantic text this principle was final or dominant. For Fichte, we remember, the function of imagination is to present a finite world through which the I may become itself, and this continuous becoming reflects the I's assertion of its infinitude. The imagination has a purpose, the creation of the possibility of real self-assertion. The mind cannot rest in the theoretical synthesis of imagination. If we examine that synthesis, we see that as with the principle of interdetermination, there is an essential instability. Within the imaginative synthesis is a built-in tension, a tendency to leap outside the synthesis, to experience the infinite, to encompass the thing-in-itself.

Like Kant, Fichte sees this as an impulse of theoretical reason to overleap itself. The imagination seeks through consciousness to hold fast the infinite spontaneity and finite passivity of the I. Imagination is the active principle that mediates between the passive mode of perception and the endlessly reflexive mode of self-consciousness. Fichte's ego never becomes fully aware of itself as creating its world through this mediating activity. Yet when the I does focus on its infinity *in itself*, it then seeks to posit something "further out," beyond the synthesis of imagination. The I would posit itself absolutely, but at the same time sees it cannot do so without the check of the finite to allow it to reflect back upon itself, to *know* itself as infinite. Yet the I must posit all reality in itself: to do this, it must see itself as the true source of the activity of the check (*GWL*, pp. 232ff). It must deny reality to the check itself. The I knows that it cannot do this and also be self-conscious, cannot finally subsume the check to itself without destroying its ability to be itself through finitude.

There are now *two* activities within the I that must be synthesized: first, the I's imaginative creation of a finite world through which it may know itself; and second an activity that seeks to be infinite in itself, to subsume the not-I completely in the absolute assertion of the I. The I thus attempts on its own to push back the boundaries created for it by the imagination. Another way to see this is that the I comes to posit itself through the finite, and Fichte calls this activity of self-reversion *centripetal*. Yet the I would assert itself "simply *for itself"* as it would be without this finitude; Fichte calls this activity *centrifugal* (*GWL*, p. 241). If the I reflects upon the first activity, it encounters the synthetic act of imagination, the creation of the *real*. But if the I seeks to encompass all things in itself, it goes beyond the real to things as they *ought* to be, toward the *ideal* (*GWL*, p. 244). The I demands that the two activities, centripetal and centrifugal, belong to it itself. But this can be the case only if these activities are alike, are congruent (*GWL*, p. 229). They are not, in fact, alike, because the activity of the check infinitely opposes the I; hence the I must demand and demand *infinitely* that they *ought* to be alike. This infinite demand would be impossible without a world to demand against; the imagination thus creates a world for the I to attempt to overcome. Fichte calls this infinite struggle of the I to overcome the world it creates the principle of *striving* (*GWL*, p. 231).

In the synthesis of imagination, the I comes to know itself as it *is*, vis-à-vis the world. Striving enables the I to extend itself "beyond the actual world to a world as it *might* be and become."[19] This demand conflicts with the harmonizing power of imagination. Idealist striving plays a crucial role in the teleological unfolding of nineteenth-century romance.

This synthesis is, in a manner of speaking, a "temporalizing" of magic, a transforming power directed at a world acknowledged as "other." The mind comes to know itself only by engaging the world; but that engagement is itself a continuous struggle to idealize and to transform. We may state this as a principle of romance, a still higher level of synthesis than the first two: *the world must become what I desire, and desire is infinite; yet the world is precisely what resists me, and I cannot realize my desire to become what I am without this resistance. My relation to the world is thus a striving within time and finitude.* We have thus derived the romance principle of *quest*.

As Hegel was the first to point out, Fichte's synthesis of striving is by no means a comforting resolution; rather, it reflects an "alienation" of the I from the world and from itself. The striving is impossible of fulfillment on its own terms, yet for Fichte this struggle after the ideal gives meaning to the temporal mission of the I as it grows toward self-consciousness and a greater sense of its freedom. For Fichte, as for Kant, the primacy of the realm of the ideal placed a demand upon man that he struggle to awareness of his freedom within the finite world. Again, man as the being who is free within

finitude takes precedence in idealism over man as the passive per-
ceiver of mental images.

Yet for many thinkers in Fichte's age, the core of alienation in his
version of idealism led to an untenable devaluation of actual, finite
experience. The I must realize itself in the actual, yet this actual is
continuously to be overcome or "sublated" into a mere ground for the
I's assertion. The dialectic that seems inescapable is that the I strives
to overcome the alien reality in the name of self-fulfillment, yet the I
cannot become itself apart from the defining opposition of the real.
The reality once overcome, the I can no longer strive against anything and so has no ground for fulfilling itself. The I can fulfill its
demand for self-knowledge only in *activity* for Fichte, never in theoretical reflection, yet it is precisely the demand to know itself trans-
parently as the creator of its experience that initiates the theoretical
reflection. The transparency is demanded but never achieved; only
in continuous practical striving does the I find its "home." We are left
with the well-known romantic irony of man's need to find his home
simultaneously in the actual, finite world as well as within his infinite
freedom. This dialectic reflects a deep schism between the harmonizing circle of imaginative interchange and the principle of the
quest for self-realization. This Fichtean dilemma, the final result of
*Wissenschaftslehre*, provides us with one of the most complete (if implicit) explorations of romantic irony ever articulated in the romantic period, a theoretical insight that the Schlegels would develop
and reformulate into a central critical principle of contemporary
literature.

## Conclusion: Romantic Irony

The canny psychologist Søren Kierkegaard understood well how his
own generation continued to read Fichtean idealism as a guide to
psychological understanding rather than as transcendental analysis.
By 1841 the German-speaking world was well saturated with the
loose Fichteanism of Novalis, Tieck, and Schlegel, and in this year
Kierkegaard unleashed a diatribe against "Irony after Fichte." He
identifies this irony with "romanticism and the romanticist" in general. Following Hegel's lead, he eloquently attacks the infinite negativity of the ironist in relation to the actual:

> As the ego is merely formally [the I = I] hence negatively conceived, Fichte essentially got no further than the finite, elastic *molimina* [exertions] towards a beginning. He has the infinite longing of the negative, its *nisus formativus* [formative struggle], but has it as a divine and absolute impatience, as an infinite power which yet accomplishes nothing because there is nothing to which it can be applied. It is a potentiality and an exaltation mighty like a god, which is able to lift the whole world but has nothing to lift.[20]

If Kierkegaard is less than patient with Fichte's faith in continuous striving, it is because he had seen a generation confound "the empirical and finite ego with the eternal ego" and so conclude that the world existed not in itself but only to provide an arena for the finite ego to create those myths it desires for itself. Authentic life is then the life of genius, the life of continuous dramatic re-creation. Idealism, after all, could license the belief that life and fiction are equally products of the symbol-making mind. For Kierkegaard this led to a self-assured devaluation of historical actuality and an inability to commit oneself to the real experience of human life.

Nevertheless, Kierkegaard knew his debt to Fichte and knew, too, that the edge of irony is truly double. There was, for Kierkegaard, a "cleansing baptism of irony that redeems the soul from having its life in finitude through living boldly and energetically in finitude."[21] This is close to what Fichte himself hoped would be a living synthesis of imagination and striving. His notion of imagination is ultimately practical, a creative activity engaged with the world. The double power of irony stems precisely from its negativity, its capacity to free man from the actual while simultaneously embracing it: "If [irony] allowed anything to stand it knew it had the power to destroy it, and it knew this at the same moment it allowed it to endure."[22] Yet a truly complete irony recognized man's need to commit himself to the world both *despite* and *because* of the fact that it is his own creation. The positive moment of irony allows it to *reappropriate* the actual while still remaining creatively free. The negative moment allows man to free himself from his creations. This redemptive irony is truly dialectical, allowing in its duplicity a "mastery" of the real and the ideal.[23]

The great artists of the romantic period in England, particularly those of the second generation of poets, felt deeply this challenge of irony as the problem of heroism and of love in the modern world.

A mastery of the moments of irony allows the hero in an idealist cosmos both to retain his free, creative integrity and to commit himself to the moral life of man. For those who followed Fichte in the development of idealism—notably Schelling—the task now was to develop more clearly the possibilities for uniting human freedom with love for the human and the natural world. For those whose poetic project was to make central the story of the growth of the modern mind toward heroism and love, the task now was to cope with the immense dangers, alienation and despair, of an infinite negative irony. To see that infinite negativity as only one moment in the productive double action of irony is to approach a heroic and imaginative engagement with man's finitude. For writers of romance, this engagement is more a task unfolding than a resounding faith. The terms of romantic irony having been established, the mind turning in one direction or the other created or destroyed itself, became heroic or desperate, through these very same terms as seen from one existential perspective or another. This was a dangerous game enough, and the rewards at its commencement must have seemed uncertain; yet despite much wistful yearning, the safer games of the past were gone and their treasures reduced to flitting ghosts of gilded ages and securer faiths. Heroism and love would heal now in a romance forest of idealism and modern irony, or they would heal not at all. Never before, one feels, had a whole generation of poets felt so vitally expectant—or so alone.

# PART III

## The Quest for an Adequate Symbol: The Unconscious and the Creative Imagination in Schelling and Coleridge

# 6

## Schelling's Idealism and the Development of Romantic Quest

Fichte's protégé Schelling was the center of a circle of poets and thinkers at the turn of the century who thought of themselves as articulating the modern sensibility they dubbed "romantic." Fichte himself was uneasy among them, and even young Schelling, strongly influenced by the *Wissenschaftslehre,* can only loosely be connected with this movement before about 1801. Still, Josiah Royce's judgment that although Schelling, Novalis, and the Schlegel brothers "were rather speculative metaphysicians than true poets, they were nevertheless rather romancers than soberly constructive philosophers"[1] is instructive. Although Royce surely misjudges Schelling's long and serious philosophical career, there is an important core of truth in the broad distinction he makes. The philosophical system of Transcendental Idealism informed the romantic movement and paralleled it in many fundamental structures, but (with the exception of the mature—post-1806—work of Schelling) the outcomes of the philosophers' systems were quite distinct from the dark perplexities and only tentatively intuited or longed-for resolutions of the romantic poets.

The idealist project, unlike the cultural movement known as romanticism, valued an organic system of Reason that pointed to a clear teleology. The goal was to exhibit the priority of Practical Reason—the ideal realm of Ends—over phenomenal knowledge (*Verstand*). For the soberly constructive Fichte, philosophy as *Wissenschaft* could clearly define the limits of human knowing and the meaning or destiny (*Bestimmung*) of moral striving. Although knowledge does not, as we have seen, bring spiritual wholeness or overcome our alienation from the ideal, Reason can nevertheless develop a systematic account of its evolution from the fundamental intuition of self-consciousness. Yet even those romantic poets and essayists who, like Novalis and Coleridge, knew and accepted the fundamental premises and paradoxes of an idealism developed from absolute self-consciousness could not approve the Fichtean conclusion that the empirical ego must strive in the single direction prescribed by the moral ideal. Fichtean irony had opened a gap between the real and the ideal that no clear course of ethical development could close. Indeed, even at the peak of his enthusiastic reading of German philosophy Coleridge could still write to Southey, "There does not exist an instance of a *deep* metaphysician who was not led by his speculations to an austere system of morals.—What can be more austere than the Ethics of Aristotle—than the systems of Zeno, St. Paul, Spinoza (in the Ethical Books of his Ethics), Hartley, Kant, and Fichte?"[2]

For Schelling, too, Fichte's philosophy of moral striving failed to rise to the systematic wholeness that could explain and overcome the rift between the absolute self-assertion of the I and the finitude of the world. Schelling believed, in his earliest works, that originally consciousness and nature were one self-reflecting activity; only philosophical reflection had disrupted this unity once expressed in the childhood of the race through myth.[3] Although like Fichte's, Schelling's philosophy began with the free act of the "I am I," quite unlike Fichte he asks whether this act may not be considered a unifying act of *Being* in which Being reflects upon itself.[4] Philosophy must recover the meaning of this primordial unity.

Romantic poetry, on the other hand, is better characterized through the Fichtean dialectics that begin with the assertion of man's autonomy and leave problematic his relation to Being or nature. Without the idealist's faith in philosophical system, the romantic is left with the principles of imaginative quest as conflicting moments in the evolution of the self. These principles, we have noted, play against one another in ironic oscillations between faith in the magical autonomy of the self and anxiety-ridden confrontations with, or even surrender to, nature as an organic unity subsuming the self. In general one must agree with Harald Höffding that at least in contrast to systematic idealism, "the romantic school was in a state of constant oscillation. Romanticism oscillates between overweening self-pride (where the pure ego is made identical with the empirical ego) and the mystical surrender of the self (where the empirical self disappears in the pure infinite ego)."[5]

Yet this view ought not to be carried so far that we forget that the great achievements of romantic art proclaim this oscillation to be the inevitable cost of the mind's assertion of itself as the creative source of its own experience and that far from permitting a centrifugal explosion of a divided self, romantic quest seeks in contradictions themselves the clue to a dynamic psychic wholeness. "Contradiction is life's mainspring and core," the mature Schelling would assert.[6] We again recall the double principle of romantic irony: man can free himself from, stand apart from, the paradoxes created by his own free self-assertion, as well as from those very resolutions of conflicts that threaten his integrity as a free being. These resolutions are themselves deeply felt moments of triumph in romantic art: we need think only of the famous identities of mind and nature in Coleridge's "Joy," "the One Life within us and abroad," or Wordsworth's "something far more deeply interfused, / Whose dwelling is the light of setting suns," or even the physical-spiritual transport of Keats's "Pleasure Thermometer."[7] Yet in all of these instances a deep distress, the often-noted rift between self-consciousness and nature in these poets, plunges the mind into self-created alienation. Could this alienation be seen as but a negative image of the mind's struggle to be integral and free both *from* and *through* its own creations? Could this "fall" be seen—as the Wordsworth of the "Immortality" ode explicitly hopes—as the originating point of a romantic humanism that allows man to love the world, even as he frees himself from it and the myths he creates and recreates in the course of his evolving relations?

In a moment of graceful irony Byron quips, "If people contradict themselves, can I / Help contradicting them, and everybody, / Even my veracious self?" No romantic poet so willingly embraced irony as a humanizing and liberating principle, and of Byronic irony I shall have more to say. The panache of Byronic assertion, however, was not available to other romantics; Coleridge, for instance, was perhaps too much aware of his constitutional resistance to irony. "Thy Being's Being is contradiction," he groans in a particularly despondent poem.[8] For Coleridge, at his most hopeful, contradictions are the tensions that force imaginative growth, and his humanism hopes to build from these tensions a world of relatedness and love.

The present section will be concerned with the development of idealism in Schelling and with the poetic works of Coleridge, the only English romantic directly acquainted with the German idealists. I will not claim that—as was the case, for instance, with Novalis— Coleridge wrote poetry in some clear way "influenced" by Fichte or Schelling. There is no doubt that his theoretical articulations about the work of poetic imagination were informed by these and other philosophers. But it is more fundamentally true that he was drawn to idealism in 1799–1801 because he sought to give explicit form to structural principles already germinating in his own poetry and thought. We may, I believe, largely take him at his word when in 1825 he pleads to John Taylor Coleridge that he came to differ greatly with Kant, Fichte, and Schelling, though implying that they served the development of his own thought's tendencies: "All the elements, the *differentials* as the Algebraists say, of my present Opinions existed for me before I had ever seen a book of German Metaphysics later than Wolff and Leibniz, or could have read it if I had."[9]

Much has been written about Coleridge's "indebtedness" to the Schelling whose work he so freely plagiarized in the *Biographia*, and much of what has been said has glibly elided the philosophical differences between the philosopher and the poet or avoided the difficult question of why Coleridge was drawn to Schelling in the first place. The scholarly disarray has only in recent years been set in order by the labors of Gian Orsini, Daniel Stempel, and Thomas McFarland.[10] McFarland and Orsini conclude that Coleridge was drawn to Schelling's reconciliation of mind and nature in absolute self-consciousness, but recoiled when he saw this unification endangering the integrity of the individual imagination.[11] About three years after the composition of the *Biographia*, Coleridge attacked the Schelling of the *System of Transcendental Idealism* (1800) in a long letter to J. H. Green, asserting that Schelling was wrong to imagine that nature (the not-I) could be posited as one "Pole" of the absolute "I am

I": "From the tendency of my mind to confidence in others I was my-self *taken in* by [this doctrine], retrograding from my own prior and better Lights, and adopted it in the metaphysical chapters of my Lit-erary Life. . . . Fichte was far nearer the truth than Schelling."[12]

Indeed, as we shall see, the tensions and irresolutions of Cole-ridge's work are far closer to the ironies and paradoxes of Fichte's sys-tem of imagination. From the evidence of Coleridge's dissatisfaction with Schelling's cosmic principle of imagination, from the evidence of the above letter and an 1801 letter in which Coleridge actually translates the "I = I" passage of the *Wissenschaftslehre* for Dorothy Wordsworth, and from a close study of the poetic imagination at work in "Dejection: An Ode," Daniel Stempel concludes that "Coleridge owed more than he ever admitted to Fichte, perhaps as much or more than he owed to Kant, and certainly more than he owed to Schelling."[13] Stempel is, I believe, substantially correct so far as Coleridge's poetic theory and practice are concerned; but that Cole-ridge systematically and consciously understood this debt is only conjectural, given the evidence to the contrary in the letters and notebooks. Despite his indebtedness to Fichte, he displays as much hostility to Fichte's systematic idealism as to Schelling's. In the letter to Green, Coleridge asserts only that on *this* fundamental issue—the absolute autonomy of the "I am"—Fichte was "nearer the truth"; and in the translation of 1801, Coleridge is actually writing a grotesque parody of Fichte, whose speculation he compares with his young son Hartley's, sneering after his translation that "nothing in Touchstone ever equalled this."[14]

Coleridge rejected the moral striving in Fichte that saw nature as only a not-I posited for the sake of spiritual assertion; in the *Biogra-phia* he concludes (rightly or wrongly) that this implies "a boastful and hyperstoic hostility to NATURE, as lifeless, godless, and alto-gether unholy," while Fichte's ethics culminate in "an ascetic, and al-most monkish, mortification of the natural passions and desires." And Coleridge constantly fears that Fichtean idealism identifies the "I am" of human knowing with God, the principle of all being.[15] Cer-tainly—from the earliest charges of plagiarism against him—there has been no lack of scholars to brand all of Coleridge's disavowals the special pleading of a thinker beset by the guilty knowledge of his derivativeness. But contemporary scholarship now must grant the complex reasons, philosophical and psychological, both for

Coleridge's embracing of transcendental premises and for his rejection on moral, psychological, and theological grounds of systematic idealist philosophy. This ambivalence was no condemnation of Coleridge as a thinker to the one man who knew both Schelling and Coleridge so well, Henry Crabb Robinson: Coleridge "metaphysicized à la Schelling while he abused him."[16]

I will examine Schelling's idealism and Coleridge's response in more detail; here I have set out the scholarly situation with a clear purpose—to establish that the unified system of idealism was not necessarily compatible with the efforts of the romantic poet to define the psychological fact, the experience in its elusive richness, of living out the dilemmas bequeathed by that very idealist revolution. Coleridge was still hopeful in 1818 that he might somehow "proceed with all the vigor in my power . . . to my system of constructive Philosophy. But the *Form* perplexes my choice—A novel or *romance* seems better adapted to the analytical elucidation of a system so abstruse."[17]

Having acknowledged the points of romantic divergence from idealism proper, we can nonetheless assert that the psychological principles elaborated in Chapter 5 are consequences of idealism that presented themselves as problems for romanticism, or as nodes between the forces contending in the open-ended struggles of poetic romance. Despite the often conscious divergence from the ultimate implications of systematic idealism, then, the complex dilemmas of idealist assertion nonetheless stand behind the structure of nineteenth-century romance. My methodology here faces a test: can it be shown that structural affinities actually do exist between the terms of romantic quest I have elaborated from idealism and the poetry of Coleridge, and can these terms be effectively applied to romantic culture? In Coleridge's case, the affinities were—ambivalently or not—elected. But affinities need not be influences in the narrow sense to be illuminating; from Coleridge my terms may be broadened to include the major quests of the second generation of English romantics, who knew little of German speculation beyond what was transmitted to them by Madame de Staël and the Schlegels—and, of course, Coleridge himself.

This is not an entirely novel expectation. Crabb Robinson remarked that "Wordsworth represents, much as, unknown to him, the German philosophers have done, that by the imagination the mere fact is exhibited in its connection with infinity."[18] How "unknown" this connection really was—given Wordsworth's attentive ear to Coleridge in the early years—is perhaps questionable. But the fact remains, that as A. C. Bradley noticed long ago, "Europe saw a magnificent outburst of imaginative literature in England and of philosophy in Germany. Account for the poets and philosophers we cannot in the least; but we can observe a certain community of spirit among them, certain differences between one and another, certain influences which operated on them in various ways."[19] The nebulous adjectives exempt Bradley from much further definition, though he does outline in his essay "some particular affinities between Wordsworth and Hegel" and suggests largely temperamental or generally thematic parallels between Byron and Schopenhauer, Shelley and Schelling. Despite the dangers of such generalizations, a clear account of the philosophy and the literature need not content itself with merely impressionistic parallels. More recently, E. D. Hirsch, despite his reliance on the superficial notion of "Enthusiasm" to connect Wordsworth with Schelling, argues cogently that methodologically the investigation of what he calls the common "Weltanschauung" can yield a "type" of romantic outlook. "Such a type," he observes, "may function as a guiding idea, which permits the student to examine minutely an individual mind in all its complexity without losing sight of the whole."[20]

Whatever we may think of the pious buoyancy of his "Enthusiastic mystic pantheist" reading of the Wordsworth canon, Hirsch's "typological" method—applied flexibly with a clear sense of how articulated philosophical positions may provide clear structural, if not explicit thematic, guides for reading major long poems—can provide psychological, cultural, and aesthetic insights. I emphasize "structure" rather than "idea" because, unlike Hirsch, I see little to be gained by finding common explicit *ideas* or *concepts* between philosopher and poet. If we wish to be edified by Schelling's ideas (or Spinoza's, or Leibniz's, or Plato's) we might learn as much intellectually by reading the philosopher as the poet—though I do not mean to despise Sir Philip Sydney's conviction that we may be more morally moved by the beauty and rhetoric of art. But rather than seek out only common "ideas" between romantic poets and idealist philosophers (though there are many), my aim is to assert the implicit assumptions about mind and its object shared in the romantic era,

assumptions that develop through explicit concept *or* poetic metaphor into either philosophical constructions of consciousness-in-
general or psychological principles forging metaphors for the mind's
understanding of its evolution in the world.

Scholars, we have seen, have begun to sort out in the case of
Coleridge a clear need for an idealist account of consciousness. In
the preceding chapter, I outlined this account and suggested some
psychological principles that a study of idealism may provide to the
study of romantic literature. Can these shared needs and intuited
affinities be further developed into a more comprehensive assertion
of the romantic sense of mind, of the successful and unsuccessful
strategies for advancing the psychological conviction that the mind
is the imagination flowering; that the world is a symbol, still "un-
ravish'd" and expectant; that the perfected expression of art and
beauty is the true home of the questing human spirit—"home" only
because it is ever receding behind, always glimpsed in the distance
ahead?

## Schelling, the Unconscious, and an Idealism of Uncertain Resolutions

"The unruly lies ever in the depths as though it might again break
through. . . . Out of this which is unintelligible intelligence in the
true sense is born. . . . Man is formed in his mother's womb; and
only out of the darkness of unreason (out of feeling, out of longing,
the sublime mother of knowledge) grow clear thoughts." This is not
Freud, but Schelling in 1809 defining a romantic version of the
unconscious.[21] What is distinctly un-Freudian about Schelling's unconscious striving is its destiny in imaginative redemption, not endless sublimation: "The Word which is fulfilled in man exists in nature
as a dark, prophetic Word. . . . Man is the beginning of the new
covenant through whom, as mediator, since he himself is connected
with God, God also accepts nature and binds it to himself [*verbinden*].
Man is thus the redeemer of nature towards whom all its archetypes
strive."[22]

Schelling's unconscious, of course, is not the repressed memory
of the individual; it is rather the continuing process through which
consciousness comes into being in opposition to the world. The

original unity of I and not-I is not directly available to awareness, even though it must be posed to explain the possibility of self-consciousness. Here Schelling follows Fichte, but more directly confronts the unconscious as both separate from and necessary to consciousness. For idealism, unconscious process is the ungrounded activity of free self-assertion, the energy of self-constitution, which Schelling calls "the Absolute." This absolute self-assertion, both subject and object at once, reveals itself not, as with Fichte, as an impulsion toward a moral ideal (an "ought"), but rather in the systems of symbolic *meaning* we give to the world.

Again, Schelling's unconscious contrasts with the essential pessimism of Freud's: symbolic meaning for the idealist is not a continuous displacement of frustrated desire or the memory of unresolved conflict; it is the ongoing elucidation of spirit, the humanizing of the opaque into the transparent. Overcoming the selfhood bounded by memory (experience) and nature through *die geistige Welt* enables the human mind to reconstruct its physical experience as a series of relations within the unfolding of the ideal.

Man's natural history and his physical embodiment do not (as with Freud and modern psychology generally) determine the contours of spiritual evolution; rather, the experience of nature and indeed the whole sensory realm are determined by the need of the Absolute to construct itself in time and finitude. Man remains free to determine and elucidate his experience through imaginative recreation despite the resistance of the dark unconscious ground or apparent "givenness" of the sensory. These are merely "epochs" or stages in the self-revelation of the ideal. In his long career, Schelling sought this ideal within those finite orders man feels compelled to conceive teleologically, according to ends or "meanings" never completely understood and only asymptotically approached by the finite mind: within art, mythology, and the organization of a dynamic yet scientifically conceived nature.[23] Indeed, all such systems present within "fixed" limits the evolving relations of ever-active intelligence: "The intelligence," Schelling asserts, "is thus an endless endeavor towards self-organization."[24]

We note, then, a profound ambivalence in Schelling's thought, a tension between the ongoing clarification of spiritual activity and the dark unconscious ground that generates the world. Ultimately, for Schelling, these two activities are both aspects of the Absolute:

"The same activity which is *consciously* productive in free action, is productive *without consciousness* in bringing about the world."[25] The unconscious remains as the absolute principle of opacity, of real limitation, yet a limitation *within* and acting through consciousness. Schelling's unconscious "is the opaque knot of actuality in the self," explains a recent commentator, Michael Vater, "the productive or realizing intuition which opposes the limitant activity (which is the self's) to its properly intuitive activity of cognition and keeps them thus tied together." Yet this productive activity, Vater continues,

> remains hidden, unconscious and its workings remain forever enigmatic. Idealism, thinks Schelling, is forced to admit such an unconscious production and actualization in spite of its allegiance to self-consciousness. For it can in no other wise explain the distinction of inner and outer activity, i.e., of the experiential self and the experienced "thing," except by analogy to a kind of actualizing intelligence which loses itself (and self-awareness) in its productions, just as the inspired artist loses himself in his work.[26]

In other words, as the activity enters the world it becomes unable directly to reflect upon itself, to know itself, as the creator of the world. In the original absolute intuition, the I returns upon itself, becomes object to itself. That object is a subject, and as a subject it contemplates *itself* as its object, and so on in perfect identity.

This absolute "I am" is most felicitously explained by Coleridge in the *Biographia*, paraphrasing a passage in Schelling's *System*:

> In this [I am], and in this alone, object and subject, being and knowing, are identical, each involving, and supporting the other. In other words, it is a subject which becomes a subject by the act of constructing itself objectively to itself; but which never is an object except for itself, and only so far as by the very same act it becomes a subject. It may be described therefore as a perpetual self-duplication of one and the same power into object and subject which presuppose each other, and can exist only as antitheses.[27]

This identity, however, is only intuited and becomes conscious only through division and limitation, through the succession of representations in time and space. In the evolution of Schelling's doctrine, self-consciousness is identified as a centripetal activity, and consciousness of the limit (the not-I) as a centrifugal activity. When consciousness "feels" itself opposed by the not-I in such a way that it cannot immediately return upon itself, it feels itself limited by *sensations*. The mind cannot at the same time be conscious that the I and the not-I are polar aspects of one activity—otherwise the not-I would collapse into the I. Hence it feels sensation as coming from "outside" itself, as "other" than itself.[28] The philosopher cannot *demonstrate* the original unity but can only point to it; it is only as the mind contemplates itself through the symbolic world—in art, for example—that it returns mediately to a knowledge of the unity of the world known in sensation and the ideal world of the "I am." The symbol, Coleridge wrote (clearly echoing Schelling), "is characterized by a translucence of the special in the individual, or of the general in the special, or of the universal in the general; above all by the translucence of the eternal through and in the temporal." For Schelling, the mind of man produces the real world when the primary imagination creates without consciousness; it produces the art work when the secondary imagination produces a real world consciously: "For art this opposition (between real and ideal) is an infinite one in regard to *every single object*, and infinity is exhibited in every one of its products."[29]

Schelling would thus avoid the problem of the "cause" of our sensations: the sensed world is an activity within mind and reveals itself as such through the higher functions of consciousness, through our awareness of the lawfulness of nature and of symbolic meaning in art. As I have noted of the idealist position, the fundamental problem to be explained is that causality alone cannot explain our awareness of the world: billiard balls may strike each other endlessly and not become conscious that they are struck. Schelling's explanation is a complex monism (recalling Leibniz) in which sensation and the consciousness of sensation are moments in the single unfolding of the timeless activity of absolute self-consciousness. Schelling insists that (unlike Leibniz) he begins not with mind or substance as *beings* but with a free activity of dynamic spiritual self-assertion. His system, he maintains, begins with human freedom.

Yet, as Thomas McFarland remarks, that notion of freedom is more formal than actual, more an abstraction about the human spirit than a moral possibility for the individual. This is true, I believe, although in his 1809 essay *Of Human Freedom* Schelling clarifies the way in which our feeling of freedom actually brings us closer to the ground of all beings, to the God who is manifest through our freedom.[30] This is an immensely complex and, in Schelling's own day, passionately debated issue. I shall consider the problem from the point of view of the symbolic world-view I have been discussing.

The problem of the symbolic perspective is not original to Schelling, though certainly his systematic development of it throughout human knowledge is. Let us offer as an example a traditional problem: "Jesus remained silent, and Pilate condemned him." From a causal point of view, Jesus' choice caused his doom. But viewed symbolically we eliminate the causal and indeed the temporal dimension: Jesus' freedom is not even at issue; instead we would say that *both* his silence and Pilate's sentence are aspects of a single, atemporal, spiritual *meaning* that worked itself out in the silence and the condemnation. Jesus was not *determined* by this spiritual meaning, since it is manifest only after the fact of his choice; yet his freedom existed only in a moment of time, and from the symbolic perspective we transcend that moment to see the choice as only an element in the necessary evolution of a symbolic history. The viewpoint is the same when choice is not involved: "Jesus died and the skies darkened." Whether or not we wish to say that the death "caused" the darkness, both aspects of the incident are manifestations of a single spiritual revelation. Thus, only *historically* does meaning become clear, only in *past* acts and already constituted forms of order do we realize the working of the Absolute.[31] From the most primitive act of sensation, to the creation of art, to the unfolding of history itself, the act of the individual ego is the assertion of the Absolute in space and time, its progressive coming-to-awareness of itself in and through finitude. That finitude acts as a resistance to the absolute assertion, but from the higher perspective—beyond separation, time, and causality— this negative activity is itself an aspect of the One Absolute.

This last point Schelling attempts to clarify in a famous passage in *Of Human Freedom*. The finite individual is in God, but this does not diminish its uniqueness *qua* individual: "A single organ, like the eye, is possible only in the organism as a whole; nevertheless it has a life of its own." Only if the Absolute is seen as a fixed, static being (as in Spinoza) would the individual be part of a mere mechanism. But Schelling's Absolute does not exist apart from the finitude through which it endlessly *becomes* itself: "God can only reveal himself in creatures who resemble him, in free, self-activating beings for whose existence there is no reason save God, but who are as God is. . . . Though all the world's creatures were but the thoughts of the divine mind, they would on this very account necessarily have life." Schelling's God is no Being, but the continuous becoming of self-consciousness as it reveals itself in the symbolic actions of men: "God is not a God of the dead but of the living."[32]

This attempt at resolution did not go very far toward mitigating what many of Schelling's contemporaries saw as the pantheism of the system: "Still the old questions return, and I find none but the old answers," wrote Coleridge in a long note on his copy of Schelling's essay on freedom. "The question is," he continued, "do not these single wills, so included in the one '*Urwille*' become '*Things?*'"[33] And, interestingly, Coleridge objects to the abstraction of Schelling's "I" in a note to a passage in the *System* that directly follows the one he paraphrased in the passage of the *Biographia* cited above. In this later paragraph, Schelling asserts that the I does not exist in itself but only in the act of being revealed through the construction of its symbolic meaning, in the systematic self-comprehension of the Absolute: the I "*exists* at all only in being constructed, and has no more existence in abstraction from the construction than does the geometer's line." But in the margin of his copy, Coleridge attacks the geometry metaphor in a manner implying that the I is "diverse" from the system that reveals it, and he snipes that "the *Spinosism* of Schelling's system first betrays itself."[34]

The Schelling of the 1809 *Of Human Freedom*, however, struggles differently with the problems of pantheism from the Schelling who raised those problems in the world-system of 1800. The difference is crucial, for what emerges from Schelling's development is a delineation of a key romantic ambivalence about man's place in an ideal system of spirit. In 1800, Schelling imagined the Absolute as indifferent between subject and object, intelligence and matter, and saw the unconscious as progressively revealing itself through the human spirit. In 1809, the Absolute seems to *require* a dark ground (the *Urgrund*) to articulate itself, and Schelling conceives of this darkness as in some sense radically sundered from the activity of the Absolute. In 1800, Schelling sees the unconscious merely as a "negative activity" within us, and it appears to us as the shadow of Kant's thing-in-itself, as the "resisting" quality of objects we project as outside us, ignorant as we are that it is we ourselves at the source of two activities, positive and negative, centrifugal and centripetal:

We find the I's activity to be intrinsically positive, and the ground of all positivity. For it has been characterized as a striving to expand out to infinity. The activity of the thing would thus have intrinsically to be that which is absolutely and by nature negative. . . . [But] what appears to us from the present standpoint as activity of the thing-in-itself, is nothing else but the ideal self-reverting activity of the I, and this can *only* be presented as the negative of the other.[35]

But in 1809, Schelling seems less certain that the dark ground can actually be fully taken up into the human mind, and "the unruly" seems closer to Being itself—Being as the necessary separate ground for the becoming activity of the Absolute. Now man occupies a middle state in which he may choose to live in the finite, to *reduce* spirit to the dark ground, to *fix* himself as a being and deny the activity of the Absolute. This is the act of *individuation*, and Schelling defines the sin of *selfhood* as man's choosing to violate the endless act of creation through him, and instead to live in the dark ground of fixed Being, bending his will toward selfhood instead of toward the "center" of creation. That center is the absolute activity of evolving spiritual self-awareness.

Yet, Schelling insists, God's love would be powerless without the dark ground of individuation through which to act: becoming requires Being. Man's fate is to will his particularity, but his doom is the temptation to usurp the active spirit and raise selfhood above it:

That principle which rises up from the depths of nature and by which man is separated from God, is the selfhood in him. . . . The *angst* in life itself drives man out of the center in which he was created; for the latter as the lucid and pure essence of all will, is consuming fire for each particular will; in order to be able to live in it man must mortify [*absterben*, "die away from"] all egotism—which almost makes necessary the attempt to leave [the spiritual center] and to enter the periphery [the dark ground] in order to seek peace for his selfhood there.[36]

Schelling identifies the source of sin, of egoism, in *fear* (*angst*) of the endless creative becoming of life. The consequences of retreating to "the periphery," to a fixed realm where, as in Blake's Beulah, "Contraries are equally true," where man may seek rest from the endless strivings of spiritual creation—"great Wars of Eternity, in fury of Poetic Inspiration"—the consequences are, ironically, that the displaced (or "repressed") forces return in a chaos of conflicting desires and destructive passions:

> But hardly does self-will yield from the [spiritual] center which is its position, than the bond of forces also yields; in its place a merely particular will rules which can no longer unite the forces among themselves as before but must therefore strive to form a special and peculiar life out of the forces that have given way to one another, an insurgent host of desires and passions—since every individual force is also an obsession and passion. . . . As a genuine life could only exist in the original relationship [to creative spirit], there thus arises a life which is indeed a life, but is false, a life of lies, a growth of disquiet and corruption.[37]

## The Romantic Demon and Romantic Love

As we have noted, Coleridge was unsatisfied with Schelling's explanation of the meaning of individuation and its origins. He constantly feared that in the idealism of both Schelling and Fichte, the absolute I of finite knowing was confused with the Absolute Being, the God of the created universe and origin of individual life. In his copy of *Of Human Freedom*, opposite the definition of selfhood (given in the first sentence quoted above), Coleridge wrote, "We will grant for a while, that the principle [of selfhood] evolved or lifted up from this mysterious *Ground* of existence, which *is* and yet does not exist, is separate (*geschieden*) from God; yet how is it separate from the Ground itself? How is it individualized?"[38] The tension in poetic creation between the principle of personal integrity (freedom) and the imagination as the creative manifestation in man of "the One Life" is characteristic of Coleridge, long before his reading of Schelling, as early indeed as "The Eolian Harp" (1795), the poem in which the problem of the One Life is first broached.

From this tension in Transcendental Idealism, first developed by Schelling, we may deduce a psychological dilemma common not just in Coleridge but in romantic quest generally. As we saw with Fichtean idealism, we can ask how problems raised by transcendental philosophy were felt as psychological imperatives by romantic poets. From Schelling's idealism, we can deduce two further principles of romantic quest. As noted in Chapter 5, our last principle, of *quest*, is—as all these principles are—unstable. The world, by this principle, must become what I desire; yet I can realize this desire only through a world that infinitely resists me. The self desires a return to the state of *magic*, in which the ego and the world are mutually responsive, the world being the spontaneous creation of the ego. But the way back is blocked by a "fall," by the growing awareness of the ego's peculiar need for the not-ego in order to realize itself. The two principles can be reconciled in a certain sense, but only, it will turn out, with the introduction of further instabilities. The move back to pure magic blocked, the self may simply set above itself another, greater mind that *does* produce the world and also produces or guides the quest of my mind toward itself: this creative principle authors the narrative that appears as my world. My struggle to recreate the world, my "quest," is a moment in the higher creation of this greater mind. Thus *my own mind creates the form of the world in order to realize the larger desire (power) that fundamentally moves behind my mind and the world, both of which are only aspects of its creation.* We may call this the principle of *pantheism* (a more exact term than E. D. Hirsch's "enthusiasm").

But what, then, is this "me," this "my own," this principle of individuation that will not factor out of our equations? We saw that from the principle of magic the principle of imagination inevitably evolved as soon as otherness, *discreteness,* was seen as necessary both to creating the world and asserting the self. We recall that the dialectic of imagination began with an act of alienation that then enables the mind simultaneously to assert itself and to create a world: the world discloses itself in the creative act, but this act presumes the world as other. Our next principle evolves in a similar way from the principle of pantheism, but now the discreteness of the *self* (as freedom) is asserted. That freedom must be asserted absolutely so long as the pantheism is asserted absolutely, for any attempt to mediate self and power would only show that at a certain point—wherever that may be located—the self merges into the power, and this is initially what must be resisted. The absolute assertion raises the self even beyond its magical role as dreamer, for in that role the self defined itself not absolutely and independently but through its spontaneous creation of the world. But the absolute assertion goes beyond the simple interchange of mind and its creations; it is not dialectical, like magic, where world and mind are eternally united in the creation of symbol.

It is rather the assertion of self as imbued with all power to assert itself against and apart from all other meaning or spiritual activity. The world is not my dream but simply my assertion, for I am powerful whether I choose—and my power to choose is infinite—to create a meaningful world or a nightmarish, incoherent one. We may express this extreme but inevitable response to pantheism as: *it is my desire that creates the world; I am diminished by any greater spiritual power, and I am greater in my freedom and separation from this power than the power itself.* This is, of course, a species of narcissism expressed in modern psychoanalysis as the assertion of libido against the introjected father. Romanticism did understand the power of sexuality as an aspect of revolt but as only one aspect of the self's drive toward freedom and integrity. As in Schelling, there is an ambivalence in this principle: seen as one moment in the creative growth of the soul it is an assertion of the energy of self-integrity and may be called the principle of *freedom.* But seen as an absolute principle of life, it is given a better name by romantic culture itself—the *demonic.*

The demonic principle stands behind that most characteristic of romantic emblems, the Wanderer, Cain, the *poète maudit,* and the symbolism testifies to the romantics' own fear that this was the most unstable principle of all. The cultural source of this romantic theme is not, of course, in idealism, but in the long history of figures descended from Milton's Satan. But Satan's tormented but defiant stance that "the mind is its own place" does assume new resonances, profoundly troubling ambivalence, in a culture increasingly influenced by idealist premises.

The word *demonic* is itself strangely ambivalent and entails its own denial. For the demonic implies the infinite assertion of self-will; but as Schelling insisted, the self can never actually clarify itself to itself: there will always intrude a dark *un*conscious remainder. What emerges, that is, in self-assertion is something more than the self could know—this was a commonplace of the economics of the unconscious long before Freud asserted it. The presence of the unconscious, of desires unknown and motives inconceivable, assures that the freedom of self-will will turn to become its opposite, the "possession" of the self by a higher power. Thus the demonic begins in free willing but deflects toward its root meaning, the surrender of the self to a *daemon.*

The final principle of romance is a dialectic similar to that of imagination, but it is seen from the perspective of the mind's interchange with spiritual power, rather than with the world as material for aesthetic form. This principle is no "resolution" of extremes but rather an attempt at dynamic harmony between self, the unconscious, and the other. This dynamic must assume the reality of otherness. But the other is not simply an opaque boundary that resists me. The other appears like me in that it too is *spirit*, is continuous self-creative assertion, but also like me it is free and integral. I may thus engage in relation to this other not as if it were an "it" but as a "thou." The relation is larger than myself yet depends upon a free act of my selfhood; the relation is a spiritual interchange with otherness that is an activity of creative imagination. As in the synthesis of imagination, this other becomes real to me through my own creative act, yet this act itself depends in turn on my recognition of the free spiritual activity of the other. I retain my integrity by asserting myself *through* this relation (as the artist does through his work). We may summarize this dialectic: *in asserting my relation to the other-as-spirit I assert my own free integrity; to go out to this other is to find myself.* Perhaps it should not surprise us that this principle is only suggested by the idealist philosophers; we would expect its fuller articulation from poets. This principle of romance we may call simply *romantic love*, a particular romantic understanding of *eros*. For Schelling, this eros is the bond that joins all beings: "This is the secret of love, that it unites such beings as could each exist in itself, and nonetheless neither is nor can be without the other."[39]

The overcoming of selfhood, the turning away from falsely raised gods and numinous powers, and the transcendence of alienation through imagination and love are seen by Harold Bloom as the goals of all romantic quest, though each romance creates a different path:

> There are thus two main elements in the major phase of the romantic quest, the first being the inward overcoming of the Selfhood's temptation, and the second the outward turning of the triumphant Imagination, free of further internalization—though "outward" and "inward" become cloven fictions or false conceptual distinctions in this triumph, which must complete a dialectic of love by uniting the Imagination with its bride, who is a transformed ongoing creation of the Imagination rather than a redeemed nature.[40]

It is a difficult, at times cryptic, sentence, yet one is struck by how apt a description it is of the complex dialectic of romantic quest. But Bloom's theory raises a number of philosophical questions that are indeed implicit in the whole field of quest romance so conceived. Chief among these are problems that confront any cultural movement that seeks to build on idealist assumptions: just what kind of marriage is this, if the bride is the offspring of the groom? What kind of world is it that is only my dream? Who am I if I am only the world's dreamer? Yet what kind of love is *not* the imagination's return to itself through the other? What active mediation is finally to be found between incestuous marriage and uncanny encounter?

As Bloom recognizes (and as we may know without the aid of poets and philosophers), romantic love is fraught with instabilities. Not the least of these is what Bloom calls the "natural Selfhood," the retreat from imaginative dialectic to a fixed self demanding its completion in the fixed other: "Romantic love . . . is not the possessive love of the natural heart, which is the quest of the Freudian Eros, moving always in a tragic rhythm out from and back to the isolated ego. . . . Desire for what one lacks becomes a habit of possession, and the Selfhood's jealousy murders the Real Man, the imagination."[41] Selfhood may interpret imaginative relation as a threat to integrity and freedom; conversely, the will to integrity may endanger relation. Again, absolute centrifugal union (ecstasy) or absolute centripetal assertion (alienation) annihilates the dialectic of imagination or love.

For philosophical idealism in the period, questions of the mind's responsibility to (and love for) its world could be answered only progressively, in stages of continuing analysis and synthesis. Our six principles are stages upon life's way, no one of them finally synthesizing the others, though indeed imagination and love provide the greatest opportunities for creative interchange between self and other. But desire is infinite, and the fundamental irony is that desire without finitude is meaningless as finitude without desire is sterile and dead. The principle of quest assures us that life must always oscillate between infinite assertion and finite otherness in endless ramifications.[42] In fact, to arrive at any single understanding of these relations—magic, imagination, quest, pantheism, the demonic, love— impels us through inherent instabilities on to the next term, or back in a new way to a previous one. To seek some static reconciliation is itself a denial of the one premise that generates all these principles derived from idealism: that the mind is an endless activity of developing self-awareness. Assuredly, imagination and love are consummate visions; yet romantic irony, I have suggested, is the dialectic that allows the mind to have its visions and float above them, the dreamer aware of himself in the dream. The mind finds that it wakens itself from its visions in the name of some awakening that becomes its new sleep. The achievement of romantic poetry is not a simple therapeutic vision but the warp and woof of a fabric like a progressive version of Penelope's shroud—woven every day with a renewed hope, unwoven every night to prevent a death or a capture.

We will now turn to romantic quest itself, beginning with Coleridge, confronting the dilemmas of transcendental idealism not as abstractions but as psychological facts felt and experienced by the living man. It is not incidental that Coleridge's greatest published philosophical work is a biography, a "Literary Life."

# 7

## Theory in the Biographia and Coleridge's Early Poetry

The *Biographia Literaria* is a difficult book to read—and an easy one to misread—if only because Coleridge pursues his apologia through aesthetics, anecdote, admonition, metaphysics, and morals, forcing many readers to see large sections as peripheral and some others as central, or most revealing, or most interesting. The scholar may take the book as a useful filing cabinet of Coleridge's views on education, Jacobinism, German metaphysics, Wordsworth's poetry, or the poetic imagination. And although some scholars have recently found Coleridge's translations from Schelling to be elements in a personal, dynamic metaphysic, many more have dismissed his thinking as merely derivative. In 1955, René Wellek wrote, "Much that has impressed I. A. Richards and Herbert Read—the discussion of the subject-object relations, their synthesis and identity, and the appeal to the unconscious—is simply the teaching of Schelling and cannot be the basis of a claim for Coleridge's philosophical greatness."[1] But more recently, Thomas McFarland, in his detailed and erudite study, has traced the intricacies of Coleridge's involvement with the post-Kantian idealists and concluded that Coleridge found Schelling and the German metaphysicians ultimately pantheists, their philosophy incompatible with his own dialectical view of the creative imagination.[2] Coleridge emerges as a more original critic of contemporary idealism, one who sought continuously to reconcile philosophical theory with his own experience of the poetic act.

In light of the debate and the range of approaches to this protean work, I would like simply to reassert the central principle of the book (it is too easy to forget that it has one) and examine, along lines first suggested by McFarland, the philosophical context of Coleridge's attempts to see the imagination as the great "reconciler" of mind and nature, subject and object.[3] This theory, McFarland notes, never proves quite satisfactory, and in Chapter XIII Coleridge introduces his famous definition of imagination in effect to rescue both himself and poetry from the Schellingean metaphysic so liberally drawn upon in Chapter XII. There are doctrinal reasons for this retreat. McFarland is painstaking and expert, going further than any critic in a century and a half of Coleridge criticism in reconstructing the often forbiddingly subtle context of post-Kantian idealism and the intricate, idiosyncratic, often contradictory responses of Coleridge the poet, moralist, and metaphysician. Every Coleridge critic must confront the difficult fact that, from his early flirtations with Spinozism to his fully evolved Trinitarianism, Coleridge presses doctrine into the services of his evolving self-understanding— metaphysics as autobiography. This statement is not meant as a psychological reduction—we can agree with Nietzsche's observation that as a thinker, one should speak only of self-education. Yet probably no thinker has left such a tangle of autobiography, meditative poetry, fragmented notebooks, and compendious essays, each pleading in its special way for support from the other genres, each struggling to pull everything into a canon, a coherent *authorship*, the organic biography Coleridge saw as the soul's destiny.

I will suggest that for Coleridge, the theory of imagination functioned not only in the metaphysical sense McFarland elaborates; it also implied the ultimate reconciliation of the conscious mind with its unconscious sources. Yet the problem of pantheism and individuation required Coleridge to assert the freedom of the artist from the forces that drive and enable his creativity. Further, I will try to show that the tensions and contradictions that forced Coleridge to abandon Schellingean transcendental resolution had been at work all along in the early poetry. In viewing imagination from a *psychological* perspective, Coleridge very early conceived it as a conduit—though an active, organic one—between unconscious drives and conscious creation. In pursuing this path, Coleridge unleashed possibilities for the most exalted spiritual harmony but also for the most sublime terror. In pursuing the theory beyond psychology, into the transcendental and metaphysical formulations in the *Biographia*, Coleridge carries along with him the paradoxes and dilemmas that power his greatest poems.

The *Biographia Literaria* is a justification for the creative life as the most existentially authentic relation between man and his world and for the imagination as a redemptive force bringing man into immediate but personal relation to God. In the familiar Coleridgean theory, the creative artist exercises a power of mind analogous to the power that posits the world itself. Moreover, the power that posits the world does so in order to reveal *itself* to itself (this is a Fichtean theme elaborated in Schelling).[4] The great and ancient mystery of artistic creation has affinities on the one hand with the infinite self-consciousness that creates the world and on the other hand with each man's spontaneous reflexive *awareness* of that world and of himself *as* aware. Thus the imagination is a repetition in the poetical mind of an epistemological principle in all men that unites them with Infinite Mind. The *Biographia* is an epistemological version of the central romantic myth, the growth of the individual mind struggling toward paradisiacal communion while retaining the integrity of self-consciousness in its fullest sense.

This would seem congruent with the Schellingean principle of the mediating power of the aesthetic symbol. But to Coleridge, Schelling's reconciliation of the subject-object duality in an absolute self-consciousness threatens to annihilate the creative act. For what the imagination creates is *duality*, and only through dualities can the self ever come to know itself as a discrete coherent "it," know the world as object, know one object from another, understand the distinctions necessary for language or for poetry. On the other hand, self-consciousness is the mode of reconciliation, the creative source (the I am I) that posits the dualities to begin with. The I am I is to be the unity of free subject and finite object, but as soon as this unity is grasped and articulated it is no longer absolute but only a relative object of the understanding. The unity at the basis of idealism can be intuited, but once the mind operates to understand unity it does so only through its finite categories. In other words, the critique of the idea of self-consciousness is built into the idea itself. How can the idealist project ever begin, if self-consciousness is to come to understand itself as absolute, unitary, unconditioned, although it can create objects of understanding only through the finite and the relative?

This paradox may seem to be a question of emphasis (on either the dualities or their source), but it was a vital question for Coleridge. For the early Schelling, self-consciousness implied a paradisiacal reconciliation with a cosmic I AM, but to Coleridge this implied self-annihilation and a universe that tends toward *stasis* and *silence;* Coleridge understood imagination as a reproduction of this eternal reconciling principle in a finite mind, a mind that grows to know itself and *speak* itself through the distinctions and dualities it creates.

Coleridge is, as Daniel Stempel has noted, closer to Fichte than to Schelling in seeing imagination as creating images both real and ideal but holding them in separation and oscillating between conflicting demands. Hence Coleridge adopts the Fichtean conception of "centripetal" and "centrifugal" forces on the self, the mind flying ever inward to understand itself in its own distinct integrity, flying ever outward toward the world that grounds it.[5] The imagination may act as a redemptive force within finite man, pulling us toward a paradisiacal vision of the power that generates the dualities and the necessary distinctions of our existence and intelligence. And the subtler the imagination, the more finely it presents the finite world of distinctions through which the creative mind may, expanding, erect ever-larger paradises of reconciliation, or, turning in upon itself, become trapped in an ever-unfolding hell of contrariety, paradox, and incoherence. The poet at either pole becomes mute, the self in either a pure transcendentalism or a pure solipsism unable to "actualize" itself in thought, act, or word.

As we have seen, in the Schellingean metaphysic that Coleridge reproduces in Chapter XII of the *Biographia,* the self-consciousness that unites man with the creative principle of the universe is in fact that very cosmic principle working through man; but for Coleridge, as McFarland notes, "on the contrary, imagination mediates between a nature of *real* objects and a *real* 'I am,' creates poetry, not the world."[6] He believes that Coleridge breaks off the metaphysic of Chapter XII because he sees Schelling leading him to a Spinozan monism. To Schelling, we recall, natural lawfulness, or the order of physics, geometry, and so on, is an order of mind within nature, and is the *same* principle of self-consciousness, of matter becoming conscious of itself, as is found within the organizing human mind. In the *System*, Coleridge's source for Chapter XII, the young Schelling writes:

> How both the objective world accommodates to presentations in us, and presentations in us to the objective world, is unintelligible unless between the two worlds, the ideal and the real, there exists a *predetermined harmony*. But this latter is itself unthinkable unless the activity, whereby the objective world is produced, is at bottom identical with that which expresses itself in volition, and *vice versa*. . . . The ideal world of art and the real world of objects are therefore products of one and the same activity.[7]

This is indeed a position that Coleridge initially assumes in Chapter XII. Yet in his own copy of this work he has written, on the title page, a response to this passage: "The Percept[ion] grounds itself on the assertation 'es ist allerdings eine *productive* Thätigkeit, welche im *Wollen* sich aussert,' in the very same sense of the word 'productive' in which Nature 'im produciren der Welt productiv sey': only that the former is 'mit' the latter 'ohne Bewusstein productiv'— Now this is merely *asserted*. I deny it: & for the reasons above stated." Coleridge goes on to attack Schelling's apparent monism, although he has written, following the above remarks, "A book I value, I reason & quarrel with as with myself when I am reading."[8] McFarland argues that Coleridge recognized Schelling's position as depending upon an untenable equation of mind and the real world, an equation that could not survive the Kantian objections that Coleridge well knew.[9] Kant's *ding-an-sich* stands "behind" natural law, and time and space are creations of our own phenomenal perceptions. Man creates natural law; the "things-in-themselves" are real, but beyond intellection. Hence the Kantian objection to Schelling is that we cannot make self-consciousness the ultimate cosmic principle because such a principle would be noumenal, beyond our ability to categorize it even as mental or not mental. The ultimate unity of mind and world must forever elude our knowledge. For McFarland, Coleridge always remains loyal to Kant. This is correct, and I would emphasize that Coleridge abandons the Schellingean position because, in the context of the *Biographia* as a self-justification, he needs to retain the imagination as the creator of the artist's integral, *finite* experience in all its breadth and complexity, as well as the power by which that experience may be transcended. For Coleridge always roots the imagination in an individual, integral response to the world.

Hence the imagination may be said to create the artist's perceptual experience, to create the artist's subjectivity. But it also "objectifies," organizes, and reifies that experience into a coherent "I AM." In this sense, the imagination is the "power," as Coleridge puts it, which creates the finite self—itself its own subject and object.

To the extent that the imagination harmonizes the irreconcilable jumbles of experience in accord with a parallel principle in nature, we meet God. But to the extent that human imagination is its own creator and interpreter, we are free to create our own order or to create no order at all. The Kantian bias in Coleridge is the freedom of human knowing from any ultimate principle behind man and nature. Thus in the definition of imagination in Chapter XIII as a *"repetition* in the *finite* mind" of the infinite I AM, we are given the freedom to see our imagination as our own. Imagination creates an "I" founded on a self-consciousness as free and undetermined as God's. But the finite mind retains its integrity (is untranslatable and "primordial" in Husserl's phrase) and always stands independent, vis-à-vis God. The intuition of an undetermined "I" remains the act of an irreducibly finite mind. We can now understand how Coleridge's epistemology reproduces the romantic myth of a paradise regained by an integral self-consciousness. But we can also understand how the free imagination can (centripetally) create its own solipsistic Self of irreconcilable tensions, or (centrifugally) attempt to annihilate itself by seeing itself as identical with and *hence determined* by a single cosmic principle.[10]

Schelling himself recognized that his early system endangered the reality of individual freedom. The brilliant polemic of 1809, *Of Human Freedom*, failed to convince Coleridge that individuation and pantheism were reconcilable, but it does take up the tensions in man in a way distinct from Schelling's earlier attempts. Schelling here confronts the demonic principle derived from individuation, all the while insisting on a pantheistic ground (*Urgrund*) that subsumes oppositions. Despite this insistence, this is a very different Schelling from the author who stands behind the essential optimism of the *Biographia:* here Schelling writes of man's struggle with primal darkness in a manner strikingly reminiscent of the dual vision, of heaven and hell, in Coleridge's early poetry. The unconscious here is a primal desiring, which man may choose to see as impelling him to creations of light, or pulling him downward into selfhood, confusion, and darkness:

> The unruly [*das Regellöse*] lies ever in the depths, as though it might again break through, and order and form appear nowhere to have been original. . . . This is the incomprehensible basis of reality in things, the irreducible remainder which cannot be resolved into reason . . . Man's conceit opposes this origin from the depths [*Grunde*] and even seeks out moral reasons [*Grunde*] against it . . . only out of the darkness of unreason (out of feeling, out of longing, the sublime mother of knowledge) grow clear thoughts. This primal longing moves in anticipation like a surging, billowing sea, following some dark uncertain law, incapable in itself of forming [*Bildung*] anything that can endure. . . . Every being which has arisen in nature in the manner indicated [through a tension between forces], contains a double principle which, however, is at bottom one and the same. The first principle is the one by which they are separated from God or wherein they exist in the mere basis [*Grund*] of things. The principle of darkness, insofar as it was drawn from the depths [*Grunde*] and is dark, is the self-will of creatures.[11]

At this point, I would go further than McFarland and insist that Coleridge's affinity with this formulation of the dual, or "mediating," nature of imagination was not simply the product of his metaphysical positions evolving as the *Biographia* was written in 1815. Indeed, it is possible that the theory of imagination was being formulated as early as 1803.[12] But the polarities, I would argue, had been defined implicitly throughout Coleridge's poetry, beginning in 1795 with "The Eolian Harp." The terms in which he conceived the problematic nature of imagination (and its relation to his own pursuit of the creative life) were never so clear as in 1815, nor were they so confidently, almost triumphantly, asserted. But the problem itself, and his own ambivalent responses, had been with him for twenty years. Further, the ambivalence over individuation, over pantheism and the demonic, is not peculiar to Coleridge's early thought, but occurs in Schelling as he independently develops his idealist system. Imagination in Coleridge's poetry reproduces the tensions among psychological principles that I have suggested are common to romantic idealism.

## The Quest of the Ancient Mariner

The early poems explore the singular perversity of the human condition that, given a choice, we will *choose* annihilation or fragmentation. But in a way we have no choice at all, driven by inner forces that block a dynamic balance between our own evolving creation and God's. This is certainly the case with the *Ancient Mariner*. In this poem the vision of redemptive cosmic harmony is either uncertain—he blesses the water snakes "unaware," and we have only the gloss of 1817 to assure us that the spell is broken (line 187)—or ineffective. We are never certain that the sin was a sin from any point of view but the Mariner's. The experience can be "read" however the superstitious crew pleases: "Then all averred, I had killed the bird / That brought the fog and mist" (lines 99–100).[13] There are only two poles: either a universal order that determines the Mariner's fate, plays dice for his soul, and makes expiation—the spontaneous will to be free of a sinful past, to remake one's life—impossible in a predetermined world; or a universal disorder onto which we project our deepest guilts and fears. In neither case is the Mariner free from his own visions. His imagination creates a hell of incoherence, a universe of uncertain justice and causality, or a heaven in which the free and integral human consciousness (complete with its dark, unconscious motivations) has only an uncertain place.[14]

For some critics this is no more than the Mariner deserves. A. M. Buchan, for instance, sees the Mariner as a "passive victim of forces more active than he"; his actions are "caught up in a chaos of unwilled movement, and he himself is an alien speck of human purpose tossed meaninglessly about in the roaring winds of fate."[15] In one sense this is true: the Mariner's world is a chaos; but it is only so from the point of view of the eye that beholds it. There is also beauty and perhaps even beneficence in the world the Mariner comes to bless. Why, then, does he "pass, like night, from land to land" (line 584)? Why the "agony" that compels him "on certain hour" (line 582)?

Many critics recognize that the Mariner's alienation in the mysterious world of the poem is a product of his mind's disease. Yet they often argue, with James Boulger, that if he would but see it, the Mariner lives in a universe of "religious" mystery that includes all life in one organic whole. But it is not for finite man to grasp the meaning of this religious truth (Boulger seems, in fact, to identify the "religious" with a vague cosmic mystery), and the Mariner must learn that what his imagination intuits is how *little* he can know about the cosmos.[16] In a similar vein Irene Chayes has somewhat more subtly argued that the Mariner's crime is "false mysticism," that is, the attempt to intuit spiritual truths from the mere data of nature. The shooting of the albatross, "an act of destructive metaphysical trespass," is an attempt to define the unknown through *fixing* it in images of sense.[17]

Common to all these arguments is the assumption that the universe is the way it is and that the Mariner is punished for recklessly ignoring this fatal necessity. Such a view, however, leaves us little more enlightened than the Mariner himself, who prays for deliverance to saints, the Virgin, or "the dear God who loveth us," despite the capriciousness of these powers, the fate they have inflicted upon the ship's crew, and the endless misery to which they condemn the luckless sailor. Edward Bostetter reminds us of the "capricious irrationality" and "utter ruthlessness" of the powers that humble the Mariner and rejects any implication that he is punished for his blindness to some cosmic order: "Instead of the 'One Life' we are confronted at the end of the poem by the eternally alienated Mariner alienating in his turn the Wedding Guest [who is] forced to share the disillusioned wisdom and guilt of the Mariner." Thus the Mariner's failure is not a moral flaw but a symbolic vision of Coleridge's own fear that the recalcitrance of the world was far greater than the transforming power of the imagination to overcome it. Bostetter is near the truth when he sees the *Ancient Mariner* as a psychomachia within Coleridge's mind: "What [Coleridge] wanted to believe in and increasingly devoted his intellectual energies to asserting was a universe of order and benevolence in which man possessed freedom of will and action to mold his own destiny; what he feared was a universe in which he was at the mercy of arbitrary and unpredictable forces. The *Rime* envisions such a universe."[18]

But the dialectics of imagination are more complex than this. The Mariner is defeated—and this is truly Coleridge's fear—by a failure of imaginative vision and not by the higher powers of a ruthless universe. The point is that such powers have force only to the mind that surrenders to them, to the mind that indeed creates them. The

Mariner, like so many failed romantic questers, chooses isolation and flees persecution; he turns fearfully away from imaginative relation at the moment the albatross falls from his neck. From this relation of natural and spontaneous joy, the Mariner, I will argue, surrenders his responsibility for both this joy and his later despair to self-projected gods who are superstitiously feared.

The real pessimism of *The Rime* is not the malignity of the universe so much as the Mariner's impulsiveness, his helplessness before his own unconscious will. He does not, finally, *choose* to deny imaginative regeneration (his impulsive state drives him to do so), but he fails to interpret his own tale as a symbol of his mental state. This is, presumably, why the poem is a tale *told*: it is for the Wedding Guest, or perhaps for the ideal hearer never found, to perceive the story's symbolic warning. The Mariner will remain trapped in the causal chains forged by his own will until he can rise to the symbolic (in Schelling's sense) perspective: that what he saw and did reflected what he unconsciously willed, that his tale is a text that he has authored. Yet by implication he can never reach this point. He is compelled to tell the tale just as he was compelled to shoot the bird. The Mariner suffers for us, his hearers, to display symbolically the dilemma of human will and individuation. The "will" here corresponds not to conscious choice but to Schelling's unconscious drive that oscillates between self-centeredness and love, between evil and good. That this is the core dilemma of the tale has recently been asserted by Laurence Lockridge, who first notes the striking congruence between "self-will" in Schelling's *Of Human Freedom* and will in Coleridge's poetry, concluding of *The Rime* that "the poem portrays the weakness of the moral virtues . . . relative to the arcane movements of the will, which is evil in its nature. At the same time we can assume it is the will that energizes and defines the Mariner as *that one* who has been alone on the wide wide sea. . . . Is there not a suggestion that the Mariner is punished because he has literally distinguished himself? Is not this the punishment implicit in the act of individuation itself, which inevitably gives rise to suffering and alienation?"[19]

It is certainly true that, as Lockridge admits, the human will may also mysteriously return to the principle of love, for the Mariner blesses the water snakes as impulsively as he shoots the albatross: "Both alienation and reunion are acts of will, both originate from sources below what can be known either by Mariner or by reader." Yet Lockridge concludes that the moment of communion here is less enduring than the act of alienation, the act that defines and dooms the Mariner.[20]

In the moment of communion the world of the magic voyage that inspired only superstitious awe has become responsive to the joy of a human heart. The Mariner loves the beauty of an alien world, and in his new-found respect for its otherness a new relation is formed. The cool "hoar-frost" light of the moon falls on the "sultry" sea, and the living things shine alternately with flakes of "hoary" white and flashes of "golden fire." From this moment of united forces the Mariner retreats: the "spring of love," a moment of human sympathy and joy, he attributes to some supernaturally induced "blessing." The Mariner twice asserts his belief that he "blessed them unaware," "sure" that a saint had pitied him, the double assertion reflecting his need to persuade himself. The Mariner's action, in retreating to a superstitious theism, symbolizes the flight of the mind from the freedom of imaginative relationship to a conception of itself as bound by externally projected forces, by judging gods.

Even the one act that can be called free, the Mariner's biting his arm to suck the blood and call out to the crew, ironically announces only the arrival of the Death Ship. As Humphry House noted, this central irony underscores the man's helplessness, that his one deliberate action is to signal death for the crew and involve him "in a tangle of error, incomprehensibility and frustration."[21] But more than this, the act is symbolically ambivalent. It is a moment of deliberate sacrifice, a bloodletting counterpoised to the slaying in that it is undertaken out of love for the others, "The many men, so beautiful!" On the other hand, as an emblem the bloodsucking denotes self-consuming vampirism, the isolation of Life-in-Death in which the Mariner is reborn only by turning to the endlessly internal recoursings of his own blood. His act is a ghoulish adumbration of the sterile cycle of introspection he will come to live.

This cycle is presided over by the *belle dame*, Life-in-Death:

> *Her* lips were red, *her* looks were free,
> Her locks were yellow as gold:
> Her skin was white as leprosy,
> The Night-mare LIFE-IN-DEATH was she
> Who thicks man's blood with cold.   (lines 190–94)

Like other such figures in romantic quest, Life-in-Death is a vision whose enchantments prevent a true marriage, isolating the hero from imaginative union. Her "free" looks promise more than the blushing bride of lines 33−34, but only to those who succumb to the false enchantment of experience that she really is, cold agent of the dull round of nature, of empty causality, chance, and death. In Life-in-Death, all process and change, all becoming, is a game of dice and man the passive victim. The Mariner begins his never-ending quest by seeking a return to natural innocence from the "Hermit of the Wood," whose altar is "the moss that wholly hides / The rotted old oak-stump" (lines 521−22) and whose isolation reflects the Mariner's own. But like Keats's Endymion or his knight-at-arms, the Mariner has already been led beyond nature to an enchanted world.[22]

Inevitably, the enchanted mind is enthralled only with itself, or more accurately, with the magic responsiveness of the world to the ego's desire. But the danger, as our study of idealism has shown, is that the dream world threatens the integrity of the free ego that would assert itself independently of its creations. In the extreme of demonic assertion, however, creation is impossible: the I asserts itself as independent, but turned in upon itself becomes fixed as a "Selfhood." As one critic remarks, "The daemonic in Coleridge is profoundly debasing, as the repressed part of the self which becomes the daemon grinds the rest of consciousness into spellbound compliance or helpless remorse."[23] At the same time, the world contracts away from the ego and presents its own resistance. Out of this anxious retreat to Selfhood, the I projects the "reality principle" as its sad shield against enchantment. The world of enchantment, then, threatens to engulf the I, while the counterassertion of self-will may make the I (and the world) a fixed, dead otherness. The "solution," I have suggested, lies in accepting the otherness of the changing world and uniting with this unfolding through imagination and love. *Becoming* is itself, then, not a cold, dead process but the evolution of a spiritual life. The primitive enchantment of magic idealism yields, Harold Bloom has theorized, either to the anxious resistance of Selfhood or to the "higher" creativity of imagination or love.[24] The deeper issue is freedom: can the ego at once remain free, accept process and change as its own creations, and yet love the world both despite and because of that otherness which lets the ego be itself?

This complex goal should by now be familiar as a consequence of idealist theory. I have identified it as a spiritual mobility often appearing as irony. It is also clearly what Coleridge's Mariner cannot do. His response to the magic of the early voyage is to destroy the bird loved by the "Polar Spirit," who seems magically to split the ice that imprisons the ship (lines 68–79). The albatross allows the ship to move, the journey to continue. The Polar Spirit, who later takes revenge by moving the ship "onward from beneath," is primarily an image of spiritual movement: the word "pole" for Coleridge often implied a node among shifting forces, a point at which motion culminates and is driven on.[25] As many critics have noticed, the Mariner has lashed out to "fix" the bird in death, an act of self-will.

The ship is soon becalmed, "fixed" by the Sun:

> All in a hot and copper sky,
> The bloody Sun at noon,
> Right up above the mast did stand,
> No bigger than the Moon.
> Day after day, day after day,
> We stuck, nor breath nor motion:
> As idle as a painted ship
> Upon a painted ocean.   (lines 111–18)

Later, when the Polar Spirit abandons them for a moment, this fixing at a single point, a pole without motion, is made explicit: "The Sun, right up above the mast, / Had fixed her to the ocean" (lines 383–84). In the well-known theory of Robert Penn Warren, these are instances of the symbolism of the "two lights," the Sun of fixed, dead Understanding and the Moon of Imagination.[26] Although I do not mean to add yet another "symbol cluster" to the many claimed to be central to this poem, I would suggest that the most pervasive metaphors for the spiritual condition of the hero are the broad kinetic patterns of *movement* and *stasis*.

The Mariner's doom, of course, is to be always moving yet always spiritually paralyzed. The direct contrary to this state is to "sojourn, yet still move onward," and the Mariner himself, the gloss tells us, yearns to transform his state to that symbolized by "the moving Moon":

> In his loneliness and fixedness he yearneth toward the journeying Moon, and the stars that still sojourn, yet still move onward; and every where the blue sky belongs to them, and is their appointed rest, and their native country and their own natural homes, which they enter unan-

nounced, as lords that are certainly expected and yet there is a silent joy at their arrival.

What is interesting here is the interplay and counterpoise of movement and stasis. Every movement home is a further journey beyond. The moon "no where did abide" and seems to the Mariner an alien like himself; yet the cold face of the moon and the scattered dust of the stars are always arriving in joyful communion at a home that always slips away from them. Their integrity is not incompatible with communion.

The Mariner looks up to the moon from the depths of aloneness and self-hatred:

> Alone, alone, all all alone,
> Alone on a wide wide sea!   (lines 232–33)

Sounding in the expanse of those repeated vowels is the cry of a self that has attempted to usurp the world and is lost without a horizon, a limit, a meaningful border. We may recall here Coleridge's extraordinary notebook entry of November 1796:

> inward desolations—
> an horror of great darkness
> great things that on the ocean
> counterfeit infinity.[27]

As he looks into the sea the Mariner sees the moon spread out a boundary, "the shadow of the ship." "The boundary is redemptive," notes one critic, "not only because it restores nature to the Mariner's vision, but because it contracts the daemonic's region of engulfment."[28] The moving water snakes that dart in and out with their living presence are the "thousand thousand slimy things" (line 238) that once served only to intensify his loneliness, guilt, and self-hatred. Now their movement is redeemed by his comprehension of the moon's motion-as-homecoming. The snakes are alien, are others observed from a distance, yet their movement suggests a spiritual kinship to the voyager after the revelation of the journeying moon. In this new relation to the world he recognizes the integrity of the "happy living things," which he violated by the killing, and a "spring of love" gushes from his heart. The albatross falls away not simply as a sin purified but more as an emblem of Selfhood overcome.

The vision does not last. The vision of the moon's journey through space was an image of the self's experience of time, and it is this image the Mariner cannot sustain. We recall Fichte's doctrine that the imagination creates space and time so that in the infinite process of discrete moments—each one infinite with potentiality yet bounded and dependent upon the series as a whole—the ego may be able to realize its infinitude through the boundaries of the finite.[29] The past is fixed yet always recreated by the activity of the imagination, and the ego "still sojourns, yet still moves onward." For the Mariner, the movement of time is not redeemed by imagination. He is a prisoner of memory.

The repressed returns—again and again. The Mariner's imagination turned inward uncovers only the fragments of the past. He oscillates wildly from surrender to an inhuman pantheistic order to isolation within a Selfhood possessed by demons of the past. His imagination creates a heaven in which individuation is a violation and a hell in which the Self is bound without choice to its darkest past. Memory here is damnation because it serves not the creative imagination but the Selfhood's anxiety for coherence. Memory in this sense creates the kind of "sick" life Schelling describes: time is not at the spiritual center of evolving life but is cast into fixed forms, what Schelling calls the "ground."[30] The Self may thus exalt its individuation, but it pays a price, a fall away from the active becoming of spirit through *life*. Life must express itself as a unity of forces in individuation. For Coleridge, man is driven back and forth between these "poles," between a communion that threatens annihilation and an integrity that threatens isolation and death. The imagination creates time and space, movement and growth, to unite these poles in a sacrament of creative life. In the *Biographia*, the imagination in man is the mediator in man's relation to the world he perceives; in the poetry, Coleridge seeks, like the Mariner, for spiritualized forms that will excite the mediation of love—love in the poetry is the mediator to the world man would "inly feel." As Lockridge eloquently summarizes Coleridge's ideal, "Love is the most intense form of knowing, and it entails the enrichment of one's sense of reality by means of the felt reality of another. . . . The self journeys outward to a symbol of the self of another, and returns through the mediation of the symbol to itself. . . . Through the act of imagination that is love, one comes home to where one has never been."[31]

## Paradise, Pantheism, and the Spiral of Imagination

Coleridge's first—and last—love poem to his wife asserts that human love is not possible if man surrenders Self to the force of some pantheistic order projected by the mind to escape the demands of creative imagination. Perhaps Sara's "mild reproof" in "The Eolian Harp" is darted not only out of Christian piety but also because her new husband's moment of blissful pantheism violates her own integrity and the possibility of real relation. (She may have sensed even then that she was embarking on one of the less successful marriages in literary history.)

"The Eolian Harp" asserts the necessary presence of active individual consciousness even as man reaches toward paradise.[32] The poet begins in a paradisiacal garden of repose. The senses are filled serenely and become attenuated into silence. But even in that repose, the poet's mind is working, Adam-like, giving names, making emblems of the jasmine, myrtle, and the "star of eve" (lines 3–7). And the world of images evoked by the harp is a world within the poet: the images are all introduced by "like" or "as," the poet giving imagined form to the music, attempting to recreate within himself the cosmic dance without. The active spiritual unity of the emblem-filled garden magically reflects his desire for Sara. But she is "pensive," and the poet is filled with his own imaginings. He moves even further, seeing not his imagination working on the harp, but both his own mind and the harp vibrating with

> The one life within us and abroad,
> Which meets all motion and becomes its soul,
> A light in sound, a sound-like power in light,
> Rhythm in all thought, and joyance every where—
>     (lines 26–29)[33]

In such a paradisiacally conceived world the self expands to "love all things" (lines 30–31), but ends in annihilation. As in *The Rime*, a magical unity contends with growing individuation, and in the end individuation is seen as a sinful falling away from a pantheist vision of the world. In the early manuscript draft the vision is straightforwardly Spinozan, a vision of a God who is

> The universal Soul,
> Mechanized matter as th' organic harps
> And each one's Tunes be that, which each calls I.
> (lines 44–46)[34]

All "I's" are united by a single "mechanism," and all matter is as much "I" as the poet. This union annihilates both the integrity of the poet and the integrity of God. For Coleridge a God who is everywhere is nowhere. To know God is to stand apart from him—Sara's "reproof" destroys the "indolent and passive" reverie and in restoring the distance between poet and God shatters the paradise of love. But this love was more adoration than *active* love, and in the shattering of a pantheistic paradise, the possibility for active love returns. So, however, does Coleridge's knowledge of "sin," our inevitable state of sunderance from God. This sunderance was present in Coleridge's paradise all along—as the poet, "a sinful and most miserable man," discovers at the poem's end.

The redemptive paradise was not so much a delusion as a disabling vision: the poet's indolently "stretching his legs" is contrasted with walking humbly in "the family of Christ." But redemption is possible ("his saving mercies healed me"), its prerequisite, paradoxically, a recognition of the *gulf* between man and God. The gulf establishes—as in the Mariner's new-found respect for living things—the integrity and reality of both.

Certainly Coleridge's terms in this poem are not idealist but traditional Christian ones, the quest for paradise and the reminder of guilt. But it is Coleridge himself who alerts us to his heterodox desire to locate paradise in the present experience of a world attuned to the human mind. The danger of pantheist self-annihilation and its opposite, the isolation of the sinner, are both aspects of the demand developed by idealism, that the autonomous human mind is the creator of its own world.

If the imagination spins the self centrifugally into annihilation, it is Coleridge's sense of sin that pulls him back (the poet is also "imagining" Sara's reproof, and he immediately feels his heresy). There is more than a tinge of the Mariner's self-hatred in the "sinful and most miserable man" who sees his individuation to be as sinful as his pantheistic retreat. The poet throws himself upon the rescuer (God, but also the merciful-mother figure, Sara) as the Mariner does upon the Hermit. The poem establishes the conditions of love, but the sense of necessary separation is shot through with an anxiety dubbed "sinfulness." Sin here is, in Christian terms, original sin, the necessity for man to choose not to be God. If we are to erect a paradise, it cannot be a pantheistic communion, but must retain our separateness from God. Yet this separateness might pull us centripetally inward, as consciousness becomes more and more cut off from creating an inner harmony reflecting or echoing a harmony without. The "Dejection" ode moves in the opposite direction from "The Eolian Harp," and the poet is again disabled.[35]

"Dejection: An Ode" is the clearest statement of the need to root the imagination in the poet's experience, the imagination moving outward to reproduce in the finite mind a vision of nature's own harmony. We cannot perceive the latter unless the imagination has built an inner harmony. The "Ode" is a poem about the failure of the poet's imagination to connect, to mediate between inner and outer harmonies. It is an absolute vision of consciousness unable to create itself or an external cosmos.

The poet arrives at a mute, dead solipsism:

> A grief without a pang, void, dark, and drear,
>     A stifled, drowsy, unimpassioned grief,
>     Which finds no natural outlet, no relief,
>         In word, or sigh, or tear. . . .   (lines 21–24)

He then affirms the power of imagination to work on the individual's experience until the individual consciousness "envelops the Earth" and is able to perceive cosmic order. Without such a movement from within we can see only an "inanimate cold" nature.

> I may not hope from outward forms to win
> The passion and the life, whose fountains are within.
>
> O Lady! we receive but what we give,
> And in our life alone does Nature live:
> Ours is her wedding garment, ours her shroud! (lines 45–49)

The imagination repeats in the finite mind the power of "Joy" that eternally creates the universe: "Joy, Lady! is the spirit and the power / Which wedding Nature to us gives in dower / A new Earth and new Heaven" (lines 67–69).

M. H. Abrams emphasizes this "Joy" as a redemptive principle, declaring that "*Dejection* concludes . . . with a passage that expresses the poet's triumph over his exclusive self-concern" even though this Joy is "forever lost" to the poet.[36] But I suggest that the emphasis is on the poet's disability, not on his hopes for the "dear Lady." The poet's vision of Joy makes all the more powerful his inability to realize it within. When his imagination does begin to work upon the "Aeolean lute," he hears "a scream / Of agony by torture lengthened out" (lines 97–98). Images of loneliness, death, groans, and warfare overwhelm the poet, and the tale "of less affright, and tempered with delight" is scarcely delightful, a tale of the screams of a lost child. When the imagination works on the joyless, cut-off self, it produces only a plethora of pain and discord.[37]

We recall the words of Schelling, quoted above:

> Man's will may be regarded as a nexus [*band*] of living forces; as long as it abides in its unity with the universal will these forces remain in their divine measure and balance. But hardly does self-will yield from the center which is its position, than the bond of forces also yields; in its place a merely particular will rules which can no longer unite the forces among themselves as before. . . . As a genuine life could only exist in the original relationship, there thus arises a life which is indeed a life, but is false, a life of lies, a growth of disquiet and corruption.[38]

This discord, this solipsism and alienation, is as much a pole of human consciousness as the paradises we build. It is our lot to build paradises we cannot live in. "Thy being's being is contradiction," Coleridge laments.[39] Even after erecting the perfect balance of Xanadu, Kubla hears voices far-off prophesy war. The voices emerge from the subterranean seas of creative energy that burst into a world ordered by the imagination. But again, the poet himself in "Kubla Khan" questions his ability to revive a lost yet still remembered paradise. The imagination that flings us outward toward cosmic order is rooted in a self with its own subterranean desires and hidden guilts. When the imagination, allied with self-consciousness, operates inwardly on the soul of man, it discovers unconscious horrors that threaten to annihilate the coherent self.

Indeed, we will not find this Freudian gloom in the theoretics of the *Biographia*. There we have the imagination mediating between two poles, absolute objective identity and absolute transcendent consciousness. Only in the poems are the horrors and temptations of the self-annihilation at both poles explored. In the poems we most often see the imagination failing to mediate.

Yet even so, what is theoretically available through imagination in the *Biographia* is offered as a practical goal in the poems—the goal of love. Love is the imagination in spiritual relation to another consciousness. In the conversation poems, however, love often is a goal that others may reach but which for the most part eludes the poet himself. Imagination, it seems, is powerful not only in intensifying the poet's alienation but also in projecting over against this a lost paradise, and this projection makes matters even worse. Again, memory is a curse for Coleridge when, as in the "Dejection" ode, it reveals only a fixed past inevitably sundered from the static prison of the present. Even stormy despair is longed for if only it will make the soul itself "move and live." Self-consciousness in Coleridge often appears as memory; his wish for love for *others* is as far as he can go to overcome the Selfhood that his imagination too often offers as its proudest creation.

"Frost at Midnight" is virtually unique in Coleridge's poetic canon for its masterful creation of a mind that moves to establish itself through overcoming itself.[40] It is his only successful love poem. Even here, Hartley will triumph where the poet failed, yet Coleridge's imagination triumphs in prophecy nevertheless. The prophecy foretells a spiritualized world, but not a world of primitive superstitious desires or fears. The central image of the poem, the "stranger," is an emblem of superstition and of days when the world was instinct with magic. But that hope for magic is blasted by the reality of the dull classroom in the "dim" city. Hence, in an early printed version (1808) Coleridge dismisses the superstition as one of the "wild reliques of our childish Thought," as the mere projection of the mind's need to see life in any moving thing rather than be still and alone.[41]

But Coleridge later omitted these lines. The superstition was not so foolish after all—its meaning was only improperly understood. For the world of magic gives way to a world responsive in a higher, *symbolic* way: the stranger has arrived, and it is Coleridge himself, coming home through love for his son and the recreation of memory into prophecy. Memory here is taken up by imagination and seen as consisting of images to be realized in symbolic tales for the active, interpreting spirit. The poem is a symbolic unity, as House has said, that "as a whole leaves us with a quite extraordinary sense of the mind's *very being*, in suspense, above time and space; the mind with all its powers of affection and memory, and its power of reading nature as the language of God." Lockridge explicitly contrasts the "sinister magic" of *The Ancient Mariner* to the benevolent spiritual power that here carries the mind onward to its productive center. And in his thorough and sensitive reading of the poem, Reeve Parker too suggests that "the significant movement in the poem is from the willful and superstitious solipsism of a depressed sensibility, toying with a companionable form, to the apprehension of a regenerate companionship, based not on superstition but on substantial belief."[42]

Memory, once cold and frozen, stirs into crystalline life, and like the frost thaws and grows as "all seasons" transform it. The "secret ministry" of frost is the secret of time, time regenerated through the free imagination. The structure of memory is fluid though intricate as a crystal sustained by the opposition of forces: the movement of the "stranger" stirs the mind into movement, first to a memory within a memory, the dream of his "birth-place"; then to past school-days when the boy's imagination, "presageful," yearns for companionship in the future; then to rebirth through the babe whose breath enters thought as a rhythm of life like the rhythm of the seasons that nurture the child at the poem's end.

This lyric represents the triumph of the symbolic imagination over memory and of sympathetic love for another over Selfhood and alienation. The growing spiritual life of the child through time reflects, but is not slavishly subject to, the growing revelation of symbolic meaning in nature—"the lovely shapes and sounds intelligible / Of that eternal language." So the poet has grown in realizing to himself the symbolic evolution of his own past, its evolution into a prophecy of love. In this apotheosis of memory through imagination critics have found a faith like Wordsworth's at the close of "Tintern Abbey"—though, to be sure, without his sonorous intensity.[43] But the particular greatness of "Frost at Midnight," for me at least, is that the continuities Wordsworth begins and ends with in nature Cole-

ridge builds up from the isolated mind itself. There is indeed alienation and grief in Wordsworth's great lyric—that "nature never did
betray / The heart that loved her" is more an urgent hope than the
poet's true experience—but he returns again and again to certain
*given* continuities, no matter how far away from them the mind has
fallen. In Coleridge, the mind is most radically the maker of its own
meanings.

Yet, of course, the world must come alive in reciprocity—and
from the Fichtean themes of magic and quest to the active romantic
engagement with imagination and love, we have seen that the ego's
creative freedom requires otherness to enable its activity. Coleridge,
perhaps more than any other romantic poet, felt this most deeply as
a Fall. But he understood the Schellingean principle that declares the
Fall powerful only as the creative energies of the ego are transferred
to the boundary (the "ground") itself, only as the ego comes to define itself not as infinitely free but as infinitely opposed. The ego
then applies its energy to creating a Selfhood set against the world as
"reality principle."

The alternative to such a Fall is realized in "Frost at Midnight":
the mind creates a continuous eddying, a relation to a recreated
world instinct with spirit and articulating itself through symbol. The
psychological principle of "quest," that the world shall become what
I desire even as it infinitely resists me, is given a spiritual meaning in
this poem. For the young Coleridge's desire for magical gratification
is not fulfilled: the relative does not appear in the schoolroom door,
the playmate sister (an image of himself in innocence, "both clothed
alike") does not return. But the "stranger" *does* announce an arrival—
the formative power of the poet's imagination, the redemption of experience in love, the symbolizing of memory into prophecy. "What"
the ego desires is now clear, and it is a spiritual not an objective fact:
the ego desires a continuing revelation of itself through its own created symbols. Coleridge sees a "stranger" that is at first as alien and
lonesome as he, though it is a "companionable form"; the mind's superstitious desire presages a reunion; the mind is penetrated by the
spirit ("breathings") of another who symbolizes the growth and love
that regenerate the world. A door has opened and the reunion with
the stranger does take place: it is Coleridge who enters and comes
home to himself.

What is remarkable is how rare such homecomings are for

Coleridge: we think of the Mariner's vision of the moving moon and realize that this is precisely the kind of resolution that is withheld from his memory-tormented soul.

In the *Biographia* we see the imagination as the most powerful force for integrating man and his universe. In the great lyric, "Frost at Midnight," imagination and love create new symbolic meanings that integrate mind with itself and with others. For these are fundamentally optimistic works, and the imagination here is able dynamically to reconcile inner discord by pointing inward to the very center of creative life where the dualities are created. In the same way, it points outward to an eternal creative power that generates dualities in nature. Thus the mind grows to larger and larger self-awareness, at each step able to perceive greater order without. The greater the ability to comprehend order without, the greater the ability to comprehend order within, and vice versa. The principle is like the principle of spiral growth in nature, the organism spiraling ever outward, as it attempts to move forward but is deflected in widening circles by forces within and without.

The possibility of collapse or annihilation is explored in the early poems. Imagination is not often able to bear the strains that tear it outward away from the self or inward away from the cosmos. But in the *Biographia* and "Frost at Midnight," the creative spirit is portrayed as able to retain its integrity as a growing, organic unity, mirroring in infinite but expanding coherence the eternally created order of the universe.

# PART IV

*From Infinite Enchantment to Dialectical Imagination: Shelley's Maturing Quest*

# 8

## Alastor: *The Disabling Vision*

Although it was not until 1818 that Shelley read the English translation of *A Course of Lectures on Dramatic Art and Literature*, August Schlegel's definition, in the opening lecture, of the predicament of the modern "romantic" poet must have struck a note of recognition in the author of *Alastor* (1815):

> [Under the influence of the Christian doctrine of the Fall, the modern poet fears] that no external object can entirely fill our souls; and that every mortal enjoyment is but a fleeting and momentary deception. When the soul, resting as it were under the willows of exile, breathes out its longing for its distant home, the prevailing character of its songs must be melancholy. Hence the poetry of the ancients was the poetry of enjoyment, and ours is that of desire: the former has its foundation in the scene which is present, while the latter hovers betwixt recollection and hope. . . .
>
> The Grecian idea of humanity consisted in a perfect concord and proportion between all the powers—a natural harmony. The moderns again have arrived at the consciousness of the internal discord which renders such an idea impossible; and hence the endeavour of their poetry is to reconcile these two worlds between which we find ourselves divided, and to melt them indissolubly into one another.[1]

"Such a passage," Stuart Curran asserts, "could stand as an epigraph for Shelley's life work."[2] For Shelley, man's created images may offer ideal reconciliations that betray us, seduce us from the finitude of our nature. Like Fichte's, Shelley's image-making mind may overleap the boundaries of the not-I and returning only upon itself encounter an imageless deep. But for Shelley as for Fichte, the irony of our state is that to remain within the borders of the "given" is to betray the freedom and self-creativity that are also our nature. For Shelley, the most powerful emblem of this dangerous surrender is the fact of physical death.

These are the poles of annihilation in *Alastor,* Shelley's early quest romance. The problem he raises in this poem is typical not only of his career but also of the idealist legacy—both English and German—that so personally engaged him: does the image-making faculty create what it perceives? If it does, does imagination create only empty delusions that leave man suspended above some unknown thing-in-itself? If it does not, then does imagination again confront an utterly alien not-I, and to what extent can mind re-form and transcend the alien "Power"? The goal of idealism, and indeed of Shelley's mythopoeic quest, is what I have earlier called a "redemptive irony" (above, pp. 94–95) that raises imagination above itself, as it were, to see itself as the very creator of this oscillating dialectic, as the creator of its own dilemmas when it attempts to resolve this question finally. In Shelley's poetry, the imagination from this perspective is the creator of a higher skepticism: though the mind cannot know the answer to the riddle of itself, it can create a poetic image of itself in skeptical contemplation of its dilemmas. Thus, though the higher understanding may not be available to the speaker or main actor in a poem, it may be available to the reader as his own mind recreates the poles of possible self-interpretations. We may recognize this "gap" in perspectives as a species of literary irony, and we will call this particular romantic irony "mythopoeic" (so as, later, to distinguish it from Byronic, or "existential" irony).[3]

This higher perspective, however, is not available to the Poet whose career is portrayed in *Alastor,* trapped as he is in the Fichtean ironies of pursuing the ideal to its absolute source in the free, creative ego. Shelley would have read an explicitly Fichtean formulation of the problem I have been discussing, in a work he certainly knew, Madame de Staël's *De l'allemagne,* translated in a very popular English edition of 1813. In her chapter on post-Kantian philosophers, she attempts a synopsis of the Fichtean ego; in the course of two paragraphs, she turns from the absolute I as an identity that transcends time and physical death to the Absolute as empty and lifeless: "It is to the immoveable soul, the witness of the moveable soul, that Fichte attributes the gift of immortality, and the power of creating, or (to translate more exactly) of *drawing to focus in itself the image of the universe.* This system . . . makes everything rest on the summit of our existence, and places a pyramid on its point." For Fichte, she continues, the world is only a boundary to the creative mind, but the boundary, too, is created by the mind, "the activity of which is constantly exerted on the web it has formed." But this ideal of absolute creativity is a mixed blessing: "Idealism, stripped of sentiment, has nevertheless the advantage of exciting, to the highest degree, the activity of the mind; but nature and love, by this system, lose all their charms; for, if the objects which we see, and the beings whom we love, are nothing but the works of our own ideas, it is man himself that may be considered as the great *caelibatary* [bachelor] of the world."[4]

A more acute précis of the *Alastor* Poet's predicament would be hard to find. Like Schlegel's modern poet, Shelley's Poet "hovers betwixt recollection and hope," between the remembered image of his dreamed union with his *anima* and his hope to find his home in infinity. Can any perceived image be adequate to his own imagination's power? The Poet's soul has conjured an image of its own infinite reflection in an Other that mirrors its own spiritual self; yet that image is always receding, as two obscure points of light, the self and its double. The recession is infinite because the I is in itself infinite. The quest for the source of all human knowing leads to the infinitely creating ego, independent in itself from the finite world of its images. "It is a mysterious impulse of our inner being," said Novalis in a Fichtean dialogue upon these issues, "to expand towards all sides from an infinitely deep central point."[5] But, then, is not this infinite self-reflecting act an annihilation of the very real finite self of our experience—is not this source of all our images a kind of death?

This question is posed by Staël in her remarks on death and the pantheist notion of immortality she believes is offered by Schelling: "The school of Schelling supposes that the individual within us perishes, but that the inward qualities which we possess, enter again into the great whole of the eternal creation." But despite the nobility and stoic otherworldliness of this conception, it is an immortality "terribly like death," for

> are not the affections of the heart, and even [moral] conscience itself, allied to the relations of this life? . . . it is exactly, because we have an instinct which would preserve our existence, that it is a fine thing to sacrifice that instinct; it is because we are beings whose center is in ourselves, that our attraction towards the assemblage of all things is generous; in a word, it is because we exist individually and distinctly, that we can choose out and love one another. What then becomes of that abstract immortality which would strip us of our dearest recollections as mere accidental modifications?[6]

"Vision and Love!" cries Shelley's Poet, as his driven boat approaches a yawning cavern amid the threatening crags of the Caucasus, "'I have beheld / The path of thy departure. Sleep and death / Shall not divide us long!'"[7] But there is no reason for the reader to believe in such a consummation, at least insofar as he adopts the Narrator's admittedly limited perspective:

>         . . . —but thou art fled—
> Thou canst no longer know or love the shapes
> Of this phantasmal scene, who have to thee
> Been purest ministers, who are, alas!
> Now thou art not. . . .   (lines 695–99)[8]

The path of the Vision's departure is not upward to some mystical realm of forms but down into the endless maze of the Poet's own mind. Thought, says Shelley, can only "with difficulty visit the intricate and winding chambers it inhabits. It is like a river whose rapid and perpetual stream flows outwards—like one in dread who speeds through the recesses of some haunted pile and dares not look behind. The caverns of the mind are obscure and shadowy; or pervaded with a lustre, beautifully bright indeed, but shining not beyond their portals."[9] Shelley's imagery here recalls Plato's Myth of the Cave; however, the glimmer of ideas radiates not from a transcendent mind, a Sun beyond the cave, but from the human mind transcendentally conceived as the center of consciousness.[10] The imagery also recalls, however, the perilous quest of the Poet, whose object—the fixed reflection of his Selfhood—recedes as quickly as his pursuit hastens forward. The I is not a thing, we recall, but an activity; the source of our finite images—the "deep truth"—is itself imageless.[11]

Metaphysics, Shelley had declared, must begin with the mind as the source of its images; here and only here is certainty:

> Let us contemplate facts; let us in the great study of ourselves resolutely compel the mind to a rigid consideration of itself. We are not content with conjecture, and inductions, and syllogisms in sciences regarding external objects. . . . Metaphysics will thus possess this conspicuous advantage over every other science, that each student by attentively referring to his own mind may ascertain the authorities upon which any assertions regarding it are supported. There can thus be no deception, we ourselves being the depositaries of the evidence of the subject we consider.[12]

Certainly Shelley is here writing in the tradition of Descartes, Locke, and Hume. Yet we might also recall the opening words of Fichte's *Wissenschaftslehre*: "Attend to yourself; turn your attention away from everything that surrounds you and towards your inner life; this is the first demand that philosophy makes of its disciple. Our concern is not with anything that lies outside you, but only with yourself."[13] In his essay, Shelley asks what might lie beyond our experience. Fichte found an infinite freedom, a self-reverting assertion, but Shelley (like Hume) fears there is nothing. Fichte would agree that no *knowledge* lies beyond experience, that mind can intuit its freedom but can neither know nor speak it. This may be what Shelley means by his assertion,

> These diversities [of spatiotemporal experience] are events or objects and are *considered relatively to human identity*, for the existence of the human mind. For if the inequalities produced by what has been termed the operations of the external universe were levelled by the perception of our being uniting and filling up their interstices, motion, and mensuration, and time, and space; the elements of the human mind being thus abstracted, sensation and imagination cease.

Unlike Fichte, for whom the mind can intuit itself as the infinite source of creative energy, Shelley is skeptical that the mind can know its power directly, apart from the images it creates. "Mind," he concludes, "cannot be considered pure."[14] The imagination, Fichte had asserted, creates the finite world of space and time, of boundaries and eternal process, to save the self-reflecting ego from extinction (above, pp. 88–89). For German idealism generally, the I strove after itself as receding *ideal*, and the imagination creates finitude so the I can unfold to itself through an understanding of *moral* imperatives. Shelley would generally agree, but in his terms the imagination unfurls a world of value and of images through which the mind comes to know itself in the relation of *love*.

Yet when the imagination seeks to know the mind directly, or to create an image of its source itself, it ends in annihilation. If this is so, then does the fancy "cheat" itself, as Keats put it? Does imagination create finite forms that merely mask the ultimate reality, which is a void of self-reflexiveness? Or are the webs of natural relations perhaps after all the only paths toward active love and self-assertion; do these provide the images of interchange, growth, and duration which allow the mind symbolically to contemplate the only reality with any claim to ultimacy: the progress of self-understanding and the endurance of spiritual value amid the transformations of human life? From *Alastor*, to "Mont Blanc," to the affirmations of *Prometheus Unbound*, Shelley records the transformation of the romantic idealist quest for ultimate knowledge into the struggle to realize the ideal in the imaginative recreation of our human life and human loves.

These, then, are the poles of contradiction upon which critics of *Alastor* have, notoriously, been impaled. It would be difficult, for instance, to find two critics to agree on the central incident of the poem, the appearance of the Dream-Woman. Does she represent a disembodied ideal impossible of attainment yet nobly sought for? According to Evan Gibson, the Poet "seeks for the pattern or original of the vision itself, the antitype . . . the furies of an irresistible passion [do not] come from searching in the actual world." A more recent critic, John Bean, believes the Poet's failure is a result of his longing for fusion with the infinite, for "direct mystical union" through the erotic. Or does she represent a more naturalistic eroticism, a compulsion to carnal union which the Poet flees? For Gerald Enscoe, "she represents sensual love, biological necessity." A down-to-earth compromise is offered by Milton Wilson, who sensibly observes that she represents an ideally suitable but very real mate, whom the Poet does not flee but pursues to the exclusion of all others, and to his own destruction: "He does not seek an embodiment or earthly equivalent of an otherworldly form. He seeks the thing itself, which is simply the human object he finds most desirable. Even if he were to find her in the next world, she would be no different from what she would be in this . . . *Alastor* is anything but Platonic."[15]

Shelley's own explanation, in his Preface to the poem, of the Poet's vision is a more subtle and fertile analysis of the psychological phenomenon he has drawn than these critical attempts at a univocal philosophical interpretation:

> [The Poet] thirsts for intercourse with an intelligence similar to itself. He images to himself the Being whom he loves. Conversant with speculations of the sublimest and most perfect natures, the vision in which he embodies his own imaginations unites all of wonderful, or wise, or beautiful, which the poet, the philosopher, or the lover could depicture. The intellectual faculties, the imagination, the functions of sense have their respective requisitions on the sympathy of corresponding powers in other human beings.

Yet we cannot rest with this psychological analysis alone, for Shelley does not face the problem raised by the "vision," namely, why exactly it is so devastating. The Poet's quest, says Shelley, is for "a prototype of his conception. Blasted by his disappointment, he descends to an untimely grave." Why is this so? Shelley offers the theory that "self-centered seclusion" is responsible for the Poet's destruction, but the meaning of this statement requires elucidation.[16]

Shelley clearly interprets the vision as a narcissistic projection of the Poet's own idealized Selfhood ("he images to himself . . . the vision in which he embodies his own imaginations"). Critics have long tended to compare this imaging with the healthy state of reciprocal love Shelley theorizes about in his fragmentary essay *On Love*:

> We dimly see within our intellectual nature a miniature as it were of our entire self, yet deprived of all that we condemn or despise, the ideal prototype of every thing excellent or lovely that we are capable of conceiving as belonging to the nature of man. Not only the portrait of our external being, but an assemblage of the minutest particles of which our nature is composed: a mirror whose surface reflects only the forms of purity and brightness: a soul within our soul that describes a circle around its proper Paradise which pain and sorrow and evil dare not overleap. To this we refer all sensations, thirsting that they should resemble or correspond with it.[17]

Shelley in this essay closely approximates our principle of romantic love, that the Other is both alien and integral in its opposition to me but also an image of my own nature as a free, self-creating ego. Thus in my relation to this Other I find myself. In terms of the problems of imagination in *Alastor*, if the imagination cannot find or create in the world an image of its own power, may it not find that image, finally, in another spirit, a person, an "intelligence similar to itself"?

The danger here, however, is that the imagination will create a fixed, finite image, and so not truly encounter the Other as spirit or infinite freedom. The *Alastor* Poet, according to the Preface, "is represented as uniting these [ideal] requisitions and attaching them to a single image." It is the monocular vision, this quest for a fixed ideal, that destroys the Poet: like the Ancient Mariner, the Poet is enthralled by a belle dame, a Life-in-Death. To this extent the endless longing of Shelley's *poète maudit* is unlike the reciprocal meeting of separate but kindred souls and the infinite interchange between mind and nature described in *On Love*.

As in Coleridge's poem of failed, compulsive quest, the hero in *Alastor* does not himself realize that the images that drive him on are creations of his mind reflecting his spiritual state. That understanding of symbolic meaning is left for the reader, for the Poet himself is condemned to pursue a paradox, a real image of his own creative infinitude. He is tormented as long as he keeps that image held apart from him, not seeing that he himself is at the source of his projection. It recedes forever because of the endless recursiveness of the human mind when it attempts to know itself in the same way in which it knows the objective world. This may, in fact, be what Shelley means when he implies in the Preface that the Poet is compelled by a "sacred thirst of doubtful knowledge" and is "duped by [an] illustrious superstition." This perspective on *Alastor* as quest serves to support the conclusions of a recent critic, who cogently observes that the Poet is lured "further and further into his own mind" to the extent that he searches for "an embodied and permanent reality" that will image his mind's infinity. Hence, "the visionary's journey is an endless regress of consciousness."[18]

The Poet's pursuit, in Earl Wasserman's well-known reading, brings "a glory to the world *because* he sought to exceed it," and he is destroyed only because he strives ("demonically") for ideality in an imperfect world.[19] Wasserman recognizes that the Narrator's "natural" love and restricted perspective culminate "only in the extinction that completes the circle of man's animate life: in nature's endless cycle of death and birth" (p. 24). But Wasserman, anxious to emphasize the contrast between a "Wordsworthian" Narrator and a "Visionary" Poet, undervalues the symbolic meaningfulness of the natural landscape—he must interpret nature's images of relatedness as beautiful but seductive snares—while he overvalues the nobility of the Poet's "love." The Poet's spiritual quest "requires an infinite subject as its object," because "when the mind refuses to limit itself to any finite being it has no choice but to envision its own object in a dream, not of actual reality, but of 'hope'—an object that is only potential" (p. 19). But this is confusing: the Poet *does* limit himself, not to a finite being but to a single projected image. Wasserman assumes that the Poet's love should be read as a type of the spiritual interchange described in *On Love*, which he offers as a parallel (pp. 21–23). Yet in *On Love*, Shelley describes a spiritual interaction with a true Other, an ectype met in the world; indeed this love is prefigured by a genuine sympathy with a humanized nature not found (in fact, rejected) in the "Visionary's" quest: "In the motion of the very leaves of spring in the blue air there is then found a secret correspondence with our heart."[20]

The Poet does not at all, as Wasserman implies, engage in a true relation with "an object that is only potential," but rather attempts to pursue the infinite as if it were finite, projecting his own creative infinitude as a coveted image. A clearer statement of the Poet's predicament is provided in a remark of Bloom's that his search for imaginative power "becomes a quest for a finite and measured object of desire which shall yet encompass in itself the beauty and truth of the infinite and unmeasured conceptions of the Poet."[21] As Schelling said, in his review of the 1790 *Faust* fragment, the complex ironies of Faustian striving develop because "the subject as subject cannot enjoy the infinite as infinite, which is nonetheless a necessary inclination of the subject."[22]

Yet only the reader might come to understand the impossibility of this Faustian quest; Shelley's hero cannot. The reader's task is complicated, moreover, by Shelley's providing shifting and unclear alternatives to the Poet's doomed quest. The poem is confusing, one must admit, to the extent that the young Shelley still grapples with his characters' conflicting perspectives and tends to support them as his own. The Preface does not help matters. Here Shelley dubs the Poet one of the "luminaries of the world" who is "deluded by [a] generous error, instigated by [a] sacred thirst of doubtful knowledge." We can understand this thirst as the quest to know what cannot be known directly, the mind's spiritual power; but the Preface does not offer a clear idea of what *successful* illumination might be. In the poem itself, at least from the Poet's perspective, the only alternative to the mind's fruitless quest to know the infinite is a nature seen as complete unconsciousness, annihilation, and death. If the self-reflective in-finitude (the "bad" infinite) of the Poet's narcissistic quest is itself a kind of death, so too is the Narrator's pantheistic nature where self-consciousness has as yet not even arisen. Indeed, the Narrator intro-duces us to the Poet as a corpse, as "the charmed eddies of autumnal winds / Built o'er his mouldering bones a pyramid / Of mouldering leaves in the waste wilderness" (lines 52–54). There is cold comfort in those autumn eddies, and it is no wonder that so many critics dis-trust a narrator who feels compelled to call such a *frisson* "charmed."

The dead leaves swirl often through the poem, and as the Nar-rator later laments, all of "Medea's wondrous alchemy" will not re-trieve from extinction our mysterious consciousness "Of what we are" (lines 672, 29). The Poet's hope that "the dark gate of death [might] / Conduct to thy mysterious paradise, / O sleep" (lines 211–12) is later seen to be only a tenuous, superstitious hope (cf. lines 508–14) and is at best only what Madame de Staël called "an immortality terribly like death" (see note 6, above). Does Shelley's romance provide any way out of this perplexing clash of demonic or pantheistic annihilations? What attitude can we take toward the hero, if, as a recent critic, Ronald Tetreault, concludes, "The poem does not claim the superiority of the visionary perspective over the natural. Instead, it merely plays one against the other in order to discover the 'alastor' or avenging demon that haunts each"?[23]

Tetreault reaches his conclusions after a thorough study of the poem as a response to the Wordsworthian imagination; but we may also be reminded of the dialectics of *Faust*, and, particularly, *The Sorrows of Werther*, which T. J. Hogg tells us "fascinated" the young Shelley.[24] The dialectic Tetreault defines is certainly typical in ro-mantic quest: "Muse becomes 'alastor' as imagination dooms the Visionary to tragic self-destruction, while nature suffers the Nar-rator to be an enslaved survivor in a world that has lost its appeal."[25] As Schelling said of *Faust*: "The point of departure is the insatiable thirst to behold and, as subject, to enjoy the inner essence of things; and its initial direction is to satisfy ecstatically this insatiable desire beyond the aims and limits of reason. . . . The other way out for the mind's unsatisfied striving is that of plunging into the world, to experience earth's sorrow and happiness."[26]

If there is any suggestion in the poem of a way out of this dialectic, recent critics have hinted that it may be the creation of the narrative itself, or, better, in Shelley's creation of a nature that is not dead but is (at least from the reader's perspective) a symbolic landscape.[27] In the Preface, Shelley tells us that the Poet was initially "joyous, and tranquil, and self-possessed" not in a dead nature but amid the "magnificence and beauty" of an external world of objects "infinite and unmeasured." Is there any sense in this poem that nature is "infinite" in a way not destructive to the infinite desires of the hero?

Nature provides the artist, Schelling suggested, with the finite images through which the infinite reveals itself symbolically. The Poet himself does not understand that the Dream-Maid is a symbol projected by his mind; he pursues her as an object of desire, not seeing that she is only the creation of his need to meet love within the real world—the world, indeed, of flux and change that is transformed only when imagination recognizes that world as the necessary ground for its activity.

Nature wears two faces in the poem. It is a world of unconscious relatedness which is alien to the self-conscious striving of man. It is beautiful but blind. Yet from a higher perspective it is a landscape of romance, magically eloquent with symbols of the Poet's inner state. It is not surprising that the hero himself cannot read the landscape as symbolic: it is, after all, a long-honored convention of romance that nature seem a treacherous snare. In Shelley's modern romance, nature is in fact destructive and misleading, but, ironically, it is so only to the mind that addresses it as such. "The Visionary defines man in terms of his mortality," says Wasserman (pp. 20–29). Indeed, that is so, but Wasserman's analysis, subtle as it is, can account for only one view of nature—the Poet's. He quotes with approval the Poet's rejection of the swan, which, though it soars "scaling the upward sky," is yet always at home, exactly like the Ancient Mariner's moon and stars that "sojourn yet still move onward":

> Thou hast a home,
> Beautiful bird; thou voyagest to thine home,
> Where thy sweet mate will twine her downy neck

With thine, and welcome thy return with eyes
Bright in the lustre of their own fond joy.
   (lines 280–84)

For Wasserman, the Poet understands here that his only home is beyond the world and so must undertake a voyage to an equally uncertain goal—death.

And what am I that I should linger here,
With voice far sweeter than thy dying notes,
Spirit more vast than thine, frame more attuned
To beauty, wasting these surpassing powers
In the deaf air, to the blind earth, and heaven
That echoes not my thoughts?  (lines 285–90)

But this "understanding" is remarkable only for its blindness. As Donald Reiman notes of these lines, "The Youth has become so deluded by the desires of his own heart that everything seems inert and unreal except himself and his own imaginings."[28] The elements are blind and deaf only to the Poet who would pursue himself into infinity. Note the extraordinary eloquence of lines 280–84, the reciprocal love the Poet turns from. Even the woven sounds of the poetry here are resonant with music the Poet—though he himself speaks the words—does not hear. The swan's mate welcomes it "with eyes / Bright in the lustre of their own fond joy," one of the many images of mirror-reflections in the poem. To *turn* from such communion is itself a kind of death, and the Poet broods with a "gloomy smile" to think a "desperate" thought—that death is his only "hope" if the world has become mute to him.

Shelley allows the Poet to fear for a moment that nature, some "fair fiend," has led him to thoughts of suicide, but we are told explicitly that there was no such fiend blasting him with disappointment, "not a sight / Or sound of awe but in his own deep mind" (lines 297–98). The key word here is "deep": for the mind that will seek infinity not in the endless interchange with time and process but only as an abstraction in a fixed image, there is only the endless recession of empty self-consciousness. This is the lesson of the "good" and the "bad" infinite: the infinite becomes a receding abstract ideal when we try to fix it, to covet it as our own; the infinite is real only as we permit time and change to be Other than our Selves, even to be destructive of the narcissistic self-images we covet. The "good" infinite, then, is not an abstraction but is rather the endless spiritual creativity we may bring to the world that is not ourselves. Only then may we reach that greater wisdom—I have called it "saving irony"— in which we know the imagination was all along the creator of our finitude, that we might know ourselves not directly but in symbolic encounter with the eloquent world.

Such an encounter is a maturer vision than is available to either the Narrator or his hero-Poet. The vision is resisted by both men in the name of a compelling (but perhaps psychologically regressive) integrity. The tale is told by the Narrator as his version of spiritual assertion, as an admirable quest for the Truth. But because he remains bound to the empirical order himself, he can conceive such assertion only in finite, naturalistic terms. In the last analysis, the Poet rises little further than the Narrator beyond a Selfhood determined by memory and bounded by nature: in the end, the Poet's quest to transcend nature only takes him deeper into his own primary self-love, and—like the Narrator—he can only come to hate and fear the nature whose processes would force him to grow. Yet when he seeks the mystery of life he searches not within his own poetic powers but only after an accumulation of more and more natural history (lines 78ff.). In a similar way, the Narrator seeks the mystery "Of what we are" from the "Mother of this unfathomable world" in superstition and natural magic:

> . . . I have loved
> Thee ever, and thee only; I have watched
> Thy shadow, and the darkness of thy steps,
> And my heart ever gazes on the depth
> Of thy deep mysteries. I have made my bed
> In charnels and on coffins, where black death
> Keeps record of the trophies won from thee.
> Hoping to still these obstinate questionings
> Of thee and thine, by forcing some lone ghost,
> Thy messenger, to render up the tale
> Of what we are.     (lines 19–29)

The Narrator's search for truth betrays an obstinate literal-mindedness that leaves him liable to betrayal by the mother of his "natural piety." He is unable to fathom the meaning of the Poet's death and reaches almost frantically for some elixir to reanimate the dead; failing this, he rejects the "cold" comforts of artistic immortality (lines 707–10) and is left in "pale despair and cold tranquility" (line 718) to batter himself ruefully against a recalcitrant nature destructive to personality and indifferent to his questions. His love for nature alone leads to the maddening frustration and weary perplexity of the epilogue (lines 672ff.).

This attitude is a consequence of a perspective Shelley describes in a poem published in the 1816 *Alastor* volume, "On Death":

> This world is the nurse of all we know,
>     This world is the mother of all we feel,
> And the coming of death is a fearful blow
>     To a brain unencompassed with nerves of steel;
> When all that we know, or feel, or see,
> Shall pass like an unreal mystery.[29]

In both poems the appeal to the mother and nurse is a regressive hope for protected innocence, the longing for primal narcissistic integrity. In the face of death, the voice of the lyric can offer only stoic resignation until "the light of a wondrous day" dawns, a new Paradise that "must surely be." Shelley hints that this longing for Paradise is a fear of change, of the disruption of our innocent "love for that which we see" (line 30). There is a deep ambivalence in this poem between the poet's intimation of a glorious postmortem reward and his fear that we ourselves will not be able to enjoy it.[30] The world of change is destructive, but it is the only source we know for our images of beauty, or power, or greatness; in death (whatever it may offer) we will not live to hear or see

> All that is great and all that is strange
> In the boundless realm of unending change.
>
> (lines 23–24)

In the Esdaile MS. version of this poem, the "boundless realm" of nature is the "gradual path" of change, suggesting a contrast with the apocalyptic, absolute destruction of personality in death.[31] Shelley had explicitly asserted in the early *Essay on a Future State* that the fear of death and destruction of our cherished personality is the real source of our regressive superstitious hope for eternal life. His language there recalls the lament of the *Alastor* Narrator over the Poet's death:

> [One] contends in vain against the persuasion of the grave that the dead indeed cease to be. The corpse at his feet is prophetic of his own destiny. Those who have preceded him, and whose voice was delightful to his ear; whose touch met his like sweet and subtle fire; whose aspect spread a visionary light upon his path—these he cannot meet again. . . . How can a corpse see or feel? . . . All that we see or know perishes and is changed.

His conclusion is an apt diagnosis of the Narrator's narrow-minded superstition: "The desire to be for ever as we are, the reluctance to a violent and unexperienced change which is common to all the animated and inanimate combinations of the universe is, indeed, the secret persuasion which has given birth to the opinions of a future state."[32]

Despite the Poet's search for transcendent truth he is as befuddled about nature and about change as the Narrator. Despite his having "gazed and gazed" on the hieroglyphs at Dendera and having seen "the thrilling secrets of the birth of time," he has learned little about his own life or his relation to nature and naturalness. At a crucial moment in the poem, he turns from nature just when it would draw him into creative relation. The irony of this central scene at the well (lines 420–93) is that the "blind earth" and "heaven that echoes not" his thoughts (lines 289–90) do exactly this in a forest alive with images of love. Nature, reflecting his need for relation and "for speech assuming," is about to "hold commune with him" when he flees to chase the "two starry eyes," emblems of his self-created ideal.

The Poet enters a landscape that the Narrator portrays as a garden of innocence:

> Like restless serpents, clothed  
> In rainbow and in fire, the parasites,  
> Starred with ten thousand blossoms, flow around  
> The grey trunks, and, as gamesome infants' eyes,  
> With gentle meanings, and most innocent wiles,  
> Fold their beams around the hearts of those that love,  
> These twine their tendrils with the wedded boughs  
> Uniting their close union; the woven leaves  
> Make net-work of the dark blue light of day. . . .
>
> (lines 438–46)

The "woven leaves" and "wedded boughs," the "infants' eyes" that reach innocently for love bespeak a world of unselfconscious interchange, without radical individuation, alienation, or (needless to say) restless quests. Yet the serpents are "restless"—with the energy of natural interchange and growth. In this garden, insects are "unconscious" of the day, and when the Poet arrives we might expect him to do what poets do—give voice and meaning to the landscape. But he does not. For he enters this world of innocence fearing genuine relation, retreating to his own psychological version of innocence—a relation only to his idealized self-projection. Everything around him exists in an interchange with Otherness; the Poet enters the scene and exists only in relation to himself:

> Hither the Poet came. His eyes beheld
> Their own wan light through the reflected lines
> Of his thin hair, distinct in the dark depth
> Of that still fountain; as the human heart,
> Gazing in dreams over the gloomy grave,
> Sees its own treacherous likeness there.
>
> (lines 469–74)

This scene is intricate and subtle, and any attempt at explanation risks being reductive. I would insist, though, that we are not to admire the Poet's isolation from this landscape, imagining it as a noble escape from nature's snares. This is the Poet's view, and it is destructive to him. When he gazes into the well he sees only himself: the well, like the passive mind in a state of innocence, reflects the external landscape, but the Poet's mind seeks to reflect itself and sees only annihilation, emptiness, and death.[33] This is the beginning of the fall into experience, into the knowledge of individuation and death. The Poet seeks in the well the same unselfconscious, innocent reflexiveness that exists in nature; what he discovers is the inevitability of self-consciousness on the human plane. Like Blake's Thel, he turns away from this fall. His vision is revealed as polarized between realms of mute but spontaneously joyful innocence and self-aware but sterile experience. He is trapped in a dilemma: to remain at the well is to remain infinitely in contact with himself, but this is a precarious relation because it leads nowhere but to empty isolation. His "solution" is to project self-fulfillment infinitely far away yet in the single image of his ideal love, whose "two starry eyes" beckon him.

He does not seem to realize that his quest is only a further attempt at self-relation and dooms him again to isolation and, ultimately, annihilation.

The Poet can transcend this polarization only by recognizing his finitude as the necessary prerequisite for *articulate* relation, for recognizing and creating the landscape anew in its symbolic meaning. But finitude for him means not relation but destructive change, annihilation, and death. Ironically, only the reader of *Alastor* might see the landscape's symbolism—a call to relation and real love—while the Poet, intent upon himself, sees it only as dead, "deaf," "blind." The imagination, that is, gets nowhere trying to create out of itself only (the "ideal" realm of purely spontaneous creation); it can create images only by recognizing its finitude (Kant's "receptivity") and encountering Otherness. Mind draws its power from that which is "outside" it, even though that power consists precisely in overcoming Otherness in the creation of meaning.

A "Spirit" of Otherness, of the landscape itself, appears at the well as if it were trying to prevent the Poet's succumbing to the fate of Narcissus. The Spirit seems "to stand beside him" to draw him out of self-reflection,

> clothed in no bright robes
> Of shadowy silver or enshrining light,
> Borrowed from aught the visible world affords
> Of grace, or majesty, or mystery;—
> But, undulating woods, and silent well,
> And leaping rivulet, and evening gloom,
> Now deepening the dark shades, for speech assuming
> Held commune with him as if he and it
> Were all that was. . . .                               (lines 480–88)

The "silent well" and "evening gloom" themselves would assume speech, if the Poet would only give them voice. The Spirit is not, we are told, a superstitious emblem of the mind, a projected power clothed in "enshrining light," but is simply the scene itself in its need for the Poet to acknowledge and transform it. But in "intense pensiveness" he sees the "two starry eyes," "hung in the gloom of thought," a qualifying phrase that underscores his tragic isolation.[34]

The Poet insists on his literal-minded search, which leads him to pursue his image endlessly and impossibly. He seeks the source of himself in some clear and certain vision and, not finding it, gives up on any other kind of spiritual self-knowledge, assuming that if he cannot have his self-idealization there is nothing worth having or knowing. The world is thus forever disappointing, but it is so only because of the demands he makes upon it.

Seeing a stream that "like childhood . . . in tranquil wanderings crept, / Reflecting every herb and drooping bud" (lines 499–501), he brings to the image of innocence only the obstinate questioning of experience. He would have answers to questions that cannot even be asked, for—as Kant insisted in his theory of the antinomies—the destiny of the infinite, of consciousness, cannot be questioned as if it were finite. For Kant this was philosophical naivete; for the Poet it constitutes psychological backwardness:

> O stream!
> Whose source is inaccessibly profound,
> Whither do thy mysterious waters tend?
> Thou imagest my life.
>                     . . . the wide sky,
> And measureless ocean may declare as soon
> What oozy cavern or what wandering cloud
> Contains thy waters, as the universe
> Tell where these living thoughts reside, when stretched
> Upon thy flowers my bloodless limbs shall waste
> I' the passing wind!      (lines 503–14)

We will soon hear the Narrator's similar lament (lines 666ff.), his fear of death, and his anxiety over change and the loss of primal self-integrity.

The bitter disappointment that death will destroy the Self is shared by the Narrator and the Poet, then, and I suggest that this is not surprising since the Poet exists only in a tale offered us by the Narrator.[35] From his perspective we are natural beings, and since nature is "all that is" and mind is nursed only by nature, any attempt to grow beyond our nursemaid ends in the bitter confusion of experience. It is as if the meaning of his tale were "I have searched for nature's truths; here is one who had learned them and sought beyond them, but look, he attained no final knowledge and died like all men."

The oversimplification of this view underlines the limits of the Narrator's understanding. In the epilogue he blames death—the natural order of things in general—for the Poet's failure. But the Poet fails because he seeks the wrong thing. The infinite cannot be known or imagined because it is within mind itself, is in fact the creative activity of consciousness. He pursues a coveted image, a memory of union with a self-idealization, doing so because he fears change, fears that to encounter the world he must enter its flux and in recreating the world must transform himself. He cannot know himself or the world as he would like to, as objects with clearly defined and given destinies; he must learn to recreate himself and the world in constant interchange with Otherness. To know the world and oneself in clearly defined roles and unselfconscious relations is the state of innocence the Poet believes he has surpassed, but he has only translated that world of natural innocence into a psychological quest to retain primal self-integrity. He also knows, on some level, that this primal integrity must be ruptured—and since he will accept no other selfhood than this innocent one, all assaults upon it are thoughts which, as in Shakespeare's Sonnet 64, are "as a death which cannot choose / But weep to have, that which it fears to lose."

Death in the poem is the ultimate image of nature's threat to the Self, and the extreme fear of death is symptomatic of the fear of a fall into experience, an unredeemable spiritual loss. The cause of the Poet's death is not clear in the narrative, but symbolically the storyteller allows him to succumb to a perennial romantic hazard, death by broken heart. The Poet has asked the first question of experience: "Nature has nursed me to love myself, so why must I know that I will change and die?" He is left demanding his dream girl, and he is allowed to retain his essential innocence by dying before he must learn to accommodate the world of experience, where love does not come as easily as in dreams and the creative mind alone may transform the realm of loss and "unending change."

# 9

## The Power of Disenchantment: Fichtean Irony and the Creative Imagination in Shelley's "Mont Blanc"

In a moment of rare detachment from the mazes of logic in the *Wissenschaftslehre*, Fichte asks what kind of man is able to view self-consciousness from the liberating perspective of idealism: "What sort of philosophy one chooses depends," he believes, "on what sort of man one is; for a philosophical system is not a dead piece of furniture that we can reject or accept as we wish; it is rather a thing animated by the soul of the person who holds it."[1] The whole tone of his Introduction to the *Science of Knowledge* is a persistent questioning of "freedom"; the images we call "external" are those which arrive with a necessity that makes them seem alien to the free-ranging creativity of the mind when it reflects upon itself. Fichte insists that the task of philosophy is to establish the self as free despite its apparent dependence on the world of "Necessity":

> Our imagination and will appear to us to be free. . . . But the question, "What is the source of the system of presentations which are accompanied by the feeling of necessity, and of this feeling of necessity itself?" is one that is surely worthy of reflection. It is the task of philosophy to provide an answer to this question, and in my opinion nothing is philosophy save the science that performs this task. (p. 6)

Those who do not perform this task of self-reflection, Fichte implies, are too timid to accept the infinite creative freedom of idealism; they naively see themselves as *things,* and their self-reflection produces only something fixed and dead:

> Some, who have not yet raised themselves to full consciousness of their freedom and absolute independence, find themselves only in the presentation of things; they have only that dispersed self-consciousness which attaches to objects, and has to be gleaned from their multiplicity. Their image is reflected back to them only by things, as by a mirror; if these were taken from them, their self would be lost as well; for the sake of their self they cannot give up the belief in the independence of things, for they themselves exist only if things do.    (p. 15)

For Shelley, too, philosophy begins with the ego's assertion of its freedom and the problem of the feeling we have of the necessity of, or limitation by, external objects:

> Metaphysics may be defined as an inquiry concerning those things belonging to, or connected with, the internal nature of man. . . . [Writings on metaphysics(?)] more than suggest an association of words, or the remembrance of external objects distinct from the conceptions which the mind exerts relatively to them. They are about these conceptions. They perpetually awaken the attention of their reader to the consideration of their intellectual nature. They make him feel that his mind is not merely impelled or organized by the adhibition of events proceeding from what has been termed the mechanism of the material universe.[2]

We have concluded that Fichte's idealism does not simply assert that the world "is" ideal or is simply a product of the ego (see above, pp. 87–90). Such an assertion would merely attempt to create a finite image of an infinite process, an error that leads to dogmatism. Rather, Fichte's idealism develops systematically, dynamically, to show that the not-I is a necessary boundary without which the I would not be able to assert itself at all. Shelley's "idealism" does not develop as a systematic philosophy, but, nevertheless, the dilemmas of imaginative self-assertion force him to a remarkably Fichtean position in the course of his poetic development.

Self-assertion demands self-*reflection;* this act of reverting presupposes a boundary; but upon encountering the boundary, the ego in idealistic philosophy *does not surrender its creative energy to the not-I.* The ego in the very act of constructing an image avoids this regressive self-denial by retaining for itself the energy of creation. But again, the energy must turn outward, for only by adverting toward a not-I can the I make any assertion that it is anything at all. Finitude is necessary for assertion; what is asserted is the infinite independence of the mind. In this Fichtean circle, the infinite striving after an abstract ideal (Fichte calls this a "completed," and hence impossible-to-realize, infinite; see *GWL*, p. 238) is replaced by an infinite turning of the mind upon itself, overcoming itself and its created images, turning again to their recreation.

"Indeterminate striving," Fichte says, is infinite, but it does not create a real awareness of the world; "nor can it do so, since consciousness is possible only through reflection," and this requires a boundary, an absolute Other. "But as soon as we reflect" upon the ideal, "it necessarily becomes finite. The moment we become aware of its finitude, we continue to expand it further; but as soon as we raise the question, 'is it now infinite?' it is reduced by this very question to finitude: and so on *ad infinitum*" (p. 237). Pursuing the ideal to unite the ego with it completely is regressive and does not produce awareness of the world. Indeed, the infinite pursued as a finite goal or fixed ideal will always appear to recede, because although the goal will seem infinitely far away, in fact this striving is only the ego's futile attempt to know itself as all-powerful and infinitely independent.

The struggle of the Fichtean imagination is also endless, but it is a very different pursuit than endless self-assertion. The Fichtean circle is a constant confrontation with demystification. The irony of this circling is that the mind can reassert its creativity only within the endless process of time and the relentless assertions of the finite world. Certainly this struggle is as unrelenting as the *Alastor* Poet's pursuit; yet it offers, at least, the promise of imaginative creation on the plane of the human. "The poems of an ironist," Gerald McNiece has observed of romantic irony, "express his yearning for the infinite and the absolute and also record his somewhat disillusioning realization that the yearning must forever remain yearning"; and this disappointment, he notes, may serve paradoxically to liberate imagination into confrontation and creativity, awakening it from an infinite enchantment with itself.[3]

In "Mont Blanc," Shelley comes powerfully to realize how the power of otherness, of change and annihilation, may ironically liberate the human imagination to declare its own power to engage precisely in this struggle: to overcome otherness in boundless creativity, while yet remaining free from romantic enchantment with its own creations. As Earl Wasserman defines the epistemological terms of the poem, "the act of searching for the coincidence of thing-in-itself and mental image is itself constitutive of reality for the human mind . . . reality is neither the subjective impression nor the external thing, but the active and irresolvable mental tension between the two that is embodied in the word "'Seeking'" (p. 227). Wasserman's summary precisely defines the power of mind Fichte calls *imagination* (see *GWL*, p. 193; quoted above, pp. 88–89).

I would suggest that the central principle of "Mont Blanc" is the active recreation of this Fichtean dialectic in the imagination's self-discovery in creating the poem. The poem asserts that the finite is vacant and empty only if imagination ceases to create; yet creation in life—intellectual or physical—takes place only within the limits of process, decay, and the inexorable movements of loss and destruction. In "Mont Blanc" the imagination discovers its own power, paradoxically, by recognizing the power of the not-I to elude it. "I never knew I never imagined what mountains were before," an awestruck Shelley wrote to Thomas Peacock from the Valley of Chamonix.[4]

The advance over the destructive self-enchantment of *Alastor* is clear. In that poem, imagination pursues itself as a clearly defined ideal image (or, in more psychological terms, the self attempts to preserve the grandiosity of its primal innocence). In *Alastor* the failure to unite with this image forces the imagination to question the "reality" of its power: if it cannot know itself (through an image), can it ever know whether its creations are anything more than mere fantasies hovering over an empty void? In "Mont Blanc" the mountain itself provides a striking image that resolves the problem (though in no simple, dogmatic way). The mountaintop is a reality that cannot be imaged, a negation that calls the imagination out of itself, revealing that the mind cannot image itself to itself as a creative *activity*. The ideal is revealed only in endless dialogue with the real. The mountaintop is a brilliantly tantalizing image for the unimaginable, for the "secret strength of things" (line 139) that resists the poet in his own poem in the name of calling him to a higher confrontation with the real. What the power of the mountain teaches and reveals to the imagination is its own power to endure and recreate amid destruction, even though the mountain never allows itself to be fully imagined in the poem.

It is remarkable that, despite the obdurate opacity of the not-I in Shelley's lyric, the imagination is not annihilated but persistently and spontaneously creates. Yet it is continually frustrated when it would overcome finitude altogether and create some image of creative power (internal or external) itself:

> Some say that gleams of a remoter world
> Visit the soul in sleep,—that death is slumber,
> And that its shapes the busy thoughts outnumber
> Of those who wake and live. —I look on high;
> Has some unknown omnipotence unfurled
> The veil of life and death? or do I lie
> In dream, and does the mightier world of sleep
> Spread far around and inaccessibly
> Its circles?[5]

A virtually parallel moment occurs in *Alastor*, as the Poet hopes to pursue his lost dream in a world beyond death: "Does the dark gate of death / Conduct to thy mysterious paradise / O Sleep?" (lines 211–13). This possibility awakens "insatiate hope" (line 221) in the doomed Poet, and despite a moment of doubt (lines 292–95) he embraces and pursues this enchantment, for he will either pursue the ideal infinitely or give himself up to an emptiness he feels is his only alternative. The poet who turns to look up at Mont Blanc wonders in these lines whether his imagination might be carried by the sublimity of the mountain beyond finitude itself to an immortal world of numberless thoughts and dreams. But he realizes (as the Poet in *Alastor*, fatally, does not) that his mind only swirls around and around itself, since such an attempt at imagining the indeterminate (or, in psychological terms, of living in a world of infinite imaginative fulfillment) ends only in empty recursiveness:

> the very spirit fails,
> Driven like a homeless cloud from steep to steep
> That vanishes among the viewless gales!     (lines 57–59)

Shelley has asked whether "some unknown omnipotence" has dropped a curtain of limitation ("The veil of life and death") that halts the imagination, or whether the mind is "mightier" in creating dream-images of infinite desire.[6] But he is drawn up short; the question cannot even be asked. The spirit simply "fails" to know itself or the world as things-in-themselves, but this failure prepares the way for a new certainty, the certainty that beyond the spontaneous activity of the mind lies the stillness of a boundary. In the manuscript version of line 57, the "mind," somewhat melodramatically, "is faint / With aspiration," but the printed "fails" eliminates the suggestion that all human ideals and aspirations are negated by the mountain.[7] Mont Blanc asserts itself only to stop the mind's circling about in search of absolute knowledge: suddenly in the midst of the mind's self-questionings the relentless world implacably looms.

> Far, far above, piercing the infinite sky,
> Mont Blanc appears, —still, snowy, and serene—
> Its subject mountains their unearthly forms
> Pile around it, ice and rock. . . .
>
> . . . . . . . . . . . . . . .
>          did a sea
> Of fire, envelope once this silent snow?
> None can reply—all seems eternal now.
> (lines 60–63, 73–75)

Shelley will attempt (much as Keats would in "Ode on a Grecian Urn") to force his silent object to speak; but he thus raises the question, implicit in such rhetorical moves, of how far the mind can go to freely create such responsiveness from the boundaries it faces. Yet it remains the imagination's tendency not merely to create images but to "float" (as in line 42) above the finite mind and seek some coincidence between the mind's images and the not-I. What Fichte recognized in the organic unfolding of the *Wissenschaftslehre* is what Shelley sees, that the mind opposed *absolutely* by a not-I, or a mind infinitely, self-assertively free of the not-I, ends only in annihilation (cf. *GWL,* pp. 123–25). The only resolution, for Fichte, was a dialectical one in which the mind asserts itself to the degree it posits a boundary (or "check," *Anstoss*) and is able to posit (or be conscious of) the boundary to the degree it can assert itself: "The check occurs to the I insofar as it is active . . . no activity of the I, no check. . . . Conversely, the activity of the I's own self-determining would be conditioned by the check: no check, no self-determination. Moreover, no self-determination, no objective, etc." (p. 191). This dialectical resolution makes mind and world mutually determining and interdependent; although if the mind attempts to know the final delineations of that interdependence it would engulf the not-I and destroy the relation. To prevent this relation from thus breaking down, Fichte assigns the *imagination* the role of "hovering" (*schweben*) between the infinite and the finite, creating in its activity both meaningful images (Schelling will seize on this in his theory of symbols) and the experience of *process* or endless *time* (pp. 193–95). The moment in coming to fruition, filled with infinite potentiality, enters the stream of finitude and inevitable loss.

The Fichtean imagination thus establishes man's struggle through time even while allowing the mind to assert in articulate images its independence of process.[8] For Shelley, too, the mind knows itself to be defined in a complex interdependence with the not-I, even though it cannot achieve certainty about what lies beyond itself in the world. For Shelley, too, the imagination's capacity to "float" above its creations allows it, however tentatively, to confront the gaps between its images and reality while yet retaining its power to recreate actively the meaning of the world. Lloyd Abbey argues that the essential "maturity" of "Mont Blanc" consists precisely in this double potential of imagination that can create new understandings without needing to achieve transcendent illumination; in "Mont Blanc" imagination "does not perceive a spirit's vision but creates and destroys its own," enabling man to endure mutability without creating the traps of superstition and idolatry.[9]

The poem's opening clause testifies to the complex ironies of epistemological perspectives:

The everlasting universe of things
Flows through the mind. . . .

By conjoining an eternal procession of *things* with its inevitable course through the mind, Shelley "formulated a syntax which, by fusing the externalizing subject (universe of things) and the internalizing predicate (flows through the mind), denies both that 'things' are mental fictions *and* that there is any real distinction between thing and thought" (Wasserman, p. 222; emphasis added). The universe of things is a universe of images—Wasserman notes the early manuscript variant of line 1, "the stream of various *thoughts*"—images that both "reflect" the gloom of the ravine (the mind) and also "lend" to the mind that which is not the mind's own. We are prepared, then, for the following image of the mind itself as the site of a meeting of waters, a confluence of its own imageless creative energies and the persistent incursions of the vast energies of the world: it is in the mind "where from secret springs / The source of human thought its tribute brings / Of waters,—with a sound but half its own" (lines 4–6).[10] The mind creates its thoughts, its images of the world, spontaneously; that creation in its turn depends on the mind's receptivity to the not-I, to a boundary or check to its activity. Beyond this interrelation knowledge cannot penetrate to the mind or the world in themselves. This view of the mind, I have argued, is not simply "skeptical" in the strong (Humean) sense or idealistic in the Berkeleian sense. It is Shelley's version of Transcendental Idealism which, in "Mont Blanc," concludes with a dialectical imagination closely parallel to Fichte's.[11]

Imagination does not, however, appear in the opening section of the poem. The section raises a question only through its assertion that the mind's images are "but half" its own; to what extent does the mind have power and independence? Shelley's early notebook manuscript betrays some ambivalence: he had first written (in pencil) that the mind brings its tribute with a "voice," altering this to the more powerful but less intelligible "wild sound" before adopting "a sound." The mind's images have, it seems, only the power of a "feeble brook" compared to the "vast river" that "raves" beyond them; nevertheless, the mind's fountains do have an energy that is independent of the river, and so in their way they are equal to the might of the world in their integrity, if not their power.[12] Yet the question still remains, and the rest of the poem will introduce and define the imagination as the mind's power to know and to recreate itself in a world of mutability and destruction.

The metaphor of the Ravine in Section II carries on the logic of the problem raised in Section I. Within the Ravine are "clinging" pines that lend their scene to the "chainless winds," which in their turn listen to the sounds of the trees that the winds set in motion. Amid this "harmony" of interrelation (reminiscent, indeed, of the "woven" boughs in *Alastor*, lines 430ff.) crashes the relentless Arve, which the Ravine may "echo" but cannot "tame" (lines 30–31). What is the role of the mind in its interchange with the world?

Dizzy Ravine! And when I gaze on thee
I seem as in a trance sublime and strange

To muse on my own separate phantasy,
My own, my human mind, which passively
Now renders and receives fast influencings,
Holding an unremitting interchange
With the clear universe of things around. . . .

(lines 34–40)

Imagination receives and creates but also declares itself free of the mind, able to ask the transcendental question, What is the true relation of mind as repository of images to the things it claims to image? The poet, in the closing lines of Section II, seeks (*Alastor*-like) for some image of the mind itself, some image that will clarify imagination's power to itself and answer the question of the true "reality" of its images. At this point in the poem, the imagination attempts to raise up some clear image of its own power; the mind is "One legion of wild thoughts," whose wings float above the Ravine's

       darkness, and now rest
Where that or thou art no unbidden guest,
In the still cave of the witch Poesy,
Seeking among the shadows that pass by
Ghosts of all things that are, some shade of thee,
Some phantom, some faint image. . . .    (lines 42–47)

The last line of this section, as Judith Chernaik remarks, represents the mind's assertion that the things of the world are its own creation: "till the breast / From which they [mental images] fled recalls them, thou art there!"[13] That is, the images of the Ravine ("thou") as a metaphor of mind itself resides in the cave of Poesy ("there"). Yet, as Section III opens, this boundless assertion of imaginative power is questioned. Imagination may be able to float above its own creations or choose to descend to recreate a world; but it may not, I have argued, know itself directly or pierce "the veil of life and death" to subsume the not-I completely. The looming mountain of lines 60–75 calls the imagination from its task of imaging its own infinite powers, reminding it of its finitude, calling upon it to address the world of process and change.

This section, lines 75ff., marks the emergence of Shelley's Fichtean irony: the imagination must both strive to give human meaning and continuity to the not-I and be able to perceive the gap between its creations and the ever-evolving world. Else, the mind may become idolatrous of its own creations, may not know that its understandings are only its own creations. In turn, when mind sees the world as *merely* its own projection, then the world is no longer a world, a not-I, which can enable the mind to keep striving (as it must, as infinite activity). The world must again be alienated to begin again the cycle of recreation. Hence, Mont Blanc has a voice "to repeal / Large codes of fraud and woe"—false idolatries that assume some other mind than man's is the source of meaning in the world. Moreover, that voice is itself, in part, created by the rhetoric of the poet ("Thou hast a voice, great Mountain"), who demands speech and by attending to silence hears a tale of human limitation. Gerald McNiece has clearly summarized the moral implications of what he recognizes as Shelley's "Romantic irony" in the poem:

> Mountains, glaciers, deep ravines do distract the attention and stem the thirst for the abstract and the miraculous. So men must control the transcendental passions, get back to the sources and springs, consider imaginatively the process of mind from stimulus to perception to conception to assessment of value, watching themselves shrewdly and ironically all the way, aware of their myth and symbol making tendencies so essential to healthy hopefulness but so easily degenerating into secure and stable creeds.[14]

Though trapped in the circle of finitude, man nevertheless retains his imaginative freedom. The mountain teaches neither cold skepticism nor sad resignation but an active "faith" through which man may be "with nature reconciled" (lines 77–79).[15] Nature here is the world of process, loss, destruction, and recreation described in Section IV, the coil of mortal change with which the *Alastor* Poet obstinately refuses to be reconciled. Throughout this section the mountain indomitably stands as an emblem of endurance behind the cycles of our finite life. As one critic acutely observes, nature's eternal "process comes to symbolize in Shelley's mind that change is not annihilation, for in all animate things there is a life, a force, a Strength, which as in the model of Mont Blanc, enables them to ultimately survive the chaos."[16]

For man, that strength is the endless cycle of imaginative struggle to articulate a world. Shelley's mind would pierce to the top of Mont Blanc through the cloud-ceiling that obscures it. The snows fall but "none beholds them there"; the winds contend, "but silently!" (lines

131–32; 134–35). The imagination knows no vacancy, no absolute not-I. For as soon as it tries to conceive a world without human thought, that world is already conceived and imagined. Yet the mountain's very otherness is what calls upon the mind to create, creativity being nothing without boundaries to act upon. At the moment of imaginative activity the boundary has receded; the next act is impossible without a new real boundary opposing the mind. The activity is Fichte's active imagination: as he puts it, when the mind reflects upon the boundary ("the independent factor"),

> the independent factor again becomes a product of its own power of thought, and thus something dependent on the I, insofar as it is to exist for the I. But in order for this new account of the first explanation to be possible, we again presuppose already a real consciousness, and for this to be possible, we again presuppose that something on which the I depends . . . merely posited *further out*, and so we might proceed out indefinitely, without it ever being eliminated (p. 247).

Like Shelley, Fichte sees this circle as liberating for finite man; any attempt to escape it produces "*dogmatism.*" The play of mind whereby it asserts its infinitude only through the finite boundaries it confronts; in Fichte's words, this "interplay of the I" whereby it "posits itself at once as finite and infinite . . . this is the power of *imagination* (p. 193; cf. pp. 191–92). This is the "secret strength of things / Which governs thought," and which the mind itself attributes to the mute mountaintop. "What were thou," Shelley demands of Mont Blanc, "If to the human mind's imaginings / Silence and solitude were vacancy?" (lines 142–44).

Precisely by receding as an opaque not-I, the mountain draws the mind to a new understanding of its own power. The mountain teaches its meaning by veiling itself, the mind learns truths about itself in what it cannot know. Mont Blanc does not provide imagination with its absolute demand, an image of itself. Instead it shows the mind that it can know itself only as a process that endlessly reaches after congruence between itself (the ideal) and the not-I (the real). Imagination may see itself, like the mountain, as the source of the streams of its creations and so be, though ever in motion, a principle of endurance and strength. Unlike the mountain, the human mind is mobile and articulate in its creation and is thus perhaps greater than the opposing silence it nevertheless depends upon to enable its speech.

This circling of the imagination into the world is the awakening before a new, higher enchantment of the real can be possible. In this study we have arrived at the principle that the disenchantment of the mind from itself is prerequisite to successful quest. Yet the mind need not trap itself in cynical experience or despair: even this comes to be seen as another of the mind's creations. The goal of romantic quest is a mobility greater than enchantment or disillusionment. Realizing its dialectical interdependence with the world, imagination may free itself from rigid realities or from its own disabling illusions. The point of this freedom was not, for the great romantic poets, congratulatory self-assertion but an energized struggle to create new images that, in their turn, might more fully articulate the human meaning of the world and the power of the mind to endure.

# PART V

## "Spirits Which Soar from Ruin": Byron's Pilgrimage from Idealist Quest to Heroic Stance

# 10

## Encountering the Actual: Childe Harold and the Limits of Idealism

Pleasure disappoints; possibility never. . . .

The unhappiest man . . . alone he stands in the wide world. He has no past to long for since his past has not yet come; he has no future to hope for, since his future is already past. . . . In one sense of the word he cannot die, for he has not really lived; in another sense he cannot live, for he is already dead. He cannot love, for love is in the present, and he has no present, no future and no past; and yet he has a sympathetic nature, and he hates the world only because he loves it. . . . Strange that boredom (itself so staid and solid) should have such power to set in motion. . . .

Boredom is the daemonic side of pantheism. . . . Boredom depends on the nothingness which pervades reality; it causes a dizziness like that produced by looking into a yawning chasm, and this dizziness is infinite.

—Søren Kierkegaard, *Either/Or*

Byron's romantic heroes—Childe Harold, Manfred, Conrad, the Giaour, Cain—face psychological and existential dilemmas, paradoxes of self-assertion and freedom that have, in this study of idealism, been seen to be typical of romantic quest. Indeed, those who are destroyed are often defeated by the instabilities I have pointed out within romance principles, such as daemonic assertion or romantic love. Instabilities arise from the intrusion of finitude upon the mind that would deny finitude its place within human nature or attempt to place finitude at a distance from the growth of the self-conscious mind.

Byron insists, however, that despite these paradoxes the only chance for true heroism lies within this fallen world, and life itself calls man to greatness only in the very language of contrariety, evil, and sin. That greatness lies in the courage of one's responses and not in any fanatic attempt to reshape the world according to fixed moral ideals. In this world love dies, and beauty may be tainted with moral evil. In this world what seems great heroism may take place on behalf of a transient, defeated, or less-than-worthy cause; what seems a great and noble civilization may be equally transient, or, worse still, be founded on bloodshed, exploitation, and cruelty. Nonetheless, it is in this world and through the dilemmas of our very real experience that Byron locates heroism—not in Eden, or in the Giaour's demands for moral purity, or in Conrad's bower of love, or in Harold's weary longings for peace amid the "peasant girls, with deep blue eyes" in the "paradise" of Drachenfels.[1]

In an earlier chapter, I argued that contradictory psychological strategies evolve from the Fichtean dialectic in which self-assertion demands that it create the world, while the presence of a world is a condition for any assertion at all. The ego demands its paradise of endless fulfillment but demands as well its absolute self-integrity (see above, pp. 113–15). Having created a prelapsarian dream we turn our own hands upon it to destroy it: this is man's nature and his fate. Having destroyed it, we feel now that the world is a prison (to use one of Byron's favorite images), that no further action has meaning. We cherish guilt toward ourselves, resentment toward the God we project as the author of our four-cornered paradox: we desire the salvation of our created paradise-myth, yet we must destroy it to become ourselves; we desire greatness in this world yet feel the guilt of destroying Eden.

Byron's poetic response to this predicament is a further species of romantic irony. Byron's is an irony in which the creator of the romance takes responsibility for his own created self-understanding, for creating and destroying his own myths. He recognizes at the same time the power of the actual to force the mind to new self-understandings at the expense of its memories, myths, and expectations. The mind asserts its *existence* as infinite responsiveness, a continuous growth to, beyond, and again into the flux of actual experience. This is the existential irony termed "the mastered moment" by Kierkegaard, writing at the end of—and as a critic of—the romantic tradition he believed had been initiated by Fichtean dialectics. Romantic desire for a regenerated cosmos may become merely a "sickly longing . . . to have the perfect before its time." But, Kierkegaard insists, self-assertion is not given up in accepting the finite component of the soul; rather, the self comes to assert not a fixed demand for regressive self-fulfillment but its endless capacity to appropriate and to "master" the actual: "If [irony] allowed something to stand, it knew it had the power to destroy it, and it knew this at the same moment it allowed it to endure." But the poet must also make each creative moment a response to his own experience, to the finitude his mind cannot overcome or destroy. Kierkegaard's example of such dialectical irony is Goethe:

> [The] master over irony . . . will see in the particular poem a [real] moment in his own development. It was in this respect that Goethe's existence as a poet was so great: he succeeded in making his being as a poet congrue with his actuality. . . . Irony as a mastered moment exhibits itself in its truth precisely by the fact that it teaches us to actualize actuality. . . . There ought to be, in every human being a longing for a higher and more perfect. But this longing must not hollow out actuality.[2]

The idealism Kierkegaard criticized, which demanded that the world be seen as the unfolding of the human spirit, had made problematic our relations with those boundaries that define us, with the given contours of finitude or (as the spirit of change appears in *Faust*) "the Earth." If Goethe had tested the limits of romantic *Sehnsucht* in *Werther*, his long *Faust* project went further, overcoming (and outgrowing) the "sickly longing" of the ego for absolute knowledge and autonomy. Byron's own *Faust*-like drama, *Manfred*, certainly pushed the romantic narrative of self-assertion to its breaking point, raising the issues of heroism and self-transformation that would not be resolved until the later works, *Childe Harold III* and *IV* and *Don Juan*.[3]

What Kierkegaard calls "actuality" is precisely what Manfred insists his own mind can infinitely control and overcome. Manfred, like Faust, invokes the Earth magically, though in Manfred's case the

Erdgeist appears as a series of spirits, from mountains to oceans to winds, each restless with the most powerful energies of flux and transformation—"I am the rider of the Wind, / The stirrer of the Storm" (1.1.100–101). Like Faust he claims a kinship with these spirits: "The Mind—the Spirit—the Promethean spark, / The lighting of my being is as bright, / Pervading, and far-darting as yours."

Manfred's boasts of Promethean power do have a hollow ring, since whatever power of will he may exert over the Earth-spirits, neither they nor he can transform his guilt into forgiveness as long as he insists on absolute self-integrity and isolation. Such spiritual transformation requires an openness to accept that the power of Earth to heal the self is even greater than the self's mournful demand for a life without loss or disappointment. The Earth may destroy or heal. Like Shelley's Demogorgon or Blake's Spectre of Urthona, the power of change seems creative or destructive depending on the heart that beholds it. The Erdgeist in *Faust* "fashions the living garment of God" and according to a remark of Goethe's in a letter of 1819 ought to have "nothing grotesque and repulsive" in its appearance to the appalled Faust. This creative possibility is what one critic calls the rejected "cosmic rhythm" in *Manfred*, a power like the Easter chorus that offers Faust renewed life. The first act of *Manfred* ends not with resurrection but with an Incantation that reflects Manfred's Satanically self-lacerating mind: ". . . by thy brotherhood of Cain, / I call upon thee! And compel / Thyself to be thy proper Hell" (1.1.249–51).[4]

Manfred's remorse is for the death of his incestuous lover, Astarte, which he did not cause, though he feels responsible for it. Astarte represents that common romantic figure, the sister- or mirror-love, the perfect union and identity of consciousness with itself: "She was like me in lineaments—her eyes— / Her hair—her features—all, to the very tone / Even of her voice, they said were like to mine; / But softened all, and tempered into beauty: / She had the same lone thoughts and wanderings . . ." (2.2.105–9). In this idealized, regressive hope for union Manfred is not Manfred, not individuated; yet from the opposite pole, his icy peak of Promethean self-assertion, he cannot overcome himself and become Manfred, the actor in human life.

Manfred's cosmic self-assertion leads only to self-accusation and destructiveness, in Peter Manning's words to "solipsism," and his death confirms "the bankruptcy of his Titanic pretensions." "And why not live and act with other men?" asks the Abbot, whose question reflects not empty piety but the central challenge to Manfred's isolation. He can only respond that "Like the Wind, / The red-hot breath of the most lone Simoom, / Which dwells but in the desert, and sweeps o'er / The barren sands . . . such hath been the course of my existence . . ." (3.1.24–33). Manning is right, I think, to see Manfred as crippled by his demands, and though he seems to be acting he is only carried along by tides of inner conflict and turmoil.[5]

Manfred rejects human finitude because he fears it destroys the perfectly self-contained ego. Yet without openness to time and finitude, indeed without openness to the menacing flux of the Earth Spirit, the ego cannot grow to see itself anew, cannot overcome itself and so remains trapped in sterile inaction: "We are the fools of Time and Terror: Days / Steal on us and steal from us; yet we live, / Loathing our life; and dreading still to die" (2.2.164–66).

The Spirit of Earth, of activity, cannot grant oblivion; but it can offer a realm of constant change that may mean regeneration to the self that is open to it. Such a possibility is suggested in *Manfred* by the Witch of Alps, the spirit of the waterfall who transforms into endlessly renewed rainbows the craggy "perpendicular" onrush of waters. In her "calm clear brow" is "glassed serenity of Soul, / Which of itself shows immortality" (2.2.25–27). But Manfred turns from her offer of help and insists in his last moments that "The Mind which is immortal . . . is / Its own place and time." One of the key outcomes we have noted in the development of German idealism, in its ultimate result as a philosophy of moral action, was that the mind cannot know itself in itself, though it makes a demand to do so in declaring itself free and undetermined. The mind of man can overcome this apparent dilemma, can truly live, only in and through the world of activity, becoming itself in active interchange with the unfolding Earth.

In idealism proper, of course, the world of actual experience exists only to be overcome, to allow for a new self-consciousness. But though Byron is certainly committed to the freedom of the self, actuality for him comes to have its own separate presence, an opacity that no amount of spiritual power can ever clarify, an *excess* that no mental ordering can contain. We recall Kierkegaard's "master over irony," who grows in self-consciousness through living within the actual:

> Actuality in this way acquires its validity—not as purgatory, for the soul is not to be purified in such a way that it flees blank, bare, and stark naked out of life—but as a history wherein consciousness successively outlives itself, though in such a way that happiness consists not in forgetting all this but becomes present in it.[6]

Byron's "romaunt," *Childe Harold's Pilgrimage*, is such a history—of "Consciousness awaking to her woes" (1.92). The very title rings with irony, though of a bitter sort. Harold is no knight errant, and the pilgrimage, initially, leads nowhere. And we soon find that as we travel further into the ruins of European civilization there seems indeed no place to go. Harold, in the first of two cantos, wanders through a mad carnival of enslaved nations, scenes of carnage, sacked temples; the final cantos bring images of ruins, tombs, and words that echo despair over the impossibility of heroism in the modern world. And yet, though the movement is slow and hesitant, the poem concludes with an assertion of life and of endless *possibility* raised within a desert of stultifying illusions and death.

Byron thus discovers a species of heroic consciousness, and in this sense the pilgrimage is a success. From the self-mocking, despairing irony of loss and paralysis that opens the poem, Byron arrives, nearly eight years after the poem was begun, at those saving self-conscious assertions with which the poem ends: the stanzas on the tomb of Cecilia Metella, on St. Peter's, and the famous concluding address to the Ocean. I agree with Jerome McGann's conclusions on the fourth canto: "From the continuous alternation of joy and pain, hope and despair, and all of life's contraries which so madden and exhaust the spirit, is born the unreluctant consciousness of these ambiguities and conflicts; and it is upon this consciousness that Byron balances the polarities of the poem."[7]

What is indeed remarkable is that the poet does not turn from his original commitment to radical freedom and self-assertion, even though it is just this modern freedom from imposed moral absolutes that generates Harold's malaise. With the world all before him, Harold is bored and weary before his journey even begins. The essential terms of the quest remain the same throughout: the complex, experienced relations among time, human freedom, and our created ideals ("images of Eternity," 4.183). Yet the narrator (if not Harold), reconceiving the meaning of human freedom in a finite world, understanding self-assertion in a more mature way, and without receiving any apocalyptic revelation, struggles purely with his own mind's conflicting demands and reaches not resignation but dynamic affirmation. The narrator-hero begins and ends with his subjective experience but comes to embrace the relentless, implacable currents of being that he himself, as this man in this place, shares with the world. It is in this sense that we may call *Childe Harold's Pilgrimage* the romance of the first existential hero in English literature.[8]

## Nature as Actuality

The tenuous balance of self-consciousness, between the inward-turning imagination and the desire to "lose" the self amid the projected peace of "nature," reaches a critical point in the third canto of *Childe Harold*. The poem, finished in July 1816 at Geneva and copied out by Claire Clairemont, was written, it is well known, during Byron's first acquaintance with Shelley, who "dosed" the poet "with Wordsworth physic."[9] Byron was not unaware of the clashing poles of pantheistic communion and feverish self-assertion that raise conflicts not fully comprehended until the last canto. Of the third, Byron says it was "a fine indistinct piece of poetical desolation," and continues in a letter to Thomas Moore written some six months after its composition, "I was half mad during the time of its composition, between metaphysics, mountains, lakes, love unextinguishable, thoughts unutterable, and the nightmare of my own delinquencies. I should, many a good day, have blown my brains out, but for the recollection it would have given pleasure to my mother-in-law."[10]

As Michael Cooke remarks, the "Wordsworthianism" of the canto is not a real struggle for communion with nature, but rather "its transcendentalism is transcendentalism manqué," a retreat to peaceful relatedness soon disabled by self-assertion.[11] However much Byron had been "dosed" with Wordsworth, the dilemmas Shelley had raised in *Alastor*—which Byron had read shortly after its February 1816 publication—rear up powerfully in the canto's second half.[12] In *Alastor* there is little to choose from between the Narrator's regressive hope to be at one with his mother earth and the Poet's endless quest to be united forever with his own projected ideal. To this dialogue—carried on, variously, through the figures of Harold, narrator, and Rousseau in the canto—Byron adds further elements, the powerful extraversion of Napoleonic heroism and his own self-assertion of boundless but undirected energies, which he shares with a nature that he soon discovers is anything but placid.

The dramatic climax of the canto is the storm sequence (sts. 92–97), which Byron added as an integral group of stanzas to the manuscript completed in June.[13] The storm is prepared for by two important contrary movements in the poet's thought: the attempt to overcome self-consciousness by "absorption" into nature, and his turn (at st. 76) to "One, whose dust was once all fire," the Rousseau whose "foolish quest" to throw "Enchantment over passion" leads to destruction in the manner of the *Alastor* Poet.

Michael Cooke has expressed one general tendency of these central stanzas of Canto Three:

> For Nature in itself is made up of elements basically in conflict with one another. . . . What survives the natural competition, what Byron sees fittest to preserve amounts to a distillation from each of the episodes of possible redemption, in which the characteristic action has taken the form of absorption, either of Byron himself into something other, or something other into himself.[14]

Cooke's "absorption," I would argue, is not as he implies the central principle of the canto, nor of Byron's whole poem; it is, rather, one strategy adopted to deal with the dilemmas of heroic assertion raised in Canto Three. The climax of the canto, the storm sequence, presents not an absorption but a confrontation with the destabilizing energies of the real, experienced world.

Both the "self-torturing sophist, wild Rousseau" (st. 77) and the narrator who seeks absorption, to be a "bodiless thought" (st. 74), resist in the manner of the Poet and Narrator of *Alastor* such a confrontation with actual nature. Byron connects Rousseau's "phrensied" idealism (st. 80) with the "Fixed Passion" of repressed desire that explodes violently in the French Revolution (st. 84). Kierkegaard's "impatience for perfection" produces, in Byron's world, far more than the *Alastor* Poet's sickly *Sehnsucht*; it produces a violent attack on the actual world that resists absolute idealism. But there is no refuge, either, in the narrator's turn, in stanza 85, to an unselfconscious communion with the "placid" lake, emblem of a static, transpersonal spiritual order. This "outward" turn, it will develop, was really not a true "meeting" with external nature, but was in fact the mind's *created ideal of nature,* a garden of sanctuary for "a green thought in a green shade."

From the violent, clashing forces of idealistic passions in stanza 84, Byron turns to Lake Geneva in tones of sibilant consonants and hushed vowels:

> Clear, placid Leman! thy contrasted lake,
> With the wild world I dwelt in, is a thing
> Which warns me with its stillness to forsake
> Earth's troubled waters for a purer spring.
> This quiet sail is as a noiseless wing
> To waft me from distraction; once I loved
> Torn Ocean's roar, but thy soft murmuring
> Sounds sweet as if a Sister's voice reproved,
> That I with stern delights should e'er have been so moved.   (st. 85)

Into this vision, where the hush of night "stirs the feeling infinite" and a spiritual truth "melts" through our being and "purifies from self," into this vision of tender night and veiled senses bursts a storm of relentless energy awakening within the poet "Soul—heart—mind—passions—feelings—strong or weak— / All that I would have sought and all I seek" (st. 97). The rejection in stanza 85 of "Torn Ocean's roar" contrasts, too, with the "welcome to their [the waves'] roar" that opens the canto (st. 2), with the famous conclusion of the poem (4.179), and with the "swift Rhone" cleaving its way through mountains like the passions of parted lovers (3.94). The storm rises with sudden intensity, with an energy unlike the de-sexualized "Sister's voice" of the lake:

> The sky is changed!—and such a change! Oh Night,
> And Storm and Darkness, ye are wondrous strong,
> Yet lovely in your strength, as is the light
> Of a dark eye in Woman!

It is not the idealized nature of the Lake stanzas, but nature as *other,* nature as strife and destructive potential, that the poet here confronts. Moreover, the growing storm without corresponds to the growing consciousness within. In a dialectic not unlike Fichtean interdetermination, Byron's turning to recognize the dynamic otherness of nature allows him a more profound sense of the conflicting energies of his own selfhood. But unlike the Fichtean idealist view of nature, nature here has a strength, an integrity, a life equal to but not dependent upon the energies of the conscious mind.

> Sky—Mountains—River—Winds—Lake—Lightnings! ye!
> With night, and clouds, and thunder—and a Soul
> To make these felt and feeling, well may be
> Things that have made me watchful; the far roll
> Of your departing voices, is the knoll [*for* knell]
> Of what in me is sleepless,—if I rest.
> But where of ye, O Tempests! is the goal?
> Are ye like those within the human breast?
> Or do ye find, at length, like eagles, some high nest?   (st. 96)

The relation between mind and nature here is not merely metaphoric: the storm does not appear as a projection of spiritual torment. It has "a soul" of its own that yet penetrates awareness and "makes" itself "felt and feeling." The storm is—the phrase is rarely so apt—an "objective correlative" for the movements both of energetic assertion and of spiritual destruction. Conceived without enchantment, nature is not, for Byron, a paradisiacal home, but a realm of powerful change and continuous loss.

And these energies, the growing power of self-assertion amid the conflicts of the mind's desires, could never be denied. Byron journeyed from Lake Geneva to the Bernese Alps some two months after completing Canto Three and again tried to overcome the gnawing bitterness and self-accusation whose specters had haunted him most acutely since the collapse of his marriage that spring. It was here, in fact, that *Manfred* was first composed. In his journal of that tour, written for Augusta, he admits that

> —the recollections of bitterness—& more especially of recent & more home desolation—which must accompany me through life—have preyed upon me here—and neither the music of the Shepherd—the crashing of the Avalanche—nor the torrent—the mountain—the Glacier—the Forest—nor the Cloud—have for one moment—lightened the weight upon my heart—nor enabled me to lose my own wretched identity in the majesty & the power and the Glory—around—above—& beneath me.[15]

Byron's "wretched identity" with all its bitterness and galling memories cannot simply be lost. The tyranny of memory, common affliction of the Romantic Wanderer, is a Spectre that demands that Selfhood be conceived as a continuous accretion into a fixed being. The self is then nothing but the record of things wrenched from it, of shadows of a dim past, and not a recreative encounter with actuality. For Byron, it is true, the past is never lost or entirely overcome, but he will come to see loss not as an offense against a jealous self-integrity but rather as the occasion for the mind to overcome the myths it has outworn. The "goal" of his quest must then be to accept the self as the growing consciousness of its own contradictions, as a continuing process of encounter and self-discovery. This is no glib resolution but is a continuous struggle of mind to take responsibility for itself and to acknowledge that finitude and loss are inevitable constituents of man's rootedness in a large world of real forces of destruction and opportunities for renewal.

As the poem progresses, "self-assertion" comes to mean more than a mere insistence that the world must be a projected form of one's cherished self-image. Self-assertion is an act of freedom, a stance of "heroic irony," a liberation of the soul despite and within a world of desolation and disenchantment. Out of the rubble of his self-pitying poses and the hubris of his ascribing cosmic importance to his personal afflictions, Byron is struggling to engage and re-envision the world heroically. But the Spectre of memory and of a wounded self-integrity dogs the narrator throughout the poem's sweeping vision of ruin and broken dreams. That Spectre generally takes the form of the romance's nominal hero, Childe Harold.

## History as Actuality

In the opening stanzas of Canto One, Byron and Harold are clearly distinct, Byron, the poet, being able to maintain a certain amused detachment from the "Childe." But as the poem develops, Byron, meditating with Harold upon the ruins of the modern world, becomes caught up in Harold's despair and confusion: these are, after all, the fragments of Byron's world as well.[16] It becomes difficult to tell poet and hero apart; by the end of Canto Two we hear more of Byron's own despair than Harold's; in the middle of the third canto,

Harold virtually disappears from the poem; from that point on, expressions both of despair and of regenerative self-assertion belong to Byron as the poem's narrator.[17]

Throughout the poem, Harold is an aspect of Byron the poet. Although much critical attention (since the first publication of the poem, in fact) has been paid to separating or uniting the poet and the hero, for our purposes we may say generally that Harold is an aspect of an overarching heroic consciousness that includes Harold and his creator. But Harold's response to the demands of existential freedom in a world of broken hopes is generally an attitude of self-pity, despair, and finally hopeless resignation—"With nought of Hope left—but with less of gloom; / The very knowledge that he lived in vain, / That all was over on this side the tomb, / Had made Despair a smilingness assume" (3.16)—yielding at last to a weary, dreamy kind of love among the gardens, feudal castles, and simple peasant girls of his Rhine retreat (3.55).[18] Harold is useful for defining the spiritual problem to be confronted, as well as for providing a means for the poet to "objectify," distance himself from, his own responses to the world of his travels. But, finally, Harold must always run through his "vortex, roll[ing] / On with the giddy circle, chasing Time" (3.11), like so many failed questers chasing the infinite flux of the world to freeze it into the forms of their desires. Harold "knows" that "all is over," but the narrator must resist the temptation to see this frozen perspective as any more than what it is, a mind-forged myth of despair, a self-justifying retreat. The poet, though, is even more self-reflective than Harold, able in fact to reflect even outside of, as well as through, his own self-lacerating Harold-aspect; he thus carries his life onward while Harold is left in a weary round, a desperate limbo. For Byron's psychic health this is precisely where the Harold of his mind must remain.[19]

It is indeed remarkable that Byron can, in the last canto, assert, "There woos no home, nor hope, nor life, save what is here" (4.105), never relinquishing his initial commitment to the self-conscious mind as the maker of its own orders. It is also true that, as Harold, he begins his pilgrimage to find, amid the history and culture and terrain of modern Europe, an order to believe in. On this landscape he may encounter the real images of myths that, in his past, seemed to compose an imaginative order he *could* believe in (see for example, 2.88). In this sense, Harold races forward to encounter the mythic realities of the past. But his "awaking" consciousness reveals more and more the poverty of that European myth-world. The poem's contemporary popularity is, in part, due to the frank historicity of the quest: unlike the *Alastor* Poet's quest across Asia for the roots of all human ideals, of awareness itself, Byron quests after the source of his cultural identity as a modern man, as a European.

Harold is trapped on a treadmill: his consciousness of the world around him is expanding in search of some external coherence that will correspond to the internal sustaining myths that he has now lost. But his growing consciousness is precisely what is destroying him: it has shown his own past to be meaningless, and it is showing the European landscape to be a ruin. And so he runs to escape his advancing awareness. But the demon thought is also a step ahead, conjuring images that beckon the pilgrim on to some new ideal of glory, heroism, or triumph.

It is this dynamic "of Consciousness awaking to her woes" that impels the hero to motion and gives structural coherence to the four cantos. The cycle of consciousness reaching out for new, meaningful images, then destroying its own creations in its encounter with the landscape, reaching a spiritual void, and turning back to itself to recreate a sustaining myth becomes finally a struggle to bring life out of death.

The world of Cantos One and Two is a landscape of great natural beauty. But Harold brings to that natural world a consciousness first of the moral ruin of the men who people it, and second a brooding awareness of the mortality of the individual. Mortality and moral relativity, the two major motifs of these cantos, seem to deny to man the possibility of constructing a coherent myth or of realizing heroic action in the actual historical world. Harold, for all his wanderings, is passive and static. He can neither flee self-consciousness into a world of unshaken dreams of glory nor lose himself in rapture at the world of natural beauty.

Byron would not, certainly, be the first of his generation to seek in "old Tales, and Robin Hood" (as Keats said) some assurance that the imagination can meaningfully transform actual human experience. Yet the idealisms of the opening cantos—chivalric glory, a peaceful world, and human freedom—are not even in themselves necessarily compatible, and in practice, Byron finds, rarely are. The heroic glory that seems to conquer man's finitude by creating myth out of human history is founded on bloodlust, as he finds in the Spain of Canto One; and chivalric honor, he suspects, may well be only the ideology that justifies tyrants' ambitions "to pave their way / With human hearts—to what?—a dream alone" (1.42). From the bullfight to the "mailed splendour" of "renowned, romantic" battle, honor is written in blood: Byron was, said John Ruskin, "the first great Englishman who felt the cruelty of war, and, in its cruelty, the shame."[20]

The epic imagination, the songs that celebrate historical heroes, ignore cruel realities in their enchantment with idealized power. Yet the poet, Byron finds, must engage the actual historical world (no matter how disillusioning) or risk sinking further into illusion. Significantly, when in Canto One he turns to Parnassus (having rejected the epic romance of Spanish history), he finds no disembodied muses to sing the heroes of ancient wars; rather, he confronts modern Greece, fallen into degraded slavery. But Parnassus remains an image that calls upon the poet to face actual historical realities with the strength of renewed imagination.

His turn here in this early canto will establish a pattern—"Oft have I dreamed of thee!" (1.61)—that will recur in the poem, as imagination reaches after some ideal creation and *in that very process* discovers itself standing in place, at a spot, a location that in its reality challenges (as does Shelley's Mont Blanc) the search for enchantment: "Here let me sit upon this mossy stone. . . . / Here, son of Saturn! was thy fav'rite throne" (2.10); "Stop!—for thy tread is on an Empire's dust!" (3.17); "I stood in Venice on the Bridge of Sighs, / a Palace and a prison on each hand" (4.1).

The palace of imagination and the imprisoned mind clash on a real spot of earth where the mind confronts its dual possibilities. Unlike the Wordsworthian meditation on the "spot of time," where the self seeks in personal memory or in human history to elide discontinuities (with, for Wordsworth, varying degrees of success), Byron embraces these "interviews" (4.178) with the real dilemmas that imagination meets reflecting upon man's spatial, temporal, and historical limitations.[21] This mode of Byronic meditation leads, ultimately, to the dynamic assertions of the fourth canto, in which the mind grows larger by each reflection upon its own conflicting currents. At the spot where Byron stands, imagination encounters disenchantment. But lest imagination be "darkly bound" to an "electric chain" (4.23) of shadowy images of past time and easier faith, it must, to create anew, also be able to free itself. The spot thus calls the mind out of itself; but now, perhaps, the mind is free only to walk across a landscape littered with ruined gardens and broken dreams:

> But my soul wanders; I demand it back
> To meditate amongst decay, and stand
> A ruin amidst ruins. . . .   (4.25)

The landscape Byron confronts, after leaving Harold in self-indulgent peace at Drachenfels, is a space virtually sacralized by acts of individual heroism: Waterloo, Coblentz, Ehrenbreitstein, the Ossuary of Morat, and the banks of the Rhine are sites of last stands, of heroic final assertions. Byron is striving amid these ghosts with time, loss, and decay to preserve a meaningful image of heroic stance. He goes so far as to tell us, in a footnote, that from the Ossuary he has carried off some bones: "I ventured to bring away as much as may have made a quarter of a hero, for which the sole excuse is, that if I had not, the next passer-by might have perverted them to worse uses than the careful preservation which I intend for them."[22]

Harold's final psychological stand, amid the dreamy paradise of faded chivalric Rhine towers, is only resignation, *il faut durer*. Harold's "days / Of passion had consumed themselves to dust" (st. 53). His resignation is a negative aspect of endurance; its positive aspect is dynamic heroism, a regenerative encounter with the human paradox. The true hero of the final canto is a consciousness that is struggling to be born, an engaging of imaginative mobility with time, disenchantment, and the freedom to live in a demythologized cosmos.

In the great orchestration of the conflicting demands of consciousness that forms Canto Four, we might seek a final resolution. Indeed, the emotional effect of the canto seems as great and as life-affirming as if there were one. The conflicting relations of men to time and to ideals, to the historical world and to creative freedom, are not, however, reconciled so much as *suspended*, each supporting the other like the elements of the dome of St. Peter's. The dome, like the mind of the poet, is a vast self-sustaining balance of forces that is, at the same time, instinct with powerful upward movement. As art critics Robert Wolf and Ronald Millen have argued, the "terrible sublimity" of Michelangelo's design both drew from and threatened the Humanist terrain of sixteenth-century Roman architecture: the dome is "elongated and not calmly hemispherical, crash[ing] into the sky with the energy it sucks out of the tense double-columns and compressed windows of the drum and the colossal order of pilasters below, all straining upward to discharge their forces into the ribs that climb the surface of the dome."[23]

St. Peter's sublimity does not "overwhelm" Byron, for the mind is "Expanded by the genius of the spot." The minute particulars draw the mind along, and both the power of the actual space and the tendency of mind to grow ever outward, drawing from the tense movement of its perceptions, result in higher levels of awareness: "increasing with the advance, / Vastness which grows—but grows to harmonize" (4.156). Ultimately, man is in one sense very small, for he cannot see all at once how the universe really "is," too limited in perception to pronounce the cosmos a garden or graveyard. But this limitation, like Shelley's revelatory vision of Mont Blanc, frees the mind from its "impatience for perfection" and turns it upon itself to reveal its true infinity: this consists in the ability of the creative mind to reflect upon and assert itself as both constituted by and greater than the conflicting demands of its nature. The movement of mind from self-lacerating to liberating self-consciousness requires engagement in the slow process through which the mind grasps what is *actual* without "fevering into false creations" (st. 122):

> Thou seest not all; but piece meal thou must break
> To separate contemplation the great whole;
> And as the ocean many bays will make,
> That ask the eye—so here condense thy soul
> To more immediate objects, and control
> Thy thoughts until thy mind hath got by heart
> Its eloquent proportions, and unroll
> In mighty graduations, part by part
> The glory which at once upon thee did not dart.
>
> (4.157)

Without abandoning the notion that his mind is its own existential center, he recognizes its need to grow within and through the slow unfolding of the temporal world. Although he bemoans man's temporality, his "uneradicable taint of Sin. . . . / Whose root is Earth" (st. 126), he shakes off his brooding tone to speculate, in a more detached tone:

> Yet let us ponder boldly: 'tis a base
> Abandonment of reason to resign
> Our right of thought—our last and only place
> Of refuge; this, at least, shall still be mine:
> Though from our birth the faculty divine
> Is chained and tortured—cabined, cribbed, confined
> And bred in darkness, lest the Truth should shine
> Too brightly on the unprepared mind,
> The beam pours in—for Time and Skill will couch the blind.
>
> (st. 127)

The evolution of time, man's experience of process, brings not only decay and ruin but the possibility of liberation as well. The course of time is a reminder that what enters the world also leaves it; what the mind has created it can overcome. The image of the shining beam recurs as a symbol of the energy of the mind that animates the temporal round. The next stanza (128) begins a meditation in the ruins of the Coliseum, its circle lit by moonbeams. Its heritage is the brutal cycle of vengeance for wrongs remembered. It has, like Byron's own mind, outlived its heritage. Hence Byron calls upon "Time! the avenger" (st. 130) itself to invert the cycle of retribution and "curse" his foes with forgiveness; their inflicted wounds are, after all, by now only what his own mind creates in accusation. The pilgrimage that began in malaise and despair over the irreconcilable demands created by human freedom ends in an affirmation of possibility. This affirmation seems richer than mere pose or rhetorical gesture.

Again, Byron rejects the false hope that any historical incarnation can redeem man's social life from corruption, selfishness, or violence. The poem's vision, though always sensitive to its historical context, does remain centered on personal rather than political liberation. As McGann points out, the stanzas to Princess Charlotte, dead in childbirth, allow the poet to reaffirm that he has outgrown the tyranny of his own impatient expectations.[24] Byron's commitment to freedom in the political sphere is more implicit than Shelley's. His emphasis is on freedom as a human capacity to overcome disenchantment and tap the latent intensity of existence. Existence is fiercely dialectical to Byron, but where this is earlier a source of despair, it is now a source of creative power.

## Outgrowing the "Childe": The Transformation of Romance

The hero of *Childe Harold's Pilgrimage* is the individual mind that stands above the wreckage of its own past. The hero reflects, creates, lives, infinitely able to rise above the myths that he creates to sustain himself, able to destroy those myths yet able to draw strength and guiding ideals from them when he must. Thus the mind may be larger than its creations, larger than myths it has fed upon, larger than disillusion, larger than its own despair over a world of chaos and ruin.

The closing apostrophe to Ocean asserts this dynamic and creative supremacy of the individual with clarity and strength. Byron begins with an acceptance of the ocean as a realm of powerful abiding being, beyond man and his creations:

> Roll on, thou dark and deep blue Ocean—roll!
> Ten thousand fleets sweep over thee in vain;
> Man marks the earth with ruin—his control
> Stops with the shore. . . .   (st. 179)

The ocean is a vast and creative *source*, abiding beyond its own swells and motions, yet creating living forms even as the mind of man creates its forms.

> Thou glorious mirror, where the Almighty's form
> Glasses itself in tempests; in all time,
> Calm or convulsed—in breeze, or gale or storm—
> Icing the Pole, or in the torrid clime
> Dark—heavy—boundless, endless, and sublime—
> The image of Eternity—the throne
> Of the Invisible; even from out thy slime
> The monsters of the deep are made—each zone
> Obeys thee—thou goest forth, dread, fathomless, alone.   (st. 183)

Dread, fathomless, alone: so does Byron journey onward, the mind continuously alive but ready to reject all things, destroying and recreating but ever larger than its created forms, the living "monsters of the deep." In this sense Byron is a child of Ocean (st. 184), his own infinitely free mind akin to the depthless sea before him. But he is even in a sense greater than the vast power of unconscious being, more powerful in his infinite reflective freedom than the sea he sports with, standing above it and laying his hand upon its "mane." Just as does the process of time, the mind creates worlds of romance and imagination; yet through our created ideals we can stand outside the round of time, infinitely reflective. The mind is free to touch both real and ideal worlds or to stand within itself upon the shore, alone and free. In this self-possessed freedom we are larger—almost infinitely so—than the conflicting demands of the two realms through which we walk.[25]

The deep romantic irony, so central to Byron's art, is that there can be no image of paradise without there having been a fall, that it is only in the enduring movement of the recreative spirit that man finds his home. The infinite is not an object of striving, but is itself the energy of an endless encounter of the mind with the images, relations, and self-definitions it confronts and overcomes. This is the outcome not only of Shelley's idealism in "Mont Blanc," but also of Byron's quest in *Childe Harold's Pilgrimage*. The metaphor of expansive space the poet confronts in St. Peter's represents not a "fulfilled" quest, but, in McGann's words, "a symbol of a mode of experience and perception: the endless activity of self-discovery and renewed self-development. . . . We never 'gain' definitively the fullness of Life in our imaginatively recreative activities, but are always in the process of gaining anew, of becoming and going somewhere else."[26]

Does the endurance of the creative mind ensure the renovation of the world it engages? On this point Shelley's idealism is more self-assured than Byron's. Indeed, Byron (like Schelling before him) grapples with the paradoxes of idealist self-assertion only to be forced beyond idealist conclusions. Shelley, at his most optimistic, affirmed an essentially idealistic resolution to the problem of human finitude: the circling of the finite mind into the world is an act of love, the mind recovering in the disenchanted world the materials for human articulation and new, liberating perspectives. For Byron in *Childe Harold*, however, each new self-affirmation or movement toward liberation becomes swept up in an onrush of energetic being, being that resists human ordering or the recreative power of spontaneous love.

Byron does not, it is true, swerve from the idealist premise which claims, as Fichte put it, "That whose being or essence consists simply in the fact that it posits itself as existing, is the ego as absolute subject. . . . 'I am absolutely because I am.'"[27] Indeed, Bertrand Russell was not far wrong when he so memorably defined "the Byronic" as the mode of "Titanic cosmic self-assertion."[28] But Byron's early heroes become trapped, as do so many romantic questers, in their own willful demands that they and they alone may create themselves and their world absolutely in their own images. The world that opposes them is fixed and dead to the extent that it opposes them, alive only as it responds to them (I have called this interdetermination a desire for a "magical" relation to the world; see above, pp. 86–87).

The idealist dialectic we have developed through Coleridge's and Shelley's romances is a dialectic of love, in which finitude exists as a *creation* of mind at the same time that consciousness would be impossible without positing the absolute *alienation* of the finite boundary. But Byron, in the great affirmations of *Childe Harold IV* and *Don Juan*, achieves a different resolution. The finite is not for him, as for Shelley in "Mont Blanc," a mere boundary whose true being recedes but which (as a boundary) enables the mind to reach beyond itself and recreate the world; Byron's world is real in itself, presenting itself not as receding being but as present being. In studying Byron's development we now discover a distinction between "world" in the idealist's sense of a not-I, a horizon of possibility, and "world" in the sense of the actual locale of nature and human history. Time and space are real in themselves for Byron, and he knows this because the self has, as part of its *own* nature, reality, being, finitude. Byron's love is "erotic" in the classical sense, as a vital principle in the world that draws the self outward.

We are led here to the vision that we find in *Don Juan* of a world always in excess of the ordering mind, or storyteller. A study of that work's satire is beyond the scope of this inquiry, but we can see that the stubbornness of the world Byron encounters in *Childe Harold* is countered there by a new mobility, the mobility of the detached storyteller whose infinite capacity for reflection and recreation both satirizes the world and lets its vast energies show forth. "At the center of *Don Juan*," remarks Alvin Kernan, "is a realized sense of life as constant flow and change, in which all things, man, society, civilization, and nature are swept forward by their own pressure into new conditions of being and ultimately to oblivion."[29] Such a vision of things, is, as Kernan points out, tragic, the tragedy latent in Nietzsche's Dionysian nature whose excesses cannot be humanized. The philosopher Alphonso Lingis has suggested that Kantian idealism is part of a Western tradition as old as Aristotle, the need to contain this erotic excess within the human horizon of a rational system of exchange—of goods, of knowledge, of signs, of moral obligations: just as Aristotle's aesthetics assigns a homeostatic function to tragic art, his physics

> replaces a tragic concept of nature, that which sees the force of nature regulated according to a solar economy, an economy of expenditure without recompense, economy of horror, that of the sun, hub of nature, which produces a surplus energy which it squanders in the void, receiving no return from the minute quantity which, far from itself, engenders satellites, wandering planets, their Apollonian-Dionysian life, dreaming and dancing life—which is only burning itself out as fast as it can. . . . The happiness of the human order, its equilibrium and inner *energeia*, is, according to Aristotle, natural. . . . What is new in Kant is the demonstration that the reduction of social existence to the exchange of the equivalent is imperative. As well as the subjection of all nature to the laws of rational economy.[30]

In Byron's *Don Juan*, attempts to restrict or idealize the erotic power of life produce much of the satire. There is a comic vision in *Don Juan* as well as a tragic one, outside the tale, in the vital flexibility of the narrator. The narrator, a master of irony, responds to the tears of things with the endlessly reconstitutive energy of the storyteller. But, of course, Byron's storyteller resists the enchantments of his tale, responding to the fact of human finitude in a world of boundless and often destructive energies with an infinity of self-conscious orderings and reorderings.[31]

Finitude for Byron does not exist for the sake of the ego, and it is no creation of the ego. This energy of being, this eros, exists in the world and in the self as a shared principle of change, evolution, of growth in and through finitude. Yet the ego also exists for itself alone, as a *spiritual* principle of self-conscious assertion independent of the being of the world. Byron thus asserts simultaneously both the separate existence of being and the independent struggle of the ego to assert itself as greater than the world. The spirit finds greatness in its ability to renew itself over and beyond the cycles of change and destruction that are part of the being of nature, the loss that attends vitality itself. Byron, then, does not abandon the idealist faith that the source of man's freedom and strength lies in self-assertion, but he admits that finitude, time, and change are within us as part of the nature we share with the world. The finite is not merely the alien "out there" opposed to mind, but is constitutive of our nature, even though it vies within us with our spiritual capacity for self-liberation. As McGann writes,

> If Nature and her children seem to endure independently of all man's schemes to control his milieu, it is because they are their own reason for being, and derive their character from their existence, not from human reason or understanding. They *are*, therefore they are *what* they are. . . . By self-definition as an individual, analogous to Nature in independence and autonomy, he begins to achieve a spiritual freedom.[32]

Analogous to nature not only in autonomy but also in finitude, man asserts his spiritual freedom in *Childe Harold's Pilgrimage* and *Don Juan* only as he ceases the infinite attempt to transcend time and change, accepting finitude as one aspect of the self that struggles for freedom. This stance is an affirmation of human potential analogous to the more idealistic assertions of Shelley, but different in important respects.

If Byron accepts man's fallen state as not transcendable, he also boldly demands that the creative mind retain its integrity by adopting a certain stance, a position outside the mind's consciousness of its finitude. That consciousness, that continuous capacity to reflect upon its own thoughts (even thoughts of loss and finitude), is the mind's measure of creative freedom. At the same time, any idealism, as Nietzsche would insist, that conceives of the not-I as only the material for the creation of a spiritually meaningful ("symbolic") human landscape must deny the true being of the Dionysian energy that belongs to nature and is a part of man that mind cannot articulate or clarify.[33] We again face the opacity of *un*conscious energy that, we recall, the idealist Schelling came increasingly to believe threatened the idealist's quest for clarity through symbolic transformation (see above, pp. 106–08). Byron's romance moves to accept what Schelling was long uncomfortable with, what one critic calls "the opaque knot of actuality in the self."[34]

This acceptance of man's being-as-finite, while yet demanding the freedom of the self-conscious mind to create its own *uniquely per-*

*sonal* response to that finitude (in "rebellion," as Camus would say),
marks precisely that point at which romantic quest feeds into a later
cultural movement, existentialism. We might say that Byron's romantic self-assertion is a threshold on which the idealist quest for a
meaningful cosmos becomes an existential stance where man declares himself heroically free precisely *because* he is conscious of the
relentless coursing of finitude, change, and lost myths through his
embattled mind.[35]

For the more traditionally idealistic Shelley, Byron in *Childe
Harold* had presented a tortured vision of an unregenerate world.
Charles Robinson, in his recent study of the two men's literary
relationship, is ready to argue (along with Shelley) that despite some
"expressions of hope" in the fourth canto, "Byron fails to sustain the
Shelleyan belief that the world might be redeemed."[36] Yet too much
may be made of this contrast: what would not count as redemption
for Shelley might well count as redemption for Byron. For both men,
I believe, the general goal of a redemptive romance was a freedom
from the regressive *Sehnsucht* that nevertheless allowed man the infinite self-creative promise of his prelapsarian myths. For both men
the opacity of being, the resistance of the world, and the destructiveness of time are moments in the evolution of cultural and political possibilities.

But Shelley's hope was that the enduring power of imagination
would create symbols of love and relatedness prophesying to man the
limitless capacity of human ideals to persist amid disenchanting
struggle and loss.

> Gentleness, Virtue, Wisdom and Endurance—
> These are the seals of that most firm assurance
>   Which bars the pit over Destruction's strength. . . .
> To suffer woes which Hope thinks infinite
> To forgive wrongs darker than Death or Night;
>   To defy Power which seems Omnipotent;
> To love, and bear; to hope, till Hope creates
> From its own wreck the thing it contemplates. . . .
>                                         (*Prometheus Unbound*, 4.562–74)[37]

For Byron, the enduring power of mind meant, rather, the continuous ability of the individual to stand at his own creative center, free
even from his own expectations that human ideals might continu-

ously reenergize a corrupt social order. In *Childe Harold IV,* Byron hopes to bring from his "heated mind" forms from "the floating wreck which Ruin leaves behind,"

> And from the planks, far shattered o'er the rocks,
> Build me a little bark of hope. . . .
> But could I gather from the wave-worn store
>     Enough for my rude boat,—where should I steer?
> There woos no home, nor hope, nor life, save what is here.
>
> (st. 105)

For both men, the mind must be mobile enough to transcend its own illusions. This meant, to Shelley (at least in the period 1816–19, when he most felt his differences with Byron) that the reordering of the (cultural and political) world is guided by the mythmaking mind, and the goal of human creation is an order of *love.* For Byron, the reordering of the (personal) world is an enabling activity that permits the mind to know itself as the free creator of its myths. The goal of such creation is *heroism,* the capacity of the individual to act meaningfully in the world.

This is the only kind of heroism, perhaps, left to the self-conscious modern author, his sustaining myths crumbling about him. It is a demand not only for the *sprezzatura* of Byron's concluding stance, but also for renewed commitment to man's finitude, his community with being itself, his absolute self-responsibility for the creative imagination and the actual, historical world it engages. In reaching this heroic poise Byron confronts the most spiritually devastating fact of modernity—the assumption of existential freedom in a de-mythologized cosmos—and transforms it by a gesture, a hard-won assertion, into a source of psychic health and personal triumph.

# Coda: Romantic Humanism and Romantic Quest

> "This is Raphael's tomb—while he lived he made
> Mother Nature
> Fear to be vanquished by him and, as he died,
> to die too."

Cardinal Bembo's famous epitaph reflects the bold Humanism of *Cinque-cento* Rome. The warrior artist Raphael reposes in the Pantheon, his tomb lit by the sunlight that pours into the lofty dome. Romantic humanism would unpack the latent paradox in the motto. Nature fears extinction without the creative mind to sustain her, yet also is the mind's very real opponent while it lives.

Romantic humanism evolves as a dialectic between visionary ideals and the recognition of the absolute practical freedom of the particular individual—in his loves, in his society, in his daily life. Man is not bound to any order of nature or history except by his own act. Yet binding the romantic cosmos is eros, the impulsion that both draws man out of himself and aims at drawing in, humanizing, the otherness of universal flux, natural process, becoming. Eros is both personal and transpersonal, touching as if from the outside the nerve-center of human being, the impatient danger-filled love born of the endless striving of finite man. The beloved represents the capacity of the self to return to itself only by journeying outward, purchasing knowledge without loss of power.

Between the self-conscious individual and the resisting world, eros creates a series of relations, what romantic theory called "organism." The individual spirit (as Coleridge and Schelling saw it) is the highest expression of natural organism, while yet becoming the individual only at the price of reflecting upon and so alienating that organism. This spontaneous reflection (the "I am") is a new element, a consciousness, a freedom, a fall. Man can now reach across this gap only as creator of his world, for this activity of creation engages him once again in the real evolution of higher organic relations. This was, at least, the romantic hope.

The energy it takes to cross that chasm is again eros, now in the guise of imagination. The imagination retains its dangerous power to "sublate" (as Hegel put it) organism so as to energize and create anew the individual spirit, or to sublate the individual spirit for the sake of a higher organism. Human love, life itself, is the struggle to engage both strivings of eros, selfish and selfless, in a thorough reciprocity, where man is both creature and creator of the cosmos. The work of eros (coursing between consciousness and unconsciousness) is the ever-renewed enchantment of romance, the lonely striving that brings disillusioned isolation or inspiring vision, the pathway through the forest of our deepest fears and the castle of our most desired, most exalted loves.

# Notes

## List of Abbreviations

| | |
|---|---|
| BPW | *Byron's Poetical Works* |
| CL | *Comparative Literature* |
| CPR | *Critique of Pure Reason* (Kant) |
| EIC | *Essays in Criticism* |
| GWL | *Grundlage der Gesamten Wissenschaftslehre* (Fichte) |
| JAAC | *Journal of Aesthetics and Art Criticism* |
| JHI | *Journal of the History of Ideas* |
| Julian | *The Complete Works of Percy Bysshe Shelley*, Julian Editions |
| KSJ | *Keats–Shelley Journal* |
| Norton | *Shelley's Poetry and Prose*, Norton Critical Edition |
| PQ | *Philological Quarterly* |
| PW | *Coleridge: Poetical Works* |
| SEL | *Studies in English Literature* |
| SP | *Studies in Philology* |
| TWC | *The Wordsworth Circle* |
| SiR | *Studies in Romanticism* |

*Full bibliographical information is given in first footnote references and in the Bibliography.*

### Chapter 1: Romantic Subjectivity and the Goals of Romance

1. *Wordsworth's Poetry 1787–1814* (New Haven: Yale University Press, 1971), pp. 209–11; William Wordsworth, *The Prelude: 1799, 1805, 1850*, ed. Jonathan Wordsworth, M. H. Abrams, and Stephen Gill (New York: Norton, 1979).

2. "The Relation of the Poet to Day-Dreaming" (1908), rpt. in Sigmund Freud, *On Creativity and the Unconscious*, ed. Benjamin Nelson (New York: Harper & Row, 1958), p. 47. See also Freud's "Sexuality and the Aetiology of the Neuroses" (1905), rpt. in *Freud: Sexuality and the Psychology of Love*, ed. Philip Rieff (New York: Macmillan, 1963), pp. 12—15.

3. *The Divided Self* (New York: Random House, 1969), p. 94.

4. See, for example, A. O. Lovejoy, "The Meaning of 'Romantic' in Early German Romanticism," in his *Essays in the History of Ideas* (Baltimore: Johns Hopkins University Press, 1972), pp. 183—206; Thomas McFarland, "The Origin of Coleridge's Theory of Secondary Imagination" [on Tetens, Leibniz], in *New Perspectives on Coleridge and Wordsworth: Selected Papers from the English Institute*, ed. Geoffrey Hartman (New York: Columbia University Press, 1972), pp. 223—26; René Wellek, "The Concept of Romanticism in Literary History," *CL* 1 (1949): 1—29, 147—72.

5. Norman Kemp Smith, *A Commentary to Kant's "Critique of Pure Reason,"* 2d ed., rev. (New York: Macmillan, 1923), p. xxxix.

6. "The English Romantics: The Grounds of Knowledge," *SiR* 4 (1964): 22.

7. This effect may be far greater than anyone had expected. It was not until 1972 that the origin of Coleridge's theory of the imagination in Tetens's *Philosophische Versuche* (1777) was argued, by McFarland, "Origin of Coleridge's Theory." More recently, McFarland has developed a broad typology of influence and the problem of poetic originality in *Originality and Imagination* (Baltimore: Johns Hopkins University Press, 1985); see especially pp. 31—59.

8. Nietzsche, *Der Wille zur Macht* in *Werke*, 20 vols. (Leipzig: Kröner, 1911), 16: 248 (aphorism no. 822, my translation). The richest commentary on this aphorism (and on the Will to Power generally) is Martin Heidegger, *The Will to Power as Art*, trans. David Farrell Krell, Vol. 1 of *Nietzsche* (San Francisco: Harper & Row, 1979), pp. 74—76. The quotation from Hegel is from *Introduction to Aesthetics* [Introduction to the Berlin Lectures of the 1820s], trans. T. M. Knox (Oxford: Oxford University Press, 1979), pp. 8—9.

9. *Dark Interpreter: The Discourse of Romanticism* (Ithaca: Cornell University Press, 1980), pp. 13—14. Rajan here follows Paul de Man in seeing language as intentional (removed from being): see de Man's "Intentional Structure of the Romantic Image," in *Romanticism and Consciousness*, ed. Harold Bloom (New York: Norton, 1970), pp. 65—77.

In disagreeing with Rajan's deconstructionist aesthetics I do not mean to deny the importance of her book. I agree with her discussion on pages 99—105 of irony and romance as central problems for romantic poets. Although I will study irony and romance from a broader philosophical perspective, Rajan's reading of the ambiguity of fictions in Keats is both illuminating and congruent with my own theory of romance.

10. De Man, "Intentional Structure," p. 69.

11. For the peculiar redemptiveness of Byronic irony in *Don Juan* see Frederick Garber, "Satire and the Making of Selves," in *Literary Theory and Criticism: Festschrift in Honor of René Wellek*, ed. Joseph Strelka (Bern, Switzerland: Peter Lang, 1984), pp. 865—69.

12. *Language and Myth*, trans. Suzanne Langer (New York: Dover, 1953), p. 98. For the indebtedness of romantics, particularly Wordsworth, to Condillac and subjectivist views of language see Hans Aarsleff, "Wordsworth, Language, and Romanticism," *EIC* 30 (1980): 215—26.

13. "On Poesy or Art," rpt. as an appendix in the edition of *Biographia Literaria* by J. Shawcross (1907; rpt. Oxford: Oxford University Press, 1954), 2:253ff.

14. See Shawcross's discussion in *Biographia Literaria*, pp. lxxvii–lxxxi.

15. *Wordsworth's Poetical Works*, ed. Ernest de Selincourt and Helen Darbyshire, 5 vols. (Oxford: Oxford University Press, 1949), 5:338.

16. See *Wordsworth's Poetry*, pp. 39–45.

17. "The Internalization of Quest Romance," *Yale Review* 58 (Summer 1969); rpt. in Bloom, ed., *Romanticism and Consciousness* (New York: Norton, 1970), p. 20.

18. Annotation to Wordsworth, in *The Poetry and Prose of William Blake*, ed. David Erdman (Garden City, N.Y.: Anchor-Doubleday, 1965), p. 656. All further references to Blake are to this edition and will be inserted in the text.

19. "Expostulation and Reply," in *Poetical Works*, 4:56.

20. Northrop Frye, *The Secular Scripture* (Cambridge, Mass.: Harvard University Press, 1976), p. 61. Cf. J. G. Fichte, *The Science of Knowledge (Wissenschaftslehre), with the First and Second Introductions*, trans. and ed. Peter Heath and John Lachs (New York: Appleton-Century-Crofts, 1970), p. 194: "Imagination is a faculty that wavers [*schwebt*] between determination and nondetermination [i.e., freedom], between finite and infinite. . . . —This wavering is characteristic of imagination even in its product; in the course of its wavering, so to speak, and by means thereof it brings the latter to birth."

## *Chapter 2: The Context of Romantic Subjectivity and Transcendental Idealism: Kant's First Critique*

1. Although it does not demonstrate clear connections between Locke and romantic poets, the fullest account of the indebtedness of romantic theories of imagination to Locke is Ernest Tuveson's *The Imagination as a Means of Grace: Locke and the Aesthetics of Romanticism* (Berkeley and Los Angeles: University of California Press, 1960).

2. M. H. Abrams, *Natural Supernaturalism* (New York: Norton, 1971), p. 278; see also Melvin Rader, *Wordsworth: A Philosophical Approach* (Oxford: Clarendon Press, 1967), pp. 30–52, 159–66. It is true that Abrams's "joy" is a spiritual state associated with idealist unity with nature. Its roots are also in radical Christian millennarianism, as Abrams notes, pp. 46–70. But there are a number of critics who question whether the condition of joy is the most significant vein of Wordsworth's poetry.

3. *The Philosophic Mind: A Study of Wordsworth's Poetry and Thought, 1797–1805* (Columbus: Ohio State University Press, 1973). Grob argues (pp. 114–28) for the fundamentally Lockean premises—modified by concepts of relationship and love—of the poetry of 1798–99. He discusses Wordsworth's attraction to empiricist epistemology in the years of *Tintern Abbey* and the first books of *The Prelude*, pp. 46–71. That the later books of *The Prelude* constitute an outright repudiation of the earlier empiricist faith in nature has been argued by Edward Bostetter, *The Romantic Ventriloquists*, rev. ed. (Seattle: University of Washington Press, 1975), pp. 41–52.

4. *The Prelude: 1799, 1805, 1850*, 1850 version, p. 185.

5. That the Bedouin is a displaced image of Wordsworth's anxiety is argued by Hartman in his analysis of this section, in *Wordsworth's Poetry*, pp. 225–33. See also the recent semiological analysis and revision of Hartman's reading by Andrzej Warminski, "Missed Crossing: Wordsworth's Apocalypses," *MLN* 99 (1984): 1002–5.

6. Rajan, *Dark Interpreter*, p. 234.

7. *Wordsworth's Poetical Works*, 5:313–39.

8. *The Autonomy of the Self from Richardson to Huysmans* (Princeton: Princeton University Press, 1982), pp. 196–97.

9. *The Prelude*, p. 26, italics added. Wordsworth is here withdrawing from the pantheist excess of lines 445–64. See also the passage from MS. RV deleted by Wordsworth, reprinted in *The Prelude*, p. 496.

10. There is no necessary reason for this conservatism to have led to a decline of poetic power. For a good discussion of why it did, see Grob, *Philosophic Mind*, pp. 270–75.

11. Shelley's disappointment becomes explicit in "To William Wordsworth," published in the same 1816 volume as *Alastor*.

12. James Caldwell discusses Hartley and Keats in *John Keats' Fancy: The Effect on Keats of the Psychology of His Day* (Ithaca: Cornell University Press, 1945). See also Stuart Sperry, *Keats the Poet* (Princeton: Princeton University Press, 1973), pp. 13–15, 20–22. The best-known rejection of Hartley, of course, was Coleridge's: see, for detailed discussions, H. N. Fairchild, "Hartley, Pistorius, and Coleridge," *PMLA* 62 (1947): 1010–21; H. W. Piper, "The Pantheistic Sources of Coleridge's Early Poetry," *JHI* 20 (1959):47–59; and Rader, *Wordsworth*, pp. 10–38, 119–32. Associationist psychology by no means died out in the nineteenth century: the two great inheritors of the Hartleyan tradition were James Mill (*The Analysis of the Human Mind* [1829]) and Alexander Bain (*Manual of Mental and Moral Sciences* [1868]).

13. *Observations on Man* (London, 1749), rpt. in *Backgrounds of Romanticism*, ed. Leonard M. Trawick (Bloomington: Indiana University Press, 1967), pp. 53–61. The *OED* credits Blancard's *Physical Dictionary* (1693) for the introduction of "psychology" into English, but its circulation as a term is certainly the result of Hartley's influence; see Robert Brown, ed., *Between Hume and Mill: An Anthology of British Philosophy, 1749–1843* (New York: Random House, 1970), p. 4.

14. *Fichte* (Edinburgh: Blackwood's, 1903), pp. 109, 120–21.

15. Kemp Smith, *Commentary*, p. xliii.

16. *Kant's Metaphysics and Theory of Science*, trans. P. G. Lucas (Manchester: Manchester University Press, 1955), pp. 176–80; see also Kemp Smith, *Commentary*, pp. l–lii.

Kant discusses the impossibility of inferring the real nature of the self in "The Paralogisms of Pure Reason," in *The Critique of Pure Reason*, trans. Norman Kemp Smith, 2d ed. (London: Macmillan, 1933), A341–405 = B399–430; see esp. A363–67. Henceforth abbreviated *CPR*; following tradition, I refer to the first edition (1781), as "A," and the second (1787) as "B." Further references will be inserted in the text.

17. For the "loosening and separation of psychology from philosophy" in the nineteenth century, see Wilhelm Windelband, *A History of Philosophy*, trans. James H. Tufts, 2d ed., rev. (New York: Macmillan, 1901), pp. 634ff., and his *Ueber den gegenwärtigen Stand der psychologischen Forschung* (Leipzig, 1876). For Kant's own dismissal of empirical psychology's claims to metaphysical knowledge, see *CPR*, A848 = B876.

18. "The unconscious is itself the subjective term for what we objectively recognize as nature" (quoted in Lancelot Law Whyte, *The Unconscious before Freud* [London: Tavistock, 1962], p. 150).

19. Maine de Biran, *Essai sur les fondements de la psychologie* (Paris, 1812); Eduard von Hartmann, *Philosophy of the Unconscious* trans. W. C. Copeland, 9th ed., 3 vols. (London, 1884).

20. *Collected Letters of Samuel Taylor Coleridge*, ed. Earl L. Griggs, 6 vols. (Oxford: Oxford University Press, 1956), 2:706.

21. "Coleridge and Kant's Two Worlds," *ELH* 7 (1940); rpt. in his *Essays in the History of Ideas*, p. 258.

22. Ibid., p. 260. There were, of course, other reasons for Coleridge's disappointment with Hartley, whose initial appeal to him was most likely the meliorism and optimism of his system. For a detailed discussion of Coleridge and Wordsworth's rejection of associationism, see the references in note 12, above.

23. Martin, *Kant's Metaphysics*, pp. 7–8; McFarland, *Coleridge*, pp. 216–26, 240, n. 125. Coleridge certainly read Leibniz by February of 1801 (*Letters*, 2:702).

24. *An Essay Concerning Human Understanding*, ed. John Yolton from the 5th ed. of 1706, 2 vols. (London: Dent, 1965), 1:95, 97 (Bk. II, Ch. IV).

25. 1:138 (Bk. II, Ch. XIII).

26. According to Mach, Newton by no means needed "absolute" space to account for acceleration: he needed only "inertial Frames" moving with equal but opposite acceleration to the accelerating body. The problem of absolute motion, which engendered the nineteenth-century theory of an ether, was not resolved until the twentieth century, by Mach and Einstein. Newton, Mach reasoned, must have had other reasons—"philosophical," theological, or psychological—for postulating absolute space, since his own mechanics did not ultimately require it. See Ernst Mach, *The Science of Mechanics*, trans. T. J. McCormick (Chicago, 1893), secs. 2–6; also, Albert Einstein, "Relativity and the Problem of Space," in his *Relativity: The Special and General Theory*, trans. Robert Lawson, 15th ed. (1952; rpt. New York: Crown, 1961), pp. 135–57.

I am indebted in what follows to the discussion in Max Jammer, *Concepts of Space: The History of the Theory of Space in Philosophy* (Cambridge, Mass.: Harvard University Press, 1954), pp. 93–101. For an overview of Newton, Leibniz, and Kant, see Robert Paul Wolff, *Kant's Theory of Mental Activity* (Cambridge, Mass.: Harvard University Press, 1963), pp. 1–10.

27. *Mathematical Principles of Natural Philosophy*, trans. Andrew Motte, rev. and ed. Florian Cajori (Berkeley and Los Angeles: University of California Press, 1934), p. 6 (italics added). Cf. Jammer, *Concepts of Space*, pp. 99–106.

28. *A Treatise Concerning the Principles of Human Knowledge* (1710), in *The Empiricists* (Garden City, N.Y.: Anchor, 1974), p. 197; cf. pp. 195–98 (secs. 111–17).

29. Newton, *Mathematical Principles*, p. 544; Jammer, *Concepts of Space*, pp. 108–11.

30. *Nouveaus essais sur l'entendement humain*, trans. G. M. Duncan, in *Leibniz: Selections*, ed. Philip P. Wiener (New York: Scribner's, 1951), p. 424 (Bk. II, Ch. 18, sec. 3).

31. Third Letter, sec. 2; Fourth Letter, secs. 1–7, of "Letters of Samuel Clarke," trans. Clarke, rev. Philip P. Weiner in *Leibniz*, pp. 222, 228–29. He argues most forcefully that the idea of space as a "property" of God engenders hopeless confusion, in Fifth Letter, secs. 36–46, pp. 249–51. For a full treatment, see F.S.C. Northrup, "Leibniz's Theory of Space," *JHI* 7 (1946): 427ff.

32. From the key Fifth Letter, secs. 29, 33, 47, in Leibniz, *Nouveaus essais*, pp. 246, 247, 252–53. That these relations have ideal being in God's reason is suggested in ibid., pp. 421–22 (Bk. II, Ch. 13, sec. 17).

33. Martin, *Kant's Metaphysics*, p. 15. For the mental status of all relations in Leibniz ("Relation is not, therefore, an absolute reality of things-in-themselves, but rather a determination which thought brings to things"), see Martin's *Leibniz: Logic and Metaphysics*, trans. K. J. Northcott and P. G. Lucas (Manchester: Manchester University Press, 1964), pp. 150–52.

34. The Leibniz-Kant connection is argued by Martin, *Kant's Metaphysics*, pp. 28–41; see also Northrup, pp. 442–46.

35. Letters, 2:709.

36. Kant and the Problem of Metaphysics, trans. J. C. Churchill (1929; rpt. Bloomington: Indiana University Press, 1962), p. 31; cf. Kant, CPR, B72.

37. Annotations to Coleridge's copy of Kant, in the British Library, C. 12b, i.q., flyleaf.

38. Ibid.

39. See Kant's Inaugural Dissertation, trans. John Handyside (Chicago: Open Court, 1929), pp. 43-52 (2.3-12).

40. The case when I think of myself thinking not an object, but myself is admittedly a more difficult temporal problem, which Kant will address and Fichte take as centrally important. For the moment, however, we confine ourselves to sensible intuition of objects.

41. The fullest treatment of this issue in English will be found in Kemp Smith, Commentary, pp. 85-88.

42. It has often been suggested that the a priori character of space does not necessarily prove it to be subjective also: the a priori quality of geometry does not exclude the possibility that things-in-themselves are spatial. See Stephan Körner, Kant (Baltimore: Penguin Books, 1955), pp. 37-38. Seen in the context of Kant's metaphysical assumptions, however, it is impossible for a finite intelligence as he defines it to receive anything that belongs properly to the being of a thing-in-itself. For a divine, purely noetic intelligence, the distinction of "inner" and "outer" intuition would presumably not arise, so Kant could not attribute spatial properties to noumena. Cf. CPR, B71-72.

43. See Windelband, History of Philosophy, pp. 540-41. For Kant and Berkeley, see J. E. Erdmann, A History of Philosophy, trans. W. S. Hough from the 3d ed., 3 vols. (New York, 1890), 2:376, 386-88.

44. Heinz Heimsoeth, "Metaphysical Motives in the Development of Critical Idealism," trans. Moltke S. Gram, in Kant: Disputed Questions, ed. Moltke S. Gram (Chicago: Quadrangle Books, 1967), pp. 162-74.

## Chapter 3: Nature, Imagination, and Self-Consciousness: Kant's Transcendental Deduction

1. See Erdmann, History of Philosophy, 2:378-80; Kemp Smith, Commentary, pp. 246-47. The most concise, and for me the most lucid explanation of the relations among apperception, imagination, and the synthesis of the Understanding in Kant's Deduction is A. C. Ewing, A Short Commentary on Kant's "Critique of Pure Reason" (Chicago: University of Chicago Press, 1938), pp. 80-84.

2. Erdmann, History of Philosophy, 2:377; Kemp Smith, Commentary, p. 171.

3. Ewing, Short Commentary, p. 137.

4. R. P. Wolff, Kant's Theory of Mental Activity, p. 60, argues that if "we accept Kant's own description of the categories as 'functions of synthesis,' we are led to see that they are aspects of a mental activity," and that much of Kant's own confusion in organizing the Deduction of the Categories stems from his tendency to treat them as class concepts. See his general discussion of the logic of the categories, pp. 64-71.

5. Kemp Smith, Commentary, p. 179. For an opposing view, see H. J. Paton, "The Key to Kant's Deduction of the Categories," Mind 40 (1931):310-29. Paton shows that the forms of synthetic judgment must be thought of as given by the same agency that gives analytic judgments; it does not, however, follow that the Catego-

ries that Kant believes generate experience must correspond to his table of logical forms.

6. Flyleaf of Coleridge's copy of Kant's *Critique*, British Library, C. 12b, i.q.

7. It has been shown by H. J. de Vleeschauwer that in the years between 1777 and 1780, Kant studied Tetens carefully and in fact used Tetens's psychology of imagination in writing the Deduction. It may be that by the time of the 1787 second edition Kant believed the psychological doctrine poorly integrated into his argument; but though he had clearly transcended the limitations of Tetens's faculty psychology, the objective deduction remains rooted in the empirical analysis of awareness. See H. J. de Vleeschauwer, *The Development of Kantian Thought*, trans. A. R. C. Duncan (1939; rpt. London: Thomas Nelson, 1962), pp. 69, 82–88. A recent discussion of Tetens and Kant on Imagination is James Engell's *The Creative Imagination* (Cambridge, Mass.: Harvard University Press, 1982), pp. 118–39.

8. Kemp Smith, *Commentary*, p. 245; Ewing, p. 75.

9. Kemp Smith considers the leap from the unity of a series, or the unity of counting, to the rule-governed unity of objects "needlessly complex" and "confusing" (ibid., p. 247). But for Kant, what makes an image an *object* and not an illusion is its ability to be constructed by the imagination according to a *rule*; see Wolff, *Kant's Theory of Mental Activity*, pp. 130, 133.

10. Kemp Smith, *Commentary*, p. 246.

11. For a lengthy discussion of transcendental apperception and its importance to later romantic philosophy, see Gian Orsini, *Coleridge and German Idealism* (Carbondale: Southern Illinois University Press, 1969), pp. 117–29.

12. Kemp Smith, *Commentary*, p. 264.

13. See the discussion of the complex relation of Understanding and imagination in Ewing, *Short Commentary*, pp. 91ff., and Kant's explanation, A119.

14. Graham Nicol Forst, "Kant's 'Copernican Revolution' in Philosophy and the Romantic Revolution in English Literature" (Ph.D. dissertation, University of British Columbia, 1970), p. 20.

15. Coleridge, *Biographia Literaria*, ed. James Engell and W. Jackson Bate, Vol. 7 of *The Collected Works of Samuel Taylor Coleridge* (Princeton: Princeton University Press, 1983), 1: 255. Further references to the *Biographia* are to this edition unless otherwise noted. Coleridge is translating F. W. J. Schelling, *System des transcendentalen Idealismus*, in *Schellings Sämtliche Werke*, ed. F. K. A. Schelling (Stuttgart and Augsburg, 1856–61), 3 : 335.

16. Heidegger, *Kant and the Problem of Metaphysics*, pp. 86, 166–76.

17. Ernst Cassirer, "Kant and the Problem of Metaphysics: Remarks on Martin Heidegger's Interpretation of Kant," trans. Moltke Gram in his *Kant*, pp. 142–47.

18. Ibid., p. 141; see also Heimsoeth, "Metaphysical Motives," pp. 169–70.

19. Heinrich Heine, "Concerning the History of Religion and Philosophy in Germany" (1835), in *Selected Works of Heinrich Heine*, trans. and ed. Helen Mustard (New York: Vintage, 1973), p. 368.

20. This is the emphasis of the Heidelberg school, Rickert, Windelband, and Kroner. For the view that Kant's epistemology depends for its meaning on the doctrine of moral freedom, see Richard Kroner, *Kant's Weltanschauung*, trans. John E. Smith, with Kroner's revisions (1914; rpt. Chicago: University of Chicago Press, 1956).

21. Vleeschauwer, *Development of Kantian Thought*, p. 176.

## Chapter 4: Fichte and Romanticism

1. Adamson, *Fichte*, pp. 42–43.

2. Letter from Böttinger, May 1794, quoted in ibid., p. 44. The other two professors due were Ilgen and Woltmann, lecturers in Oriental studies and in history.

3. "Kant Romanticized by Fichte," in Korff, *Geist der Goethezeit* (Leipzig: J. J. Weber, 1923–57), 3:258; rpt. in *The Romantic Movement*, ed. and trans. Antony Thorlby (New York: Barnes & Noble, 1966), p. 111.

4. Fichte, *Science of Knowledge*, p. 99. Further references to the *Wissenschaftslehre* of 1794 (*Grundlage der gesamten Wissenschaftslehre*, abbreviated *GWL*) and to the First and Second Introductions of 1797 follow this translation and its page numbers. I have, however, translated *Ich* as "I," rather than "Self" as Heath does. This is closer to the original and is the traditional reading.

5. Coleridge, *Biographia Literaria*, 1:158; J. W. von Goethe, *Faust*, trans. Walter Kaufmann (Garden City, N.Y.: Anchor, 1963), p. 153 (line 1237). A discussion of Coleridge's understanding—and misunderstanding—of the Fichtean Ego will be found in Orsini, *Coleridge and German Idealism*, pp. 177–78; see also Orsini's useful general introduction to Fichte's thought, pp. 172–76. Goethe wrote that he "found nothing in the first sheets of the 'Wissenschaftslehre' which [he] did not understand . . . nothing which did not harmonize with [his] own mode of thinking about things" (quoted in Adamson, *Fichte*, p. 49).

6. Thomas P. Hohler, "Fichte and the Problem of Finitude," *Southwestern Journal of Philosophy* 7 (1976):17.

7. Abrams, *Natural Supernaturalism*, pp. 179–80, 217–18, 225–37. See also the remarks of Geoffrey Hartman on German philosophies of self-consciousness and the romantic myth of the fall, in "Romanticism and Anti-Self-Consciousness," *Centennial Review* 6 (Autumn 1962); rev. and rpt. in *Romanticism and Consciousness*, ed. Harold Bloom (New York: Norton, 1970), pp. 48–50.

8. See above, pp. 50–51.

9. For an analysis of the critical response to dogmatism, see Charles Griswold, "Fichte's Modification of Kant's Transcendental Idealism in the *Wissenschaftslehre* of 1794 and Introductions of 1797," *Auslegung* 4 (Fall 1977): 133–34. For Kant's explanation of the *noumenon*, see *CPR*, A251–52.

10. Kant's frankly disgusted attack on the idealism of Fichte was published in 1799 as *Erklärung in Beziehung auf Fichtes Wissenschaftslehre*, in *Immanuel Kants Werke*, ed. Ernst Cassirer, 11 vols. (Berlin: B. Cassirer, 1912–22), 8:515: "I consider Fichte's Wissenschaftslehre a completely untenable system." Fichte, for his part, had declared that "my system is nothing other than the Kantian," and he wonders whether Kant "was speaking of the Wissenschaftslehre *genuinely perused and understood*" (Fichte's italics; 1st Intro., *GWL*, p. 4; 2d Intro., *GWL*, pp. 43, 44).

11. For a discussion of Jacobi's attack on the thing-in-itself, Kant's bitter response, and the implications for romanticism, see A. O. Lovejoy, *The Reason, the Understanding, and Time* (Baltimore: Johns Hopkins University Press, 1961), Lecture I. Thomas McFarland points out, in a detailed analysis, that Jacobi saw in Kant's thing-in-itself only a weak and vain attempt to shut out a Spinozistic pantheism based not on materialism, but on absolute idealism: *Coleridge and the Pantheist Tradition* (Oxford: Oxford University Press, 1969), pp. 21ff. Jacobi came to believe that the thing-in-itself was not defensible, and so abandoned Kant, since historically (in Jacobi's words), "there was founded, through our Kant, quite in opposition to his intention, a second Spinozism" (quoted in ibid., p. 92).

12. See the discussion above, pp. 56–57.

13. *Werke*, ed. Friedrich Roth, 7 vols. (Leipzig, 1812–15), 2:304; 1:121; see Windelband, *History of Philosophy*, pp. 573–74. Windelband (pp. 576–90) provides the most complete historical survey of the debate over the thing-in-itself. Jacobi, denouncing all other positions, turned away from eighteenth-century epistemology, with its metaphors of ideas and representations. His mature fideism—which had a subtle but certain influence on Schelling, Coleridge, and, later, Kierkegaard—sought contact with Being in an unmediated intuition of God. See Lovejoy, *Reason*, pp. 4–16, 45–50. For a summary of Jacobi's long career and influence, see McFarland, *Coleridge*, pp. 289–97.

14. *CPR*, B135. See Griswold, "Fichte's Modification of Kant's Transcendental Idealism," p. 135.

15. *CPR*, B275, as amended by Bxxxix. (This argument belongs to the second edition and is difficult to reconcile with some of Kant's earlier remarks.)

16. See Orsini, *Coleridge and German Idealism*, p. 176.

17. Henrich Steffens, *Was ich erlebte* (Breslau, 1840–44), as quoted in ibid., p. 180. For a discussion of this example of intellectual intuition, see Frederick Copleston, "Fichte," in *Fichte to Hegel*, Vol. 7, Pt. 1 of *A History of Philosophy* (Garden City, N.Y.: Doubleday, 1965), pp. 59–62.

18. *The Notebooks of Samuel Taylor Coleridge*, ed. Kathleen Coburn, 3 vols. (New York: Bollingen Foundation, 1957), vol. 1, entry 921; the passage is discussed by Orsini, *Coleridge and German Idealism*, pp. 178–83, and by Daniel Stempel, who argues that Fichte, not Schelling, was the central German romantic influence on Coleridge, in "Revelation on Mt. Snowdon: Wordsworth, Coleridge, and the Fichtean Imagination," *JAAC* 29 (1971): 373.

19. *The Friend*, ed. Barbara Rooke, vol. 4 of *The Collected Works of Samuel Taylor Coleridge*, 2 vols. (Princeton: Princeton University Press, 1969), 1:521.

20. Griswold, "Fichte's Modification of Kant's Transcendental Idealism," p. 138. Cf. Fichte: "Initially I am neither the reflecting subject nor the reflected object, and neither of the two is conditioned by the other, since I am *both in combination*; though this union I cannot indeed think, since in the act of doing so I separate the reflected from that which reflects" (2d Intro., *GWL*, pp. 60–61).

21. *The Philosophy of Hegel: An Introduction and Re-examination* (1958; rpt. New York: Collier, 1962), p. 47.

22. George J. Seidel, *Activity and Ground: Fichte, Schelling, and Hegel*, Studien und Materialen zur Geschichte der Philosophie, Bd. 3 (Hildesheim: George Olms, 1976), p. 30.

23. Lovejoy, *The Reason*, p. 78. These lectures were first delivered in 1939.

24. Quoted in ibid., p. 78; the quotation is from Schelling, *Philosophische Briefe über Dogmatismus und Kritizismus* (1795), in *Schellings Sämmtliche Werke*, ed. K. F. A. Schelling, 14 vols. (Stuttgart and Augsburg, 1856–61), Abt. I, Bd. I, 318–19.

25. "Timelessness and Romanticism," *JHI* 15 (1954): 7.

26. *The Complete Works of Percy Bysshe Shelley*, ed. Roger Ingpen and Walter Peck, Julian Editions, 10 vols. (London: Ernest Benn, 1930), 1:156–57.

27. *The Difference between the Fichtean and Schellingean Systems of Philosophy (The Differenzschrift)*, trans. J. P. Surber (Reseda, Calif.: Ridgeview, 1978), pp. 40, 41, 46 (italics added).

28. *The Logic of Hegel*, trans. William Wallace, 2d ed. (Oxford: Oxford University Press, 1904), pp. 56–57.

29. "Romanticism Re-Examined," in *Romanticism Reconsidered: Selected Papers from*

*the English Institute*, ed. Northrop Frye (New York: Columbia University Press, 1963), p. 132.

30. "Romanticism and 'Anti-Self-Consciousness,'" pp. 49, 50 (I have in one case altered the sentence order of the original). Interestingly, Wellek ("Romanticism Re-Examined," p. 131) misreads Hartman as if he meant to support Hegel.

31. Findlay, *Philosophy of Hegel*, pp. 48, 49; see *GWL*, pp. 238–39.

32. Korff, "Kant Romanticized by Fichte," pp. 109–10.

33. Ibid., p. 111. This too would appear to have been Coleridge's conception (or misconception), from *Biographia*, 1:158–60 and 158n. That Coleridge so confused Fichte's meaning is shown, too, by his marginal note in Fichte's *Bestimmung des Menschen* (Coleridge's copy is in the British Library, C.43.a.12), in which he seems to accuse Fichte of "equivocating" by using "the word 'I'" to refer equally to the Absolute I and to the finite Ego. Coleridge also suggested that Fichte really meant "soul" (*psyche*) and not "I" in the *Wissenschaftslehre* and asks in a note on the flyleaf of his copy why Fichte never considers his absolute I as sometimes asleep (!) (his notes are in the British Library copy C.126.f.13, and are reprinted in W. Schrickx, "Unpublished Coleridge Marginalia on Fichte," *Studia Germanica Gandensia* 3 [1961]:184). But that Coleridge made creative use of his reading of Fichte is persuasively argued by Stempel, "Revelation on Mt. Snowdon," 376–78.

34. This point is clarified by Copleston, *Fichte to Hegel*, p. 65.

35. *Differenzschrift*, p. 39. See the discussion in Stanley Rosen, *G. W. F. Hegel* (New Haven: Yale University Press, 1974), pp. 99–100. It has been argued that Hegel misunderstood the true unity of all three of Fichte's principles, that the third principle is the real beginning of Fichte's dialectic, and that Hegel underestimates the resolutions provided by the practical, or moral, side of the *Wissenschaftslehre*: see Karl Schumann, *Die Grundlage der Wissenschaftslehre in ihrem Umrisse* (The Hague: Nijhoff, 1968), and Helmut Girndt, *Die Differenz des Fichteschen und Hegelschen Systems in der Hegelschen "Differenzschrift"* (Bonn: Bouvier, 1965).

36. See Griswold, "Fichte's Modification of Kant's Transcendental Idealism," p. 140.

37. Adamson, *Fichte*, p. 161; Adamson is paraphrasing *GWL*, p. 237.

38. References to Blake's poetry are to *The Poetry and Prose of William Blake*, ed. Erdman. Further citations, by line number, will appear in the text.

## Chapter 5: Interdetermination, Imagination, Striving: Fichte and Some Principles of Quest Romance

1. A ground-breaking study of Fichte's system of finite imagination is the lucid article by John Sallis, "Fichte and the Problem of System," *Man and World* 9 (1976): 75–90. See esp. pp. 78, 85; the term "circle of finitude," above, is taken from ibid., p. 89. An excellent discussion of system in German idealism and as the culmination of modern Western philosophy is Martin Heidegger, *Schelling's Treatise on the Essence of Human Freedom*, trans. Joan Stambaugh (Athens: Ohio University Press, 1985).

2. See, for example, M. H. Abrams, *The Mirror and the Lamp* (Oxford: Oxford University Press, 1953), pp. 201–13.

3. See Sallis, "Fichte and the Problem of System," pp. 80–81.

4. *Die Philosophie des deutschen Idealismus*, 2d ed. (Berlin: Walter de Gruyter, 1960), p. 59, as translated by Stempel, "Revelation on Mt. Snowdon," p. 372.

5. Hartmann, *Die Philosophie*, p. 59; my translation.

6. I here use *mind* to mean not "psyche," or the subject in psychology, but to mean "unity of consciousness in general."

7. *GWL,* p. 126; Adamson, *Fichte,* p. 168.

8. See Korff, "Kant Romanticized by Fichte," p. 111; Friedrich Hiebel, *Novalis,* 2d ed. rev. (Chapel Hill: University of North Carolina Press, 1954), pp. 49–53. The justification for making such a translation across a culture is to reveal common structures between texts, in the expectation that one text may by its clarity illuminate the other. There need be no clear "influence" between the texts for us to be enlightened by such a procedure. See above, pp. 7–9.

9. A detailed and illuminating explication of these positions will be found in Sallis, "Fichte and the Problem of System," pp. 81–82.

10. Ibid., pp. 87–88; *GWL,* pp. 200–201.

11. Hohler, "Fichte and the Problem of Finitude," p. 22.

12. For a persuasive account of the immense—perhaps decisive—effect of this doctrine on Coleridge (and perhaps, indirectly, on Wordsworth), see Stempel, "Revelation on Mt. Snowdon," pp. 372, 376–78.

13. *GWL,* pp. 193–95; see also Hohler, "Fichte and the Problem of Finitude," p. 22. Fichte's doctrine here elaborates Kant's famous definition of the unifying power of the productive imagination, *CPR,* A100–02.

14. Hohler, "Fichte and the Problem of Finitude," pp. 22–23.

15. The centrality of the circle of finitude in Fichte's system of imagination is defined by Sallis, "Fichte and the Problem of System," pp. 87–89, to whom I am indebted in this paragraph.

16. *Biographia Literaria,* 1:158. Coleridge may not have been entirely ingenuous in his disavowal of Fichte. Stempel believes ("Revelation on Mt. Snowdon," pp. 376–78) that Coleridge meant to disguise the full extent to which the Fichtean imagination was central to his own thought; evidence in the notebooks and letters, he believes, supports this view. Anyone who finds little to smile about in German idealism should read Heinrich Heine's good-natured clowning as he exuberantly misreads Fichte: "'What impudence!' exclaimed the good people, 'this fellow doesn't believe that we exist. . . . Doesn't he at least believe in the existence of his wife? No? And Madame Fichte doesn't mind?'" Heine himself knew better, but still he finds Fichtean philosophy harmless foolishness: "Concerning the History of Religion and Philosophy in Germany," pp. 383ff.

17. "The English Romantics," esp. pp. 22–34.

18. *GWL,* p. 202; John Keats, Letter to Benjamin Bailey, November 22, 1817, in *Letters of John Keats,* ed. Robert Gittings (Oxford: Oxford University Press, 1970), p. 37.

19. Hohler, "Fichte and the Problem of Finitude," p. 21.

20. Søren Kierkegaard, *The Concept of Irony,* trans. Lee M. Capel (Bloomington: Indiana University Press, 1968), pp. 290–91. For a full discussion of the historical development of romantic irony after Fichte, see Ingrid Strohschneider-Kohrs, *Die romantische Ironie in Theorie und Gestaltung* (Tübingen: Max Niemeyer, 1960). Strohschneider-Kohrs discusses Friedrich Schlegel in the context of Fichtean idealism, pp. 24–54; so too does Ernst Behler in his *Klassische Ironie, romantische Ironie, tragische Ironie* (Darmstadt: Wissenschaftliche Buchgesellschaft, 1972), pp. 85–137. Behler also discusses Kierkegaard's essay, pp. 127–33. A recent work in English, drawing on these German sources but extending the discussion of irony to the problem of romantic narrative strategy is Lilian R. Furst, *Fictions of Romantic Irony* (Cambridge, Mass.: Harvard University Press, 1984), esp. pp. 23–36. Anne K. Mellor's

*English Romantic Irony* (Cambridge, Mass.: Harvard University Press, 1980) offers a good discussion of irony in romantic aesthetic theory but is limited by its exclusive dependence on Friedrich Schlegel's formulations.

21. Kierkegaard, *Concept of Irony*, p. 339.

22. Ibid., p. 292.

23. Ibid., pp. 336–42. For Kierkegaard such a "mastered" life would be a life of religious faith; it would, in fact, lie outside—just outside—the borders of idealism and romance.

## Chapter 6: Schelling's Idealism and the Development of Romantic Quest

1. *The Spirit of Modern Philosophy* (New York, 1892), p. 174. Schelling would not have called himself a "romantic," though some of his contemporaries, such as Novalis, would have connected him with such elements in modern literature. In fact, the term "romantic" was originally used by the Schlegels in their lectures on aesthetics (1800–1810) to refer to all modern (postclassical) art, though they at times claimed the superiority of contemporary romantic forms. Certainly, Tieck, Novalis, and others did see contemporary art as a rediscovery of romance, and Madame de Staël enforced the growing European sense that the "new" movement in Germany was a "romantic" one (her *De l'allemagne* appeared in English in 1813). By 1800 there was gathered about Schelling a group of creative thinkers who saw themselves as leading a movement, and the inspiration of that movement was a *soi-disant* pursuit of romance themes in modern literature. The most recent survey of the intricate and various geneses of the "romantic" movement is René Wellek, "Romanticism in Literature," *Dictionary of the History of Ideas*, 1973 ed.

2. Letter of October 21, 1801, in *The Collected Letters of Samuel Taylor Coleridge*, ed. Earl Leslie Griggs, 6 vols. (Oxford: Oxford University Press, 1956–71), 2:768; hereafter cited as *CL*.

3. For a recent account of Schelling's early works, see Joseph Esposito, *Schelling's Idealism and Philosophy of Nature* (Lewisburg: Bucknell University Press, 1977), pp. 31–46.

4. For Fichte, we recall, no such leap to Being could be made from the I = I, which is simply a self-reverting act. See ibid., pp. 37–38.

5. *A History of Modern Philosophy*, trans. B. E. Meyer (New York: Dover, 1955), 2:577–78.

6. *The Ages of the World* (1811), trans. Frederick Bolman, Jr. (New York: Columbia University Press, 1942), p. 230.

7. Coleridge, "The Eolian Harp," in *Coleridge: Poetical Works*, ed. E. H. Coleridge (Oxford: Oxford University Press, 1969), p. 101 (hereafter cited as *PW*); Wordsworth, "Lines Composed Above Tintern Abbey," in *Wordsworth's Poetical Works*, 2:259; Keats, commenting on *Endymion*, 1:777–81, in letter to John Taylor, January 30, 1818, in *Letters of John Keats*, p. 60.

8. Coleridge, "Human Life," *PW*, pp. 425–26; *Don Juan* XV, st. 88, in *Poetical Works of Lord Byron*, ed. E. H. Coleridge (London: John Murray, 1905), p. 996. On Byron's use of a saving irony to liberate himself from the glib resolutions all too common in romantic culture, see Jerome McGann, *Don Juan in Context* (Chicago: University of Chicago Press, 1976), pp. 122–26.

9. April 8, 1825, *CL*, 5:421. He is, however, disingenuous if he means to suggest that his very early reading of Leibniz and certainly Spinoza (before the 1799

trip to Germany) were of little consequence. Thomas McFarland confirms the essential, long-standing elements of Coleridge's early thought, and, examining his youthful struggles with Spinoza, Leibniz, Hartley, Priestly, and Godwin (as well as his later reading of Schelling), concludes that Coleridge's "'development' entails the gradual adjustment of other sequences of thought to his own axiomatic sense of reality." See his *Coleridge and the Pantheist Tradition,* p. 175.

10. Orsini, *Coleridge and German Idealism;* Stempel, "Revelation on Mt. Snowdon."

11. Orsini, *Coleridge and German Idealism,* pp. 214−15; McFarland, *Coleridge,* pp. 147−56.

12. September 30, 1818, *CL,* 4:874.

13. Stempel, "Revelation on Mt. Snowdon," p. 378.

14. February 9, 1801, *CL,* 2:674. It is not impossible, of course, that Coleridge's disdain for Fichte is self-serving here.

15. *Biographia Literaria,* 1:158−60. The moral objection is repeated in a letter to Green, December 13, 1817: "Fichte, in his moral system is but a caricature of Kant; or rather he is a Zeno with the Cawl, Rope, and Sackcloth of a Carthusian Monk" (*CL,* 4:792).

16. *Diaries, Reminiscences, and Correspondence of Henry Crabb Robinson,* ed. Thomas Sadler, 2 vols. (London, 1869), entry for June 3, 1824, 2:273.

17. To J. H. Green, July 3, 1818, *CL,* 4:870 (emphasis added). The situation is complicated, however, because in 1818 Coleridge was working on his *Logic,* which draws freely from Kant, Schelling, and Fichte.

18. *Diaries,* entry for September 10, 1816, 1:343.

19. "English Poetry and German Philosophy in the Age of Wordsworth," 1909; rpt. in his *A Miscellany* (1929; rpt. Freeport, N.Y.: Books for Libraries, 1969), pp. 107, 114−21. M. H. Abrams has also studied the parallel development of thought in English poetry and German philosophy, attributing the sense of a common *Zeitgeist* less to direct influence than to "a common experience in the social, intellectual, and emotional climate of the post-Revolutionary age, and of a grounding in a common body of materials." See *Natural Supernaturalism,* pp. 256, 172ff., 217ff.

20. *Wordsworth and Schelling: A Typological Study of Romanticism* (New Haven: Yale University Press, 1960), p. 9.

21. *Of Human Freedom* (1809), trans. James Gutman (Chicago: Open Court, 1936), pp. 34−35. I have consulted the original—in *Sämmtliche Werke,* 7:359ff.— and have occasionally substituted a word closer to literal meaning where Gutman's translation is loose. By far the best commentary on this important work available in English is Martin Heidegger's *Schelling's Treatise on the Essence of Human Freedom.*

22. Schelling, *Of Human Freedom,* p. 92. (I have in one case altered the original sentence order.)

23. See Esposito, *Schelling's Idealism,* pp. 110−20, for Schelling's view of bodily experience as dependent upon the organization of intelligence.

24. Schelling, *System of Transcendental Idealism,* p. 123. Further references are to this translation.

25. Ibid., p. 12.

26. Michael Vater, Introduction to ibid., p. xxix. Despite the dangers of such generalizations, it may be observed that this bifurcation between unconscious activity—will and striving—and systematic consciousness (*Wissenschaft*) is venerable in German culture, reaching back at least to Leibniz (*nisus* vs. *intellectus*) and culminating, of course, in Freud. Cf. ibid., pp. 90−93.

27. Coleridge, *Biographia*, 1:273, paraphrasing loosely (though in a style clearer here than the original's) Schelling, *System*, p. 27.

28. For a detailed explanation of Schelling's derivation of time and space, and of the problem of sensation, see John Watson, *Schelling's Transcendental Idealism* (Chicago, 1882), pp. 118–28.

29. Coleridge, *The Statesman's Manual* (London, 1816), p. 437; Schelling, *System*, p. 231. Albert Gérard offers an interpretation of "symbol" in Coleridge in which he finds the poet struggling to reconcile "traditional Christian transcendentalism" with romantic pantheism through the mediating activity of symbolism. He does not, however, take into account the radical alteration of the Christian notion of symbolism effected by German idealism. See his *English Romantic Poetry* (Berkeley and Los Angeles: University of California Press, 1968), pp. 57–63.

30. McFarland, *Coleridge*, pp. 152–53. For Schelling's reconciliation of human freedom with systematic idealism, see Heidegger, *Schelling's Treatise*, pp. 62–103.

31. It is this problem which prompts Michael Vater to dub Schelling's idealism "Fatalism . . . thoroughly deterministic" (Introduction to Schelling, *System*, pp. xxx–xxxi). This is not, I believe, true of the Schelling of 1809, however. For history as an evolving world symbolic system, see *System*, pp. 210–12. Schelling here speaks of a God who is a "playwright," but who does not exist independently of the actors who "collaborate" in the production.

32. Schelling, *Of Human Freedom*, p. 19.

33. Ms notes rpt. in *Complete Works of Samuel Taylor Coleridge*, ed. W. Shedd (New York, 1860), 3:691, 693. Coleridge's copy of *Of Human Freedom* is in the British Library.

34. Ms note to Schelling, *System*, p. 29, in the British Library, C.43.b.10.

35. Schelling, *System*, p. 80.

36. Schelling, *Of Human Freedom*, pp. 39, 59.

37. Ibid., p. 41. The quotation from Blake is from *Milton*, pl. 30, in *Poetry and Prose of William Blake*, p. 128.

38. Ms note; rpt. in Coleridge, *Complete Works*, 3:694.

39. *Of Human Freedom*, p. 89. Schelling is repeating one of his earlier aphorisms (cited in *Of Human Freedom*, p. 115): "This is the secret of eternal Love—that which would fain be absolute in itself nonetheless does not regard it as a deprivation to be so in itself but is so only in and with another." This principle, for Schelling, applies to divine and human love. For some writers of the period, such as Blake and Novalis, self-annihilation in spiritual relation reenacted the Christian passion, suggesting a more theological understanding of love than we normally associate with romance of this period.

40. Bloom, "Internalization of Quest Romance," p. 17.

41. Ibid., pp. 23–24.

42. See above, pp. 92–93.

## Chapter 7: *Theory in the* Biographia *and Coleridge's Early Poetry*

1. *A History of Modern Criticism, 1750–1950,* 4 vols. (New Haven: Yale University Press, 1955), 2:152.

2. *Coleridge and the Pantheist Tradition,* pp. 147–56.

3. For a concise and generally reliable statement of Coleridge's development of a Schellingean Imagination, a transcendental power of reconciliation between na-

ture and ideas, see William K. Wimsatt, Jr., and Cleanth Brooks, *Literary Criticism: A Short History* (New York: Vintage, 1957), pp. 392–95. Cf. McFarland, *Coleridge*, pp. 306–10.

4. See, for instance, Fichte, "Second Introduction to the Science of Knowledge," in *GWL*, pp. 32–35. Cf. Schelling, *System*, p. 32: "For one cannot say of the self [*Ich*] that it exists, precisely because it is *being-itself*. The eternal, timeless act of self-consciousness which we call *self*, is that which gives all things existence, and so it itself needs no other being to support it; bearing and supporting itself, rather, it appears objectively as *eternal becoming*, and subjectively as a producing without limit." Cf. Coleridge, *Biographia Literaria*, 1:273.

5. See *Biographia Literaria*, 1:283–94. Cf. Fichte, *GWL*, pp. 240–43; Stempel, "Revelation on Mt. Snowdon," p. 373.

6. McFarland, *Coleridge*, p. 308.

7. Schelling, *System*, pp. 11–12. See above, p. 108.

8. Note in Coleridge's copy of the *System*, in the British Library, C.43.b.10.

9. *Coleridge*, pp. 152–56.

10. This is the pantheist alternative: McFarland explains Coleridge's attraction to, and rejection of, a Spinozan (determinist) cosmos, *Coleridge*, pp. 185–90.

11. *Of Human Freedom*, pp. 34–35, 38.

12. "Imagination, or the *modifying* power in the highest sense of the word, in which I have ventured to oppose it to Fancy, or the *aggregating* power"; letter to Sharp, January 15, 1804, in *CL*, 2:1034.

13. *PW*, p. 190.

14. Coleridge's gloss of 1817 seems an attempt (perhaps a dryly ironic one) to block the maddening sense that no matter how we turn, the Mariner's subjective imagination is creating the dilemma. But the glosser, in his credulous piety, adds only another voice. The psychological center of the poem remains the Mariner's predicament. For a discussion of the glosser's role, see Sara Dyck, "Perspective in the *Rime of the Ancient Mariner*," *SEL* 13 (1973): 591–604. For the view that Coleridge needs the gloss to control his perception of his own work, see Jean-Pierre Mileur, *Vision and Revision: Coleridge's Art of Immanence* (Berkeley and Los Angeles: University of California Press, 1982), pp. 67–72.

15. "The Sad Wisdom of the Mariner," *SP* 61 (1964): 678–79. For Buchan, the Mariner's plight stems from his following the "deceptive pleasures" of the senses, although it is not clear why the Mariner should be punished for this, nor does Buchan show how pleasure is deceptive or damning in the text.

16. "Christian Skepticism in *The Rime of the Ancient Mariner*," in *From Sensibility to Romanticism: Essays Presented to Frederick A. Pottle*, ed. Frederick W. Hilles and Harold Bloom (New York: Oxford University Press, 1965), pp. 444–46.

17. "A Coleridgean Reading of 'The Ancient Mariner,'" *SiR* 4 (Autumn 1964): 90.

18. "The Nightmare World of *The Ancient Mariner*," *SiR* 1 (Summer 1962): 246–47, 251.

19. *Coleridge the Moralist* (Ithaca: Cornell University Press, 1977), pp. 72–73. Lockridge reviews Schelling on pages 64–65. Lockridge's Schellingean terminology explicates Harold Bloom's intuition that the Mariner shoots the bird out of a "desperate assertion of self and a craving for a heightened sense of identity." See Bloom's *The Visionary Company*, rev. ed. (Ithaca: Cornell University Press, 1971), p. 208.

20. Lockridge, *Coleridge*, pp. 73–74.

21. *Coleridge: The Clark Lectures, 1951–52* (London: Rupert Hart-Davis, 1953), pp. 95–96.

22. I am generally in agreement here with Anca Vlasopolos in her brief but illuminating "*The Rime of the Ancient Mariner* as Romantic Quest," *TWC* 10 (1979): 365–69.

23. Lawrence Kramer, "That Other Will: The Daemonic in Coleridge and Wordsworth," *PQ* 58 (1979): 300.

24. Bloom, "Internalization of Quest Romance," in *Romanticism and Consciousness,* pp. 12–13.

25. We may think of those lines that conclude "Dejection: An Ode": "To her may all things live, from pole to pole, / Their life the eddying of her living soul" (*PW,* pp. 362–68, lines 135–36). See also his discussion of "poles" in the posthumously published "Theory of Life," in *Miscellanies Aesthetic and Literary: And the Theory of Life,* ed. T. Ashe (London, 1892), pp. 390–93.

26. Robert Penn Warren, "A Poem of Pure Imagination," in *The Rime of the Ancient Mariner,* by Samuel Taylor Coleridge (New York: Reynal and Hitchcock, 1946), pp. 89–93. Many criticisms have been made of Warren's Procrustean Sun-Moon/Understanding-Imagination equation: see, for instance, House, *Coleridge,* pp. 105–13; Bostetter, "Nightmare World," p. 241.

27. *Notebooks of Samuel Taylor Coleridge,* vol. 1, entry 273.

28. Kramer, "Other Will," p. 307.

29. See above, pp. 88–89. In an entry of about 1811, Coleridge compares the healthy, youthful, and imaginative experience of time to the moving moon: "To the [joyously active youth, time] is as the full moon in a fine breezy October night, driving on amid clouds of all shapes and hues, and blindly shifting colours, like an ostrich in its speed, and yet seems not to have moved at all"; quoted as note to the poem "Time, Real and Imaginary," in *PW,* pp. 419–20.

30. Schelling, *Of Human Freedom,* pp. 40–41. See Lockridge, *Coleridge,* pp. 177–78, on memory: "For Coleridge, the past is ghostly and returns to haunt the sinner; continuity of self is the perpetuation of guilt" (p. 178).

31. Lockridge, *Coleridge,* pp. 187–89. See also the quotation from Schelling, cited in Chapter 6, note 39.

32. *PW,* pp. 100–102.

33. These lines were added in 1818, but they serve to illustrate, rather than modify or contradict, the "What if" of lines 44–47.

34. [MS.R], rpt. in *PW,* pp. 519–21.

35. *PW,* pp. 362–68. The delicate balance beteween the imprisoned and the paradisiacal self had a venerable history, from Milton's Satan to Rousseau; for an excellent study of this literary tradition of self-autonomy that complements our study of the development of post-Kantian idealism, see Garber, *Autonomy of the Self.*

36. *Natural Supernaturalism,* p. 277.

37. For the opposing view that Coleridge is distanced from his despair and has finally recovered strength and imaginative vigor, see Reeve Parker, *Coleridge's Meditative Art* (Ithaca: Cornell University Press, 1975), pp. 196–208.

38. *Of Human Freedom,* p. 41.

39. "Human Life," *PW,* pp. 425–26.

40. *PW,* pp. 240–42.

41. [Lines 20–29], version in *Poetical Register,* rpt. in *PW,* p. 241.

42. House, *Coleridge,* p. 81; Lockridge, *Coleridge,* pp. 274–75; Parker, *Coleridge's Meditative Art,* p. 127. See also Parker's discussion of the poem as "adequate symbology," pp. 131–32.

43. See, for example, Bloom, *Visionary Company*, pp. 202, 204; Abrams, *Natural Supernaturalism*, p. 92. ("Tintern Abbey," incidentally, was written six months after "Frost at Midnight.")

## Chapter 8: Alastor: *The Disabling Vision*

1. *Lectures on Dramatic Art and Poetry*, trans. John Black (London, 1815), pp. 15–17. Shelley read this book aloud to his fellow travelers across northern France in March 1818 (see Newman Ivey White, *Shelley*, 2 vols. [New York: Knopf, 1940], 2:4). It is not impossible that Shelley first read or heard of the book as early as August 1816, since on the twenty-fifth of that month Byron received a copy at Diodati from Madame de Staël, who was staying across the lake at Coppet with Schlegel himself. Shelley visited Byron that week, before leaving for England on the twenty-ninth. See Byron, Letter to Madame de Staël, August 25, 1816; Letter to John Murray, August 28, 1816, in *Byron's Letters and Journals*, ed. Leslie A. Marchand, 12 vols. (Cambridge, Mass.: Harvard University Press, 1973–82), 5:88, 90.

2. *Shelley's Annus Mirabilis* (San Marino: Huntington Library Press, 1975), p. 33. Curran discusses the impact of Schlegel's romantic understanding of the Aeschylean Prometheus upon Shelley, pp. 34–35.

3. Angus Fletcher calls this a technique of allegory and argues that Shelley's "obscurity" actually forces the reader to adopt new visionary or "prophetic" perspectives. See his *Allegory: The Theory of a Symbolic Mode* (Ithaca: Cornell University Press, 1964), p. 277. See also his discussion of irony, pp. 229–33.

4. Madame de Staël [Holstein-Necker], *Germany*, 3 vols. in 2 (New York, 1814), 1:173.

5. Novalis [Friedrich von Hardenberg], *The Disciples at Saïs* (London: Methuen, 1903), p. 102.

6. Staël, *Germany*, 1:176–77. On her knowledge of Kant, Fichte, and Schelling (and Crabb Robinson's judgment of her), see René Wellek, *Immanuel Kant in England* (Princeton: Princeton University Press, 1931), pp. 154–57, 289, n. 45. Although Staël does not specify which doctrine of Schelling's she refers to, she may have in mind such a passage as the following, from a very early (1795) work: "The absolute I is the only Eternal; therefore the finite I, as it strives to become identical with it, must strive for pure eternity. . . . In the finite I there is unity of consciousness, that is, personality. The nonfinite I, however, knows no object at all and therefore no consciousness, no personality. Consequently, the goal of all striving can also be represented as an expansion of personality to infinity, that is, as its own destruction." See his "Of the I as a Principle of Philosophy," in *The Unconditional in Human Knowledge: Four Early Essays*, trans. and ed. Fritz Marti (Lewisburg: Bucknell University Press, 1980), p. 99.

7. *Alastor*, lines 366–69, in *Shelley's Poetry and Prose*, Norton Critical Edition, ed. Donald H. Reiman and Sharon B. Powers (New York: Norton, 1977), p. 79; hereafter cited as *Norton*. Further references to *Alastor* will be to this edition, and line numbers will be inserted in the text.

8. Cf. the Poet's own questioning of his immortal destiny (lines 512–14)—the universe will not tell him "where these living thoughts reside, when stretched / Upon thy flowers my bloodless limbs shall waste / I' the passing wind."

9. "Speculations on Metaphysics," in *The Complete Works of Percy Bysshe Shelley*, ed. Roger Ingpen and Walter Peck, Julian Editions, 10 vols. (London: Ernest Benn, 1930), 7:64; hereafter cited as *Julian*.

10. C. E. Pulos denies that Shelley was a "strict transcendentalist," citing his hostility toward Kant and his skepticism regarding a priori knowledge. But Shelley's knowledge of Kant was limited, and his skepticism was not incompatible with the Fichtean doctrine that the source of knowing is not knowable in itself. Pulos is correct, however, to point out that Shelley was early influenced by Hume's empirical view of the mind and the sources of its ideas. Yet as Shelley matured, he strained against the limitations of this empiricism, in ways Pulos does not acknowledge, to ask to what extent the imagination creates the experience it organizes. See Pulos, *The Deep Truth* (Lincoln: University of Nebraska Press, 1954), pp. 74–77.

On Shelley's lack of acquaintance with Kant, the conclusions of Wellek (*Immanuel Kant in England*, pp. 180–82) remain valid; but see also M. Roxana Klapper, *The German Literary Influence on Shelley* (Salzburg, Austria: Universität Salzburg, 1975), pp. 50–52. It is not impossible that Shelley read of Kant either in the *Encyclopedia Londiniensis* of 1812 or in the generally reliable article by H. J. Richter in the *Morning Chronicle* of March 12, 1814 (see Wellek, *Immanuel Kant in England*, pp. 208–9). Shelley's disdain for Kantian metaphysics (directly expressed in *Peter Bell the Third*, pt. 6, lines 61–75) almost certainly derives from Sir William Drummond's misreading of Kant as a mystical and muddleheaded idealist in *Academical Questions* (London, 1805), pp. 351–81. Yet Shelley remained curious about Kant, and having had difficulty with the Latin translation of the first *Critique*, he ordered a French one in the fall of 1821 (see Klapper, *German Literary Influence*, p. 52). He did not receive it, and we must assume Shelley remained ignorant of Kant.

11. *Prometheus Unbound*, 2.4.116.

12. "Speculations on Metaphysics," *Julian*, 7:342.

13. *GWL*, p. 6. One scholar, Joseph Barrell, has suggested that Shelley's thought struggled against the empiricism of his time and that his idealism approached the transcendentalism of Fichte more closely than that of Plato or Berkeley. I believe this is so; Barrell, however, makes only a passing reference and vague comparison to Fichte. See his *Shelley and the Thought of His Time*, Yale Studies in English, No. 106 (New Haven: Yale University Press, 1947), pp. 187–88, 201–2.

14. "Speculations on Metaphysics," *Julian*, 7:61.

15. Evan Gibson, "*Alastor*: A Reinterpretation," *PMLA* 62 (1947), rpt. in *Norton*, p. 549; John C. Bean, "The Poet Borne Darkly: The Dream-Voyage Allegory in Shelley's *Alastor*," *KSJ* 23 (1974): 63–64; Gerald Enscoe, *Eros and the Romantics* (The Hague: Mouton, 1967), p. 77; Milton Wilson, *Shelley's Later Poetry* (New York: Columbia University Press, 1957), p. 169.

16. *Norton*, p. 69.

17. Ibid., pp. 473–74.

18. Lisa Steinman, "Shelley's Skepticism: Allegory in 'Alastor,'" *ELH* 45 (1978): 262–63. It was a fundamental and common notion in German idealism that, as Schelling put it, "this unconditioned [ego] cannot be sought in any kind of *thing* . . . that which is the principle of all knowledge can in no way become an object of knowledge." See Schelling, *System of Transcendental Idealism* (1800), pp. 26, 27. See also Fichte, *GWL*, pp. 98–99.

19. *Shelley: A Critical Reading* (Baltimore: Johns Hopkins University Press, 1971), p. 47. Further references to this book will be inserted in the text.

20. *Norton*, p. 474. Milton Wilson points out other instances of divergence between *Alastor* and *On Love* (*Shelley's Later Poetry*, pp. 165–66).

21. *Visionary Company*, p. 285. Years after he wrote *Alastor*, Shelley would muse, in a letter to John Gisborne, "I think one is always in love with something or other;

the error, and I confess it is not easy for spirits cased in flesh and blood to avoid it, consists in seeking in a mortal image the likeness of what is perhaps eternal" (Letter of June 18, 1822, in *Letters of Percy Bysshe Shelley*, ed. Frederick Jones, 2 vols. [Oxford: Oxford University Press, 1964], 2:434; hereafter cited as *Letters*).

22. "[Review of *Faust*]," Lecture Fragment (1799?), trans. Cyrus Hamlin; rpt. in J. W. von Goethe, *Faust*, trans. Walter Arndt, ed. Cyrus Hamlin, Norton Critical Edition (New York: Norton, 1976), p. 437.

23. "Quest and Caution: Psychomachy in Shelley's *Alastor*," *English Studies in Canada* 3 (1977): 301.

24. Shelley had read *Werther* enthusiastically, sometime in 1811. It is possible that he had read *Faust* in 1814 or 1815 (as Rossetti dates his prose translations of it), but the weight of evidence is for a later date, perhaps 1821: see Timothy Webb, *The Violet in the Crucible: Shelley and Translation* (Oxford: Oxford University Press, 1976), pp. 144–45. One early critic, John Todhunter, called *Alastor* "Shelley's *Werther*" (*A Study of Shelley* [London, 1880], p. 51). For Shelley's reading of Goethe, see F. W. Stokoe, *German Influence in the English Romantic Period* (1926; rpt. New York: Russell & Russell, 1963), pp. 150–53. For *Faust*, *Werther*, and *Alastor*, M. Roxana Klapper collects what is known of Shelley's reading but throws no new light (beyond Stokoe's work) on the question of dates or specific influences: see *German Influence on Shelley*, pp. 14–16, 24–25.

25. Tetreault, "Quest and Caution," p. 302.

26. "Review of *Faust*," p. 438.

27. Lloyd Abbey, while finding that the poem fails to clarify itself on key points of a confusing dialectic, nevertheless concedes that "the long stretches of natural description are perplexing and ambiguous, but they are also a step toward one central achievement, not only of Shelley's poetry, but of romantic poetry generally, namely, the detailed symbolic portrayal of a private ontology"; see "Shelley's Bridge to Maturity: From 'Alastor' to 'Mont Blanc,'" *Mosaic* 10 (Summer 1977): 81. Lisa Steinman makes a similar point at the conclusion of her article, which takes the entire tale as an allegory presented as a "lesson" to the Narrator ("Shelley's Skepticism," pp. 260, 268). We should recall that the great romantic archetype of the symbolic narrative is *The Rime of the Ancient Mariner*.

28. *Percy Bysshe Shelley* (New York: Twayne, 1969), p. 38.

29. Lines 13–18, in *Julian* 1:204 (the title is Mary Shelley's).

30. Wasserman discusses the ambivalence of this lyric, *Shelley*, pp. 7–8.

31. The Esdaile reading will be found in the transcription of the notebook in *Shelley and His Circle*, ed. Kenneth Neill Cameron (Cambridge, Mass.: Harvard University Press, 1970), 4:969.

32. *Julian*, 6:206–8, 209.

33. See Wasserman, *Shelley*, p. 33; "Unlike nature, man's spirit is not complementarily returned to him as a reflection in water but lures him to pursue it." James C. Evans, in his general study of self-projection in Shelley's poetry, concluded that the Alastor poet undergoes "a daemonic transformation arising from the tunnel vision of single-faceted quest"; see his "Masks of the Poet: A Study of Self-Confrontation in Shelley's Poetry," *KSJ* 24 (1975): 74–75.

34. The "Spirit" may be the "Spirit of sweet love" (line 203) responsible for the original dream. The Dream-Maid's song, we are told, "Like woven sounds of streams and breezes, held / His inmost sense suspended in its web" (lines 155–56), suggesting that the dream represents his mind's need for true relation. In such a reading, the Poet misinterprets his own vision, pursuing it as if it itself were his love and not a

*symbolic* creation of his mind calling on him to seek an earthly, "human love." A reading of the dream along similar lines is suggested by Gerald Enscoe (*Eros and the Romantics*, pp. 73–74). He does not, however, fully appreciate the ambivalence of the "web" metaphor, which suggests that this autoerotic fantasy may well become a trap.

35. William Keach, in his study of the poem's key images, lends support to my conclusion that both Poet and Narrator (the Poet, that is, seen as a creation of the Narrator's limited understanding) share a regressive self-reflexive compulsion; see his "Reflexive Imagery in Shelley," *KSJ* 24 (1975): 50–55.

## Chapter 9: *The Power of Disenchantment: Fichtean Irony and the Creative Imagination in Shelley's "Mont Blanc"*

1. *GWL*, p. 16. Further references to the *Wissenschaftslehre* will be inserted in the text.

2. "Speculations on Metaphysics," *Julian*, 7:342, 62. (The break in the text represents a lacuna in the manuscript. See note to the text in *Julian*, 7:342.)

3. "The Poet as Ironist in 'Mont Blanc' and 'Hymn to Intellectual Beauty,'" *SiR* 14 (1975): 312; see also p. 315.

4. Letter of 22 July, 1816, in *Letters*, 1:497.

5. Lines 49–57, in *Norton*, pp. 89–93.

6. I agree here with E. B. Murray's reading of the word *unfurled*, in "Mont Blanc's Unfurled Veil," *KSJ* 18 (1969): 39–48.

7. Bodleian MS. Shelley adds e.16; this variant is reprinted in Judith Chernaik, *The Lyrics of Shelley* (Cleveland: Press of Case Western Reserve University, 1972), p. 290.

8. The outlines of Fichte's deduction are discussed above, pp. 87–90. A detailed account will be found in Hohler, "Fichte and the Problem of Finitude," pp. 22–23.

9. "Shelley's Bridge to Maturity," pp. 71, 75.

10. A canceled manuscript reading, "where from secret caves / The Fountain of the mind," tends to confirm that the "source" of thought is *within* the spontaneously creative ego; this renders less likely Ronald Bosco's reading of "the source of human thought" as the "universe of things." See his "On the Meaning of Shelley's 'Mont Blanc,'" *Massachusetts Studies in English* 4 (Spring 1974): 40.

In the recently discovered Scrope Davies MS. the mind brings its tribute, more tentatively, "with a sound not all its own." This copy represents a later version than the Swiss tour notebook in the Bodleian Library but differs in several places from the version published in the 1817 *History of a Six Weeks Tour*.

11. Pulos's attempt to read the poem as a statement of Humean skepticism devalues the role of imagination in the face of the unknown, deterministic "power" of Necessity. I do not in the least question Pulos's theory of Shelley's reading of the skeptical tradition in Hume and Drummond. And in a "weak" sense even Kant could be called a skeptic if this means only a belief that the ultimate source of knowledge is unknown. But in "Mont Blanc" Shelley is neither a Humean skeptic (the creative fountains of mind meet a very real, if opaque, boundary—terms not found in Hume) nor a necessitarian. Pulos's reading of the poem must contort all these terms to fit the poem, foundering at last on the final lines, which he reads unpersuasively

as the surrender of imaginative freedom to the (hoped-for) benevolence of Necessity. See Pulos, *Deep Truth*, pp. 64—66. On receptivity and spontaneity as the root terms of transcendental idealism, see above, pp. 52—57.

12. This is the argument of Charles H. Vivian, in his classic reading of the poem. "The One 'Mont Blanc,'" *KSJ* 4 (1955); rpt. in *Norton*, pp. 569—79. The notebook version is from Bodleian MS. Shelley adds. e.16, p. 3.

13. Chernaik, *Lyrics of Shelley*, p. 42. A similar reading is provided by Vivian, in *Norton*, p. 575.

14. McNiece, "The Poet as Ironist," p. 315.

15. Chernaik's explanation of this difficult line (79) is surely correct (*Lyrics of Shelley*, pp. 43—44 and p. 59, n. 10). The Scrope Davies MS. reads "In such a faith."

16. Bosco, "On the Meaning of Shelley's 'Mont Blanc,'" p. 50. The word "model" is apt here: in modern physics a "model" is formulated of what cannot be imaged, like an electron, to explain a thing through its processes, parameters, and effects on other things.

## *Chapter 10: Encountering the Actual: Childe Harold and the Limits of Idealism*

1. *Childe Harold's Pilgrimage*, 3, 55—56, in *Poetical Works of Lord Byron*, p. 193. All further references to Byron's poetry are to this text, hereafter cited as *BPW*. References to *Childe Harold's Pilgrimage* are to canto and stanza number.

2. *Concept of Irony*, pp. 241, 292, 337. (I have preferred to translate *Tilvaerelse* on page 337 as "being" rather than adopt Capel's "existence." Capel discusses this problem on page 431.)

3. For all their thematic similarities, it is true that *Faust* and *Manfred* are very different plays in structure, tone, and aim. I emphasize only their common place in the European romantic narrative of self-assertion and autonomy. The matter of Byron's actual indebtedness to Goethe has been much discussed (beginning, of course, with Byron and Goethe themselves). The classic comparison of *Manfred* and *Faust* is Samuel Chew's, in *The Dramas of Lord Byron: A Critical Study* (Göttingen: Vendenhoeck & Ruprecht, 1915), pp. 78—83, 174—78. Byron wrote the play only a few weeks after hearing at least part of *Faust* translated for him by Monk Lewis, at Diodati in 1816. If Byron knew little of the text of *Faust*, for all his disclaimers he could not but have been aware of the "Faustian" context of his poem. For Goethe's review of *Manfred*, and Byron's view of Goethe and *Faust*, see the lively presentation of the two men's literary relations in E. H. Butler's *Byron and Goethe* (London: Bowes and Bowes, 1956), esp. pp. 58—61, 74—75, 91—93.

4. Goethe's letter to Graf Brül, stage producer of *Faust I*, quoted in Eudo Mason, "The Erdgeist and Mephisto," in his *Goethe's Faust: Its Genesis and Purport* (Berkeley: University of California Press, 1967); rpt. in *Faust*, trans. W. Arndt, ed. Cyrus Hamlin (New York: Norton, 1976), p. 499. For the "comic rhythm" see David Eggenschwiller, "The Tragic and Comic Rhythms of *Manfred*," *SiR* 13 (1974): 63—77. The Erdgeist scene in *Faust* is lines 481—513.

5. *Byron and His Fictions* (Detroit: Wayne State University Press, 1978), pp. 74, 76—83.

6. Kierkegaard, *Concept of Irony*, p. 241.

7. *Fiery Dust: Byron's Poetic Development* (Chicago: University of Chicago Press,

1968), p. 92; cf. pp. 136–38. I am indebted, as all future comment on the poem must be, both to McGann's readings and to his overarching conception of the poem. For his analysis of the poem's composition, see pages 94–138.

8. Peter Thorslev speculates briefly on the relationship of Byron's heroes generally to the later development of the existential hero's commitment to radical freedom; see *The Byronic Hero: Types and Prototypes* (Minneapolis: University of Minnesota Press, 1962), pp. 197–99. By "existential" here I refer only to the nature of the narrator's ultimate assertion; I am suspicious of Robert Gleckner's broader implication that the poem as a whole must be read as an early example of an unredeemed modern wasteland, a nihilistic vision relieved only by the narrator's stoic endurance. He presents this judgment—which he does not alter in the course of his extensive analysis—in *Byron and the Ruins of Paradise* (Baltimore: Johns Hopkins University Press, 1967), pp. 43–44.

9. Byron's remark is quoted by Thomas Medwin, *Conversations of Lord Byron*, ed. Ernest J. Lovell (Princeton: Princeton University Press, 1966), p. 194. For the circumstances of Canto Three's composition, see McGann, *Fiery Dust*, pp. 112–18.

10. Letter of January 28, 1817, in *Byron's Letters and Journals*, 5:165. Hereafter cited as *LJ*.

11. *The Blind Man Traces the Circle: On the Patterns and Philosophy of Byron's Poetry* (Princeton: Princeton University Press, 1969), p. 40.

12. For Shelley's influence on the third canto, see Charles Robinson, *Shelley and Byron: The Snake and the Eagle Wreathed in Fight* (Baltimore: Johns Hopkins University Press, 1976), pp. 17–27. (Robinson does not discuss in this connection Byron's recent reading of *Alastor*, but does devote his third chapter to a comparison of *Alastor* and *Manfred*.)

13. McGann, *Fiery Dust*, p. 310; see also pages 119–20, for the change effected on the original manuscript poem by the added stanzas.

14. Cooke, *Blind Man*, p. 59.

15. Journal entry of September 29, 1816, *LJ*, 5:104–5. The same day, he wrote to Murray that "the feelings with which much of [Canto Three] was written need not be envied me" (*LJ*, 5:105).

16. Gleckner (*Byron and the Ruins of Paradise*, p. 43), takes a somewhat different view. Harold, he believes, represents archetypally exiled modern man, and the poem's narrator comes slowly to adopt his despair. Another voice, "the poet," escapes this despair in some ways, but only because he is able to create poetry amid the scenes of unredeemed wasteland (cf. pp. 82–84). Gleckner's is a dark view of the poem, allowing no regenerative vision to the poet at the quest's end.

17. Gleckner (ibid., pp. 53–56) attempts to distinguish a third voice, a narrator modeled upon Byron's companion Hobhouse, a morally condemnatory *homme moyen sensuel*. But Gleckner takes too seriously Byron's early condemning tone and not seriously enough his later very real, personal revulsion at the horrors of brutalized life in Spain and Portugal during the Peninsular War. No purpose seems to be served here by separating a particular narrative tone or pose from the "I" who is the poem's creator.

18. See Andrew Rutherford, *Byron: A Critical Study* (Stanford: Stanford University Press, 1961): "We may say then that Childe Harold, the *blasé* Cain-like Wanderer, is a projection of the author's moods of melancholy, loneliness, boredom, and disillusion, and that the narrator mirrors his more normal and attractive personality" (p. 31).

19. Byron himself knew this, as evidenced by his often-quoted assertion, to Dallas, in a letter of October 31, 1811, "I by no means intend to identify myself with Harold, but to deny all connection with him. If in parts I may be thought to have drawn from myself, believe me it is but in parts, and I shall not even own to that. . . . I would not be such a fellow as I have made my hero for the world" (*LJ*, 2: 122).

But Harold *was* a part of him. He is less than candid when he asserts in his Preface to the Fourth (September 1812) Edition that Harold is meant "to show, that early perversion of mind and morals leads to satiety of past pleasures and disappointment in new ones, and that even the beauties of nature . . . are lost on a soul so constituted, or rather misdirected" (*PW*, p. 145). Aside from his posture here of moral solemnity, both the narrator of *Childe Harold* and the author of the 1816 Journal (above, n. 15) often saw himself as just such a misdirected soul.

20. Quoted by Samuel Chew, ed., *Lord Byron: Childe Harold's Pilgrimage and Other Romantic Poems* (New York: Odyssey Press, 1936), p. 27n.

21. For this "spot of time" syndrome in Wordsworth, see the persuasive discussion by Geoffrey Hartman, *Wordsworth's Poetry*, pp. 84–89.

22. *BPW*, p. 205.

23. *Renaissance and Mannerist Art* (New York: Harry Abrams, 1968), p. 68.

24. McGann, *Fiery Dust*, pp. 90–92.

25. Cf. ibid., p. 137: "It is from this principle of absolute self-possession that he is able to draw his own objectivity toward the sequence of events that constitute Life, and his own life in particular. At the end of his pilgrimage he is freed completely from the self-lacerating passions which are the source of his anxiety and exhaustion alike."

26. Ibid., pp. 38–39.

27. *GWL*, pp. 98–99. As before, I have preferred "ego" to Heath's "self" as a translation of Fichte's *Ich*.

28. *A History of Western Philosophy* (New York: Simon & Schuster, 1945), p. 775.

29. "*Don Juan:* The Perspective of Satire," in Kernan, *The Plot of Satire* (New Haven: Yale University Press, 1965); rpt. in *Romanticism and Consciousness*, ed. Harold Bloom, p. 363.

30. *Excesses: Eros and Culture* (Albany: State University of New York Press, 1983), pp. 149, 153–54. Lingis's image of excess, the solar economy, is from Nietzsche's *The Gay Science.*

31. For an excellent discussion of this satiric mobility, of the narrator's making and unmaking of a tale in response to the "chaos" of life, see Garber, "Satire and the Making of Selves," esp. pp. 852–53, 862–69.

32. McGann, *Fiery Dust*, p. 82.

33. See, for example, Nietzsche, "'Reason' in Philosophy," in *Twilight of the Idols;* in *The Portable Nietzsche*, trans. Walter Kaufmann (New York: Viking, 1954), pp. 480–84.

34. Michael Vater, Introduction to Schelling, *System of Transcendental Idealism*, p. xxix.

35. The growing acceptance of finitude as constitutive of human nature is often seen as the key to the transformation of idealism into existentialism: my position here owes much to that important 1928 work that attempts to reconcile idealism with the phenomenology of Husserl, Max Scheler, *Man's Place in Nature*, trans. Hans Meyerhoff (Boston: Beacon, 1961). Most important to this position (especially for Heidegger) is the rejection of the Kantian doctrine of the ideality of time and

space, a linchpin of any idealist position. (Heidegger makes his intricate and difficult attack on Kant in *Kant and the Problem of Metaphysics,* see esp. pp. 178–208.)

36. Robinson, *Shelley and Byron,* p. 70. Robinson insists that Byron lacked "Shelley's faith in the imaginatively unified mind or center which could enlarge and purify the circumference of experience" (p. 8). This is true only if Robinson would insist on "purification" as essential to such a faith in the mind's power. Robinson's view of Byron is—as I hope my own reading has shown—restricted by his demand that what would count as imaginative strength and psychological health for Shelley must count equally for Byron. Robinson's account of Shelley's complex response to *Childe Harold's Pilgrimage* (pp. 68–80) must be acknowledged, however, as definitive and essential to further scholarly discussion.

37. In *Shelley's Poetry and Prose,* p. 210.

# Bibliography

Aarsleff, Hans. "Wordsworth, Language, and Romanticism." *EIC* 30 (1980): 215–26.

Abbey, Lloyd. "Shelley's Bridge to Maturity: From 'Alastor' to 'Mont Blanc.'" *Mosaic* 10 (Summer 1977): 69–84.

Abrams, M. H. *The Mirror and the Lamp*. Oxford: Oxford University Press, 1953.

————. *Natural Supernaturalism*. New York: Norton, 1971.

Adamson, Robert. *Fichte*. Edinburgh: Blackwood's, 1903.

Barrell, Joseph. *Shelley and the Thought of His Time*. Yale Studies in English, No. 106. New Haven: Yale University Press, 1947.

Bean, John C. "The Poet Borne Darkly: The Dream-Voyage Allegory in Shelley's *Alastor*." *KSJ* 23 (1974): 60–76.

Behler, Ernst. *Klassische Ironie, romantische Ironie, tragische Ironie*. Darmstadt: Wissenschaftliche Buchgesellschaft, 1972.

Berkeley, George. *A Treatise Concerning the Principles of Human Knowledge* (1710). In *The Empiricists*. Garden City, N.Y.: Anchor, 1974.

Biran, Maine de. *Essai sur les fondements de la psychologie*. Paris, 1812.

Blake, William. *The Poetry and Prose of William Blake*. Edited by David Erdman. Garden City, N.Y.: Anchor-Doubleday, 1965.

Bloom, Harold. "The Internalization of Quest Romance." *Yale Review* 58 (Summer 1969): Reprinted in *Romanticism and Consciousness*, edited by Harold Bloom, pp. 3–23. New York: Norton, 1970.

————. *The Visionary Company: A Reading of English Romantic Poetry*. Rev. ed. Ithaca: Cornell University Press, 1971.

Bosco, Ronald. "On the Meaning of Shelley's 'Mont Blanc.'" *Massachusetts Studies in English* 4 (Spring 1974): 37–55.

Bostetter, Edward E. "The Nightmare World of *The Ancient Mariner*." *SiR* 1 (Summer 1962): 241–54.

————. *The Romantic Ventriloquists*. Rev. ed. Seattle: University of Washington Press, 1975.

Boulger, James D. "Christian Skepticism in *The Rime of the Ancient Mariner*." In *From Sensibility to Romanticism: Essays Presented to Frederick A. Pottle*, edited by Frederick W. Hilles and Harold Bloom, pp. 439–52. New York: Oxford University Press, 1965.

Bradley, A. C. "English Poetry and German Philosophy in the Age of Wordsworth" (1909). Reprinted in his *A Miscellany*. 1929. Reprint. Freeport, N.Y.: Books for Libraries, 1969.

Brown, Robert, ed. *Between Hume and Mill: An Anthology of British Philosophy, 1749–1843*. New York: Random House, 1970.

Buchan, A. M. "The Sad Wisdom of the Mariner." *SP* 61 (1964): 669–88.

Butler, E. H. *Byron and Goethe*. London: Bowes and Bowes, 1956.

Byron, George Gordon, Lord. *Byron's Letters and Journals*, Edited by Leslie Marchand. 12 vols. Cambridge, Mass.: Harvard University Press, 1973–82.

————. *Poetical Works of Lord Byron*. Edited by E. H. Coleridge. London: John Murray, 1905.

Caldwell, James. *John Keats' Fancy: The Effect on Keats of the Psychology of His Day*. Ithaca: Cornell University Press, 1945.

Cameron, Kenneth Neill, ed. *Shelley and His Circle*. Vol. 4. Cambridge, Mass.: Harvard University Press, 1970.

Cassirer, Ernst. "Kant and the Problem of Metaphysics: Remarks on Martin Heidegger's Interpretation of Kant." Translated by Moltke Gram. In *Kant: Disputed Questions*, edited by Moltke S. Gram, pp. 131–57. Chicago: Quadrangle Books, 1967.

————. *Language and Myth*. Translated by Suzanne Langer. New York: Dover, 1953.

Chayes, Irene. "A Coleridgean Reading of 'The Ancient Mariner.'" *SiR* 4 (Autumn 1964): 81–103.

Chernaik, Judith. *The Lyrics of Shelley*. Cleveland: Press of Case Western Reserve University, 1972.

Chew, Samuel. *The Dramas of Lord Byron: A Critical Study*. Göttinger: Vendenhoeck & Ruprecht, 1915.

————, ed. *Lord Byron: Childe Harold's Pilgrimage and Other Romantic Poems*. New York: Odyssey Press, 1936.

Coleridge, Samuel Taylor. *Biographia Literaria*. Edited by J. Shawcross. 2 vols. 1907. Reprint. Oxford: Oxford University Press, 1954.

————. *Biographia Literaria*. Edited by James Engell and W. Jackson Bate.

Vol. 7 of *The Collected Works of Samuel Taylor Coleridge*. 2 vols. Princeton: Princeton University Press, 1983.

———. *Coleridge: Poetical Works*. Edited by E. H. Coleridge. Oxford: Oxford University Press, 1969.

———. *The Collected Letters of Samuel Taylor Coleridge*. 6 vols. Edited by Earl L. Griggs. Oxford: Oxford University Press, 1956.

———. *Complete Works of Samuel Taylor Coleridge*. Edited by William Shedd. 7 vols. New York, 1860.

———. *The Friend*. Edited by Barbara Rooke. Vol. 4 of *The Collected Works of Samuel Taylor Coleridge*. 2 vols. Princeton: Princeton University Press, 1969.

———. *Miscellanies Aesthetic and Literary: And the Theory of Life*. Edited by T. Ashe. London, 1892.

———. *The Notebooks of Samuel Taylor Coleridge*. Edited by Kathleen Coburn. 3 vols. New York: Bollingen Foundation, 1957–61; Princeton: Princeton University Press, 1961–76.

———. *The Statesman's Manual*. London, 1816.

Cooke, Michael. *The Blind Man Traces the Circle: On the Patterns and Philosophy of Byron's Poetry*. Princeton: Princeton University Press, 1969.

Copleston, Frederick. *Fichte to Hegel*. Vol. 7, Pt. 1 of *A History of Philosophy*. Garden City, N.Y.: Doubleday, 1965.

Curran, Stuart. *Shelley's Annus Mirabilis*. San Marino: Huntington Library Press, 1975.

Drummond, Sir William. *Academical Questions*. London, 1805.

Dyck, Sara. "Perspective in the Rime of the Ancient Mariner." *SEL* 13 (1973): 591–604.

Eggenschwiller, David. "The Tragic and Comic Rhythms of *Manfred*." *SiR* 13 (1974): 63–77.

Einstein, Albert. *Relativity: The Special and General Theory*. Translated by Robert Lawson. 15th ed. 1952. Reprint. New York: Crown, 1961.

Engell, James. *The Creative Imagination*. Cambridge, Mass.: Harvard University Press, 1982.

Enscoe, Gerald. *Eros and the Romantics*. The Hague: Mouton, 1967.

Erdmann, J. E. *A History of Philosophy*. 3 vols. Translated by W. S. Hough from the 3d ed. New York, 1890.

Esposito, Joseph. *Schelling's Idealism and Philosophy of Nature*. Lewisburg: Bucknell University Press, 1977.

Evans, James C. "Masks of the Poet: A Study of Self-Confrontation in Shelley's Poetry." *KSJ* 24 (1975): 70–88.

Ewing, A. C. *A Short Commentary on Kant's "Critique of Pure Reason."* Chicago: University of Chicago Press, 1938.

Fairchild, H. N. "Hartley, Pistorius, and Coleridge." *PMLA* 62 (1947): 1010–21.

Fichte, J. G. *The Science of Knowledge (Wissenschaftslehre), with the First and Second Introductions*. Translated and edited by Peter Heath and John Lachs. New York: Appleton-Century-Crofts, 1970.

Findlay, J. N. *The Philosophy of Hegel: An Introduction and Re-Examination*. 1958. Reprint. New York: Collier, 1962.

Fletcher, Angus. *Allegory: The Theory of a Symbolic Mode*. Ithaca: Cornell University Press, 1964.

Forst, Graham Nicol. "Kant's 'Copernican Revolution' in Philosophy and the Romantic Revolution in English Literature." Ph.D. dissertation, University of British Columbia, 1970.

Freud, Sigmund. "The Relation of the Poet to Day-Dreaming" (1908). Reprinted in Freud, *On Creativity and the Unconscious*. Edited by Benjamin Nelson. New York: Harper & Row, 1958.

————. "Sexuality and the Aetiology of the Neuroses" (1905). Reprinted in *Freud: Sexuality and the Psychology of Love*, edited by Philip Rieff. New York: Macmillan, 1963.

Frye, Northrop. *The Secular Scripture*. Cambridge, Mass.: Harvard University Press, 1976.

Furst, Lilian R. *Fictions of Romantic Irony*. Cambridge, Mass.: Harvard University Press, 1984.

Garber, Frederick. *The Autonomy of the Self from Richardson to Huysmans*. Princeton: Princeton University Press, 1982.

————. "Satire and the Making of Selves." In *Literary Theory and Criticism: Festschrift in Honor of René Wellek*, edited by Joseph Strelka, pp. 849–70. Bern, Switzerland: Peter Lang, 1984.

Gérard, Albert. *English Romantic Poetry*. Berkeley and Los Angeles: University of California Press, 1968.

Gibson, Evan. "*Alastor*: A Reinterpretation." *PMLA* 62 (1947). Reprinted in *Shelley's Poetry and Prose*, edited by Donald H. Reiman and Sharon B. Powers, pp. 545–68. Norton Critical Edition. New York: Norton, 1977.

Girndt, Helmut. *Die Differenz des Fichteschen und Hegelschen Systems in der Hegelschen "Differenzschrift."* Bonn: Bouvier, 1965.

Gleckner, Robert. *Byron and the Ruins of Paradise*. Baltimore: Johns Hopkins University Press, 1967.

Goethe, J. W. von. *Faust*. Translated by Walter Kaufmann. Garden City, N.Y.: Anchor, 1963.

Griswold, Charles. "Fichte's Modification of Kant's Transcendental Idealism in the *Wissenschaftslehre* of 1794 and Introductions of 1797." *Auslegung* 4 (Fall 1977): 133–49.

Grob, Alan. *The Philosophic Mind: A Study of Wordsworth's Poetry and Thought, 1797–1805*. Columbus: Ohio State University Press, 1973.

Hall, Spencer. "Shelley's 'Mont Blanc.'" *SP* 70 (1973): 199–221.

Hartley, David. *Observations on Man*. London, 1749. Reprinted in *Backgrounds of Romanticism: English Philosophical Prose of the Eighteenth Century*, edited by Leonard M. Trawick. Bloomington: Indiana University Press, 1969.

Hartman, Geoffrey. "Romanticism and 'Anti-Self-Consciousness.'" *Centennial*

*Review* 6 (Autumn 1962). Revised and reprinted in *Romanticism and Consciousness*, edited by Harold Bloom. New York: Norton, 1970.

————. *Wordsworth's Poetry, 1784–1814.* New Haven: Yale University Press, 1971.

Hartmann, Eduard von. *Philosophy of the Unconscious.* Translated by W. C. Copeland. 9th ed. 3 vols. London, 1884.

Hartmann, Nicolai. *Die Philosophie des deutschen Idealismus.* 2d ed. Berlin: Walter de Gruyter, 1960.

Hegel, G. W. F. *The Difference between the Fichtean and Schellingean Systems of Philosophy (The Differenzschrift).* Translated by J. P. Surber. Reseda, Calif.: Ridgeview, 1978.

————. *The Logic of Hegel.* Translated by William Wallace. 2d ed. Oxford: Oxford University Press, 1904.

————. *Introduction to Aesthetics.* Translated by T. M. Knox. Oxford: Oxford University Press, 1979.

Heidegger, Martin. *Kant and the Problem of Metaphysics.* Translated by J. C. Churchill. 1929. Reprint. Bloomington: Indiana University Press, 1962.

————. *Nietzsche.* Translated by David Farrell Krell. 2 vols. San Francisco: Harper & Row, 1979–80.

————. *Schelling's Treatise on the Essence of Human Freedom.* Translated by Joan Stambaugh. Athens: Ohio University Press, 1985.

Heimsoeth, Heinz. "Metaphysical Motives in the Development of Critical Idealism." Translated by Moltke S. Gram. In *Kant: Disputed Questions,* edited by Moltke S. Gram, pp. 148–99. Chicago: Quadrangle Books, 1967.

Heine, Heinrich. "Concerning the History of Religion and Philosophy in Germany" (1835). In *Selected Works of Heinrich Heine.* Translated and edited by Helen Mustard, pp. 274–420. New York: Vintage, 1973.

Hiebel, Friedrich. *Novalis.* 2d ed., rev. Chapel Hill: University of North Carolina Press, 1954.

Hirsch, E. D. *Wordsworth and Schelling: A Typological Study of Romanticism.* New Haven: Yale University Press, 1960.

Höffding, Harald. *A History of Modern Philosophy.* Vol. 2. Translated by B. E. Meyer. New York: Dover, 1955.

Hohler, Thomas P. "Fichte and the Problem of Finitude." *Southwestern Journal of Philosophy* 7 (1976): 15–33.

House, Humphry. *Coleridge: The Clark Lectures, 1951–52.* London: Rupert Hart-Davis, 1953.

Jacobi, F. H. *Werke.* Edited by Friedrich Roth. 7 vols. Leipzig, 1812–15.

Jammer, Max. *Concepts of Space: The History of the Theory of Space in Philosophy.* Cambridge, Mass.: Harvard University Press, 1954.

Kant, Immanuel. *The Critique of Pure Reason.* Translated by Norman Kemp Smith. 2d ed. London: Macmillan, 1933.

————. *Kant's Inaugural Dissertation.* Translated by John Handyside. Chicago: Open Court, 1929.

————. *Immanuel Kant's Werke.* Edited by Ernst Cassirer. 11 vols. Berlin: B. Cassirer, 1912–22.

Keach, William. "Reflexive Imagery in Shelley." *KSJ* 24 (1975): 49–69.

Keats, John. *Letters of John Keats.* Edited by Robert Gittings. Oxford: Oxford University Press, 1970.

Kemp Smith, Norman. *A Commentary to Kant's "Critique of Pure Reason."* 2d ed., rev. New York: Macmillan, 1923.

Kernan, Alvin. "*Don Juan:* The Perspective of Satire." In Kernan, *The Plot of Satire.* New Haven: Yale University Press, 1965. Reprinted in *Romanticism and Consciousness,* edited by Harold Bloom, pp. 343–73. New York: Norton, 1970.

Kierkegaard, Søren. *The Concept of Irony.* Translated by Lee M. Capel. Bloomington: Indiana University Press, 1968.

Klapper, M. Roxana. *The German Influence on Shelley.* Salzburg Studies in English Literature, No. 43. Salzburg, Austria: Universität Salzburg, 1975.

Korff, Hermann. "Kant Romanticized by Fichte." In Koff, *Geist der Goethezeit.* Vol. 3. Leipzig: J. J. Weber, 1923–57. Reprinted in *The Romantic Movement,* translated and edited by Antony Thorlby, pp. 107–11. New York: Barnes & Noble, 1966.

Körner, Stephan. *Kant.* Baltimore: Penguin Books, 1955.

Kramer, Lawrence. "That Other Will: The Daemonic in Coleridge." *PQ* 58 (1979): 298–320.

Kroner, Richard. *Kant's Weltanschauung.* Translated by John E. Smith, with Kroner's revisions. 1914. Reprint. Chicago: University of Chicago Press, 1956.

Laing, R. D. *The Divided Self.* New York: Random House, 1969.

Leibniz, G. W. von. *Nouveaux essais sur l'entendement humain.* Translated by G. M. Duncan. In *Leibniz: Selections,* edited by Philip P. Weiner. New York: Scribner's, 1951.

Lingis, Alphonso. *Excesses: Eros and Culture.* Albany: State University of New York Press, 1983.

Locke, John. *An Essay Concerning Human Understanding.* Edited by John Yolton from the 5th ed. (1706). 2 vols. London: Dent, 1965.

Lockridge, Laurence S. *Coleridge the Moralist.* Ithaca: Cornell University Press, 1977.

Lovejoy, A. O. *Essays in the History of Ideas.* Baltimore: Johns Hopkins University Press, 1972.

————. *The Reason, the Understanding, and Time.* Baltimore: Johns Hopkins University Press, 1961.

McFarland, Thomas. *Coleridge and the Pantheist Tradition.* Oxford: Oxford University Press, 1969.

————. "The Origin of Coleridge's Theory of Secondary Imagination." In *New Perspectives on Coleridge and Wordsworth: Selected Papers from the English Institute,* edited by Geoffrey Hartman, pp. 195–246. New York: Columbia University Press, 1972.

————. *Originality and Imagination.* Baltimore: Johns Hopkins University Press, 1985.

McGann, Jerome. *Don Juan in Context.* Chicago: University of Chicago Press, 1976.

————. *Fiery Dust: Byron's Poetic Development.* Chicago: University of Chicago Press, 1968.

McNiece, Gerald. "The Poet as Ironist in 'Mont Blanc' and 'Hymn to Intellectual Beauty.'" *SiR* 14 (1975): 311–36.

Mach, Ernst. *The Science of Mechanics.* Translated by T. J. McCormick. Chicago, 1893.

Man, Paul de. "Intentional Structure of the Romantic Image." *Revue internationale de Philosophie* 51 (1960). Reprinted in *Romanticism and Consciousness,* edited by Harold Bloom. New York: Norton, 1970.

Manning, Peter. *Byron and His Fictions.* Detroit: Wayne State University Press, 1978.

Martin, Gottfried. *Kant's Metaphysics and Theory of Science.* Translated by P. G. Lucas. Manchester: Manchester University Press, 1955.

————. *Leibniz: Logic and Metaphysics.* Translated by K. J. Northcott and P. G. Lucas. Manchester: Manchester University Press, 1964.

Mason, Eudo. "The Erdgeist and Mephisto." In his *Goethe's Faust: Its Genesis and Purport.* Berkeley: University of California Press, 1967. Reprinted in *Faust* by J. W. von Goethe. Translated by W. Arndt. Edited by Cyrus Hamlin. New York: Norton, 1976.

Medwin, Thomas. *Conversations of Lord Byron.* Edited by Ernest J. Lovell. Princeton: Princeton University Press, 1966.

Mellor, Anne K. *English Romantic Irony.* Cambridge, Mass.: Harvard University Press, 1980.

Mertz, J. T. *A History of European Thought in the Nineteenth Century.* Vol. 1. London, 1896.

Mileur, Jean-Pierre. *Vision and Revision: Coleridge's Art of Immanence.* Berkeley and Los Angeles: University of California Press, 1982.

Murray, E. B. "Mont Blanc's Unfurled Veil." *KSJ* 18 (1969): 39–48.

Newton, Sir Isaac. *Mathematical Principles of Natural Philosophy.* Translated by Andrew Motte. Edited and revised by Florian Cajori. Berkeley and Los Angeles: University of California Press, 1934.

Nidecker, Henri. "Notes marginales de S. T. Coleridge en marge de Schelling." *Revue de littérature comparée* 7 (1927): 736–47.

Nietzsche, Friedrich. "'Reason' in Philosophy." In *Twilight of the Idols* in *The Portable Nietzsche.* Translated by Walter Kaufmann. New York: Viking, 1954.

————. *Werke.* 20 vols. Leipzig: Kröner, 1911.

Northrup, F. S. C. "Liebniz's Theory of Space." *JHI* 7 (1946): 422–46.

Novalis [Friedrich von Hardenberg]. *The Disciples at Sais.* London: Methuen, 1903.

Orsini, Gian. *Coleridge and German Idealism.* Carbondale: Southern Illinois University Press, 1969.

Parker, Reeve. *Coleridge's Meditative Art.* Ithaca: Cornell University Press, 1975.

Paton, H. J. "The Key to Kant's Deduction of the Categories." *Mind* 40 (1931): 310–29.

Piper, H. W. "The Pantheistic Sources of Coleridge's Early Poetry." *JHI* 20 (1959): 47–59.

Poulet, George. "Timelessness and Romanticism." *JHI* 15 (1954): 3–22.

Pulos, C. E. *The Deep Truth.* Lincoln: University of Nebraska Press, 1954.

Rader, Melvin. *Wordsworth: A Philosophical Approach.* Oxford: Clarendon Press, 1967.

Rajan, Tilottama. *Dark Interpreter: The Discourse of Romanticism.* Ithaca: Cornell University Press, 1980.

Reiman, Donald. *Percy Bysshe Shelley.* New York: Twayne, 1969.

Robinson, Charles. *Shelley and Byron: The Snake and the Eagle Wreathed in Fight.* Baltimore: Johns Hopkins University Press, 1976.

Robinson, Henry Crabb. *Diaries, Reminiscences, and Correspondence of Henry Crabb Robinson.* Edited by Thomas Sadler. 2 vols. London, 1869.

Rosen, Stanley. *G. W. F. Hegel.* New Haven: Yale University Press, 1974.

Royce, Josiah. *The Spirit of Modern Philosophy.* New York, 1892.

Russell, Bertrand. *A History of Western Philosophy.* New York: Simon & Schuster, 1945.

Rutherford, Andrew. *Byron: A Critical Study.* Stanford: Stanford University Press, 1961.

Sallis, John. "Fichte and the Problem of System." *Man and World* 9 (1976): 75–90.

Scheler, Max. *Man's Place in Nature.* Translated by Hans Meyerhoff. Boston: Beacon, 1961.

Schelling, F. W. J. *The Ages of the World* (1811). Translated by Frederick Bolman, Jr. New York: Columbia University Press, 1942.

———. *Of Human Freedom* (1809). Translated by James Gutmann. Chicago: Open Court, 1936.

———. "Of the I as Principle of Philosophy." In Schelling, *The Unconditional in Human Knowledge: Four Early Essays.* Translated by Fritz Marti. Lewisburg: Bucknell University Press, 1980.

———. ["Review of *Faust*"]. Translated by Cyrus Hamlin. In J. W. von Goethe, *Faust.* Translated by Walter Arndt. Edited by Cyrus Hamlin. Norton Critical Edition. New York: Norton, 1976.

———. *Schellings Sämmtliche Werke.* Vols. 3 and 7. Edited by K. F. A. Schelling. Stuttgart and Augsburg, 1856–61.

———. *System of Transcendental Idealism* (1800). Translated by Peter Heath. Introduction by Michael Vater. Charlottesville: University Press of Virginia, 1978.

Schlegel, August W. *Lectures on Dramatic Art and Poetry.* Translated by John Black. London, 1815.

Schrickx, W. "Unpublished Coleridge Marginalia on Fichte." *Studia Germania Gandensia* 3 (1961): 171–208.

Schumann, Karl. *Die Grundlage der Wissenschaftslehre in irhem Umrisse.* The Hague: Nijhoff, 1968.

Seidel, George J. *Activity and Ground: Fichte, Schelling, and Hegel.* Studien und Materialen zur Geschichte der Philosophie, Bd. 3. Hildesheim: Georg Olms, 1976.

Shelley, Percy Bysshe. *The Complete Works of Percy Bysshe Shelley.* Edited by Roger Ingpen and Walter Peck. Julian Editions. 10 vols. London: Ernest Benn, 1930.

————. *Letters of Percy Bysshe Shelley.* Edited by Frederick Jones. 2 vols. Oxford: Oxford University Press, 1964.

————. *Shelley's Poetry and Prose.* Edited by Donald H. Reiman and Sharon B. Powers. Norton Critical Edition. New York: Norton, 1977.

Sperry, Stuart. *Keats the Poet.* Princeton: Princeton University Press, 1973.

Staël, Madame de [Holstein-Necker]. *Germany.* 3 vols. in 2. New York, 1814.

Steinman, Lisa. "Shelley's Skepticism: Allegory in 'Alastor.'" *ELH* 45 (1978): 255–69.

Stempel, Daniel. "Revelation on Mt. Snowdon: Wordsworth, Coleridge, and the Fichtean Imagination." *JAAC* 29 (1971): 371–84.

Stokoe, F. W. *German Influence in the English Romantic Period.* 1926. Reprint. New York: Russell & Russell, 1963.

Strohschneider-Kohrs, Ingrid. *Die romantische Ironie in Theorie und Gestaltung.* Tübingen: Max Niemeyer, 1960.

Tetreault, Ronald. "Quest and Caution: Psychomachy in Shelley's *Alastor.*" *English Studies in Canada* 3 (1977): 289–306.

Thorslev, Peter. *The Byronic Hero: Types and Prototypes.* Minneapolis: University of Minnesota Press, 1962.

Todhunter, John. *A Study of Shelley.* London, 1880.

Tuveson, Ernest. *The Imagination as a Means of Grace: Locke and the Aesthetics of Romanticism.* Berkeley and Los Angeles: University of California Press, 1960.

Vivian, Charles H. "The One 'Mont Blanc.'" *KSJ* 4 (1955). Reprinted in *Shelley's Poetry and Prose,* edited by Donald H. Reiman and Sharon B. Powers, pp. 569–79. Norton Critical Editions. New York: Norton, 1977.

Vlasopolos, Anca. "*The Rime of the Ancient Mariner* as Romantic Quest." *TWC* 10 (1979): 365–69.

Vleeschauwer, H. J. de. *The Development of Kantian Thought.* Translated by A. R. C. Duncan. 1939. Reprint. London: Thomas Nelson, 1962.

Warminski, Andrzej. "Missed Crossing: Wordsworth's Apocalypses." *MLN* 99 (1984): 983–1006.

Warren, Robert Penn. "A Poem of Pure Imagination." In *The Rime of the Ancient Mariner,* by Samuel Taylor Coleridge. New York: Reynal and Hitchcock, 1946.

Wasserman, Earl R. "The English Romantics: The Grounds of Knowledge." *SiR* 4 (Autumn 1964): 17–34.

————. *Shelley: A Critical Reading*. Baltimore: Johns Hopkins University Press, 1971.

Watson, John. *Schelling's Transcendental Idealism*. Chicago, 1882.

Webb, Timothy. *The Violet in the Crucible: Shelley and Translation*. Oxford: Oxford University Press, 1976.

Wellek, René. "The Concept of Romanticism in Literary History." *CL* 1 (1949): 1–29, 147–72.

————. *A History of Modern Criticism, 1750–1950*. Vol. 2. New Haven: Yale University Press, 1955.

————. *Immanuel Kant in England*. Princeton: Princeton University Press, 1931.

————. "Romanticism in Literature." *Dictionary of the History of Ideas*. 1973 ed.

————. "Romanticism Re-Examined." In *Romanticism Reconsidered: Selected Papers from the English Institute*, edited by Northrop Frye, pp. 107–33. New York: Columbia University Press, 1963.

White, Newman Ivey. *Shelley*. 2 vols. New York: Knopf, 1940.

Whyte, Lancelot Law. *The Unconscious before Freud*. London: Tavistock, 1962.

Wilson, Milton. *Shelley's Later Poetry*. New York: Columbia University Press, 1957.

Wimsatt, William K., Jr., and Cleanth Brooks. *Literary Criticism: A Short History*. New York: Vintage, 1957.

Windelband, Wilhelm. *A History of Philosophy*. Translated by James H. Tufts. 2d. ed., rev. New York: Macmillan, 1901.

————. *Ueber den gegenwärtigen Stand der psychologischen Forschung*. Leipzig, 1876.

Wolf, Robert, and Ronald Millen. *Renaissance and Mannerist Art*. New York: Harry Abrams, 1968.

Wolff, Robert Paul. *Kant's Theory of Mental Activity*. Cambridge, Mass.: Harvard University Press, 1963.

Wordsworth, William. *Wordsworth's Poetical Works*. Edited by Ernest de Selincourt and Helen Darbyshire. 5 vols. Oxford: Oxford University Press, 1949.

————. *The Prelude: 1799, 1805, 1850*. Edited by Jonathan Wordsworth, M. H. Abrams, and Stephen Gill. Norton Critical Edition. New York: Norton, 1979.

# Index